D0366930

WALKING,

The Way

DISCIPLING EVERYWHERE;
WITH A FRESH SET OF EYES

DL NEWCOMBE

 FriesenPress

Suite 300 - 990 Fort St
Victoria, BC, V8V 3K2
Canada

www.friesenpress.com

Copyright © 2020 by DL Newcombe
First Edition — 2020

Foreword by Bonnie Newcombe

All rights reserved.

No part of this publication may be reproduced in any form, or by any means, electronic or mechanical, including photocopying, recording, or any information browsing, storage, or retrieval system, without permission in writing from FriesenPress.

Scripture taken from the NEW AMERICAN STANDARD BIBLE®,
© Copyright 1960, 1962, 1963, 1968, 1971, 1972, 1973, 1975, 1977, 1995 by The Lockman Foundation
Used by permission.
www.Lockman.org

ISBN
978-1-5255-4546-7 (Hardcover)
978-1-5255-4547-4 (Paperback)
978-1-5255-4548-1 (eBook)

1. RELIGION, CHRISTIAN MINISTRY, DISCIPLESHIP

Distributed to the trade by The Ingram Book Company

"Go therefore and *make* disciples…"
Matthew 28:19

SEGMENTS

————

AS A DISCIPLE OF JESUS...

———

You will begin to know and understand, if you haven't already, when you receive by God's providential will your *"new identity;"* that you became a disciple of Jesus. As Jesus's disciple, you step into the shoes the disciple left behind. You are now the next disciple stepping into those shoes as you respond to God's *calling* on your life so you would walk *The Way* Jesus did.

Have confidence — your shoes are just like those worn in the wilderness; they will never wear out, because God designed them to be walked in by those who will faithfully carry His Word and truths in their hearts to the world!

And when *that day* comes; you like everyone before you, will step out of those shoes, and another disciple will step into them right behind you, and the truth of the Only True God and Jesus Christ will GO on and on and on!

FOREWORD

When David first asked me to write the Foreword, I thought it might be a little strange for the author's wife to write it. I'm not a published author, theologian, minister, or person with expertise in God's Word. Then God gave me understanding. It was perfectly fitting to do it. Why? Because I am an expert witness to the saving grace of God, and the blessing of new life He gives to everyone who believes!

The Lord saved us both over sixteen years ago, and we have been on a *forward* journey ever since. We are living out Colossians 1:10 by walking in a manner worthy of the Lord and pleasing Him in every respect — We are bearing fruit in every good work and increasing in the knowledge of God. What a great journey to live out! I have witnessed the life change that occurs when God gives you a new heart and puts His Spirit in you. Before Jesus saved us, our life was like many of yours or people you know— filled with strife, deceit, pride, and a plethora of other sins.

So, for me to even imagine two people yoked together with God and walking in a whole *new life* is totally amazing! I have tasted and seen the goodness of the Lord, and His work in me, and in and through David. David has laid all things aside to complete the work God has prepared for him. Believe me, in 2003, if you would have told me God would place it on his heart to write a book about discipleship, I would have laughed in your face. Why? Our hearts were as far as the East is from the West from God. Our marriage was a wreck, full of selfish desires and disregard for each other. We are so thankful for God's saving grace and mercy, yet we have only scratched the surface of the true love God has for us. What did we know about discipleship or the unconditional love of God? Nothing! But God, in His mercies restored our marriage and has allowed us to see and live the wonderful life He has intended for a husband and wife, man and woman, dad and mom, papa and grandma, and servants of the Lord.

This journey God put us on was not always the smoothest, nor was it the straightest path, yet what a blessing it has been! There have been doubts, disagreements, and anxiety during the many hours of writing and editing. However, we stepped out in faith, knowing and trusting the Lord has called us to do His work. We trust He will provide for and support us every step of the way. Why do we have such unwavering faith the Lord will do this? Because God has demonstrated His faithfulness to us so many times in the past. Reflecting back over the years, He was faithful even when we weren't. He has shown His faithfulness, and made Himself known to us by His provision, when there were no means for provision.

He demonstrated His love to us even when we were unlovable and rescued us when we were in the depths of despair and self-destruction.

I've seen firsthand the inspiration from the Lord written down on paper. Authoring a book *sounds* easy until you sit down to complete the task. I have watched David diligently ask God for wisdom as he wrote, prayed, and believed the Spirit of God was with him in his work of writing this book. I know there are many wives desiring their husband to be the spiritual leader in their family. I was one. I can tell you there was constant prayer for God to change the heart of my husband. It may sound crazy to you, but we should all desire to be married to a man who loves God more than he loves us. Why? Because the love he has for God, and God has for him, flows from God through David to me. I am the recipient of the love of Jesus through my husband. I am so thankful God has shaped David into a man of God. His life reflects the love of Jesus in how he lives, serves, and loves God and others.

Reading, editing, and discussing this book has changed my life. I have grown in my knowledge of God's Word, and what He expects from us as His disciples. I have a renewed understanding that there is so much more to a truly intimate relationship with Jesus than just reading the Bible, going to church, and trying to be a "good person." I pray it will change your life as well!

Thank you, David, for being a man after God's own heart. For being obedient, listening, being still, following the commands of the Lord, and putting down on paper all God intended, so He will use it to change the lives of many! A true imitation of God's love, as it says in 1 Corinthians 13.

I love you!

Bonnie

PREFACE

TOTALLY DEPRAVED

Hello, my name is David, a sinner saved by the grace of God. I am a man who was spiritually dead, who has been brought to life by the saving power of God. Sin ruled my life for over thirty years and consumed my thoughts, words, and deeds. My total depravity was confirmed by my actions and how I lived. Sin was a daily practice, and I was captivated by it. I did not realize, until Jesus saved me, I was blind to sin's pitfalls and destruction. Sin almost destroyed my life, marriage, and relationships with my children because it was wreaking havoc in me.

Sin consumed my life, and because of my practice of it, it became natural to live it out.

It began very slowly as it slithered into the things I liked to do. Then it creeped into all aspects of my life. I did not recognize the enormity of it at first since my lusting and desires had profound influence over my conscience. Once this occurred, I developed a tolerance for sin, just like it is with drugs. First, I needed just a little, and then more was needed to achieve the same result. It attacked my mind, creating believable illusions. Once these illusions took on the appearance of reality, I began to act in response to what I perceived was real.

This is part of sin's deception, as I began to believe I could cope with and control it, as everything seemed to be progressing normally. That, too, is deception, I could not see myself coming apart at the seams, but others could see it. I was captivated by it, and at this point, my friend, I was in sin's clutches, feeding the beast breeding within me. I wondered why some people avoided me when I came into their presence.

I will compare sin to the effects of drugs and alcohol. At first, it is fun, exciting, relaxing, and could be very enjoyable. Both drugs and alcohol continued to lure me back, essential if I wanted to have an enjoyable time. Sin is the same. It continued to beckon, and I found myself answering its call time after time. My drugs of choice were marijuana and cocaine. The deception of marijuana was that I could relax, laugh, and enjoy the ambiance. The drugs and alcohol masked the pain, so I placed them in the pleasure center of my brain. When it came to alcohol, beer, scotch, cognac, and only the strongest of bourbons were consumed when drugs were not available. I found myself using alcohol to bring me down from my cocaine high. Then, one day, I was addicted. Over time, I was always in search of it, and the deeper I went, the tighter it gripped me. I frequented places where it was available, but by then it was with me everywhere I went.

It would have been easy for me to say drugs and alcohol are the culprits, responsible for my sin, but I would be lying to you. They were just vices to satisfy my sinful desires, the lust of my eyes and flesh, and my deceitful and desperately sick heart. I am certain there are many who could testify that they've never done a shot, had a brew, smoked a joint, or done a line of coke. Of course, if you have never been a user leading to addiction, we should address the other areas of sin of the flesh leading to the same type of addictions and the sinful behavior associated with it.

It is More Than You Think It Is

Sin can be so deceitful; humanity covers it in the cloak of "habits and hang-ups." Let's be frank with one another: it's sin. Every act of sin confirms the habit, searing the conscience in it. And those around us see it and call it a hang-up. Speeding is not a big deal, until you are caught. Talking about someone is the same, until you're heard.

Look at what the Bible says about pride, adultery, immorality, impurity, anger, jealousy, envy, stealing, lying, greed, carousing, evil desires, slander, selfishness, idolatry, power, and control. If you say you do not have any of the above-mentioned sins, or will not admit to the practice of sin, sin is disguising itself, and you are being deceived, just like me.

Know this—*sin is crouching at your door.*

I hope everyone will be able to relate to sin of one type or another. Just imagine if your life was full of those sins, and then throw in drug and alcohol addiction. Can you see the bondage I was in? I needed to be rescued because I could not escape and, the truth be known, I did not want to be rescued, because I was worshiping the sin created by the god of this world, Satan.

Let me tell you how pornography, the sin created by evil desire and lust, affected my life, and what captivity by this sin of the flesh does to the one entangled by it. At first it was only a few frames of pornography and then the entire movie. I'd watch one movie and then a few hours of video. Next, it carried over to a few days. I found myself viewing it in secret as often as I could. This led to months and then years of addiction. It is so damaging it warped my mind enough to imagine these sinful acts and tried to persuade others to participate. Talk about an addiction. This is one of the worst, as these images play on and on and have consequential and lasting effects.

It is different than drugs and alcohol. Addiction to pornography is not chemically based which creates physical cravings. Porn produces millions of images flashing in your mind within seconds and it creates a mental "appetite" craving satisfaction. My mind was consumed with pornographic thoughts. Ask anyone who is or was addicted to porn, and they will testify my statements are true. At first, I thought I could shut it off, since I was a "strong willed person." I found the more I tried, the less I succeeded. It was in control and I was stimulated by it. This sin was actively working on my mind and in my heart. I found myself answering its crafty call repeatedly.

It was not always like this for me.

When I was a young boy, I lived a normal childhood, that is, until I was seven or eight, when the abuse began. The abuse was sexual, physical, emotional, and psychological and continued into adolescence. The abuse caused me to make a promise to myself. And it was, one day, all who were responsible for this physical, emotional, and psychological anguish would pay. I buried the promise of revenge deep in my heart. Little did I know that, once I set the roots of bitterness and hatred in my heart by making revenge my only alternative, those roots would grow and bind my heart. I must testify, the roots of any sin without repentance can never be pulled out by yourself, as they bind tightly in and around your heart. The older I grew, the more my heart hardened and became cold. It burned with hatred for revenge.

For years I struggled with bitterness, hatred, anger, and trust. In effect, for thirty years I used whatever means possible to mask the deep-down bitterness, hatred, pain, and anger. I could not control this rage until, in my mind, justice was carried out. If you need a picture, here's what my heart looked like before the grace of God saved me and gave me a new heart. Believe me, I did not know I needed

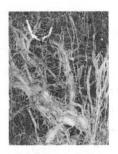

a heart bound by sin

one, but God did! Please understand, this also was not the "reason" or could I "blame" my sin on these sins committed against me.

These sinners will have to stand before the judgment seat of Christ, as all men will. I just hope God in His mercy has forgiven them, but that is between them and God. Sin has its way of continuing to gnaw away at the substance of my being. Do not be deceived. It can happen to you as well and may already be happening. Do you see the signs of emptiness, a void you cannot fill? I was living it daily, until there would be no life within me. I was just existing, living out this curse. It came to a point—either destroy myself or them. Someone had to go. Revenge was always the answer. There is no remedy for revenge. On the surface it seems a satisfactory answer, but this is the deception! Below, it is only bondage. For me to be free, I needed to forgive them—all of them—or sin would eventually choke the life right out of me. I never considered forgiveness as an answer to bondage and a way to freedom.

Sin totally obstructed my conscience and drastically effected the clarity of my thoughts. Sin deceived me into believing that anything I desired to do would bring pleasure or satisfaction, and if it did, it was good. It was evident by my choices sin clouded my ability to distinguish between good and evil. It created a mindset of "If it feels good, it must be good, so do it!"

Let me explain the extent of sin's deceptiveness in me. At one point in my young life, living a life of homosexuality seemed good. It provided relational and emotional stimulation, giving the illusion of pleasure leading to both physical and psychological satisfaction. The psychological spin by the sexual abusers was homosexual behavior was a good thing, and I needed to learn how to enjoy it. Pornography assisted and supported the abusers' influence and deception. And when this way of life was all I knew, with the pornographic images pulverizing my mind, I proceeded in a life of homosexual sin without any hesitation. I was deceived to believe this was a way of life for me because it started out so early.

An internal conflict continued for years, since I was also attracted to women. Those relations also touched the same relational, emotional, and pleasurable needs. To be quite blunt, I was a wreck, internally struggling, both psychologically and emotionally.

Looking back, I understand now why I was committing the sins of masturbation; and fornication with every willing woman as often as I could. It was my masculinity trying to regain control. Over time, the more I obsessed about sex with women, the less I desired homosexual relations. Once I approached my late teens, I attempted to put this way of life behind me as far as I could. I learned I could have "close and personal" relationships with men which did not and wouldn't involve any sexual attraction. Once the psychological and sexual abuse stopped, it was a fight for an exceptionally long time since I had lived with abuse and a secret homosexual life for several years. I was in some form of sin's bondage from eight to forty seven. *The truth; the practice of any sin is bondage, and I needed to be set free because I could not free myself!*

This life of sin was concealed and carried into my marriage. On the outside, I projected myself as a person who had it all together. On the inside, it was a different story. I was bound up tighter than a criminal in shackles. As much as I tried to live a normal life, sin continually reared its ugly head, and my spouse and children were the victims of my secret sin of pornography, drug and alcohol addiction, and pent up bitterness and anger. Not only was I incredibly angry and deceptive, I was a lying adulterer, and I created a home environment of fear by control. My wife walked on eggshells, and my children responded to me out of fear, not love. At any given moment, for anything, I could blow up like a bomb and the yelling and cursing would commence. I was quick to point out their flaws and lack of adherence to the standards I set when, the truth be known, I couldn't meet those standards myself. I was living a lie, and my life was full of hypocrisy.

It would be so easy for me, like so many others before God saved me, to think that the good things I had done in my life outweighed all the bad because the sin was not against others, it was my own. Can you see how deceptive sin can be? I was blind to the truth and could not see all the evil I was committing. So, to continue to justify my sinful behavior, I began to manipulate others to join into my masquerade, living out the deeply embedded pornographic images in my mind. You see, sin filled my heart, and it permeated my mind. All I can testify to is, my life was full of sin. It was little more than a cesspool of pus.

It is Not About Religion

If you would have asked me if I was a Christian, my response without hesitation would have been yes! I was baptized as a Catholic and had completed five of seven sacraments. I satisfied the *religious* works because this is the way to earn passage to heaven, right? In fact, the only time I would mention God was when I said His name in vain. I attended Catholic school and understood the *basics* of religion. However, I was far from living the life God intends for His people to live. I believed that if I gave the impression of living a religious life, like attending church, my family and others would believe I was a religious man. This also was an illusion.

I was so warped in my thinking, doing the ritualistic things proved to myself I would be acceptable to God, regardless of my practice of sin. Again, sin is so deceptive, it had me believing this. I even forced my children to follow tradition, making them wear head coverings when attending mass, because it was the thing to do as a "Catholic."

I had never continuously read the Bible, and during this period of my life, I never provided any biblical advice, because I did not know of any. Due to my spiritual blindness, I never considered that my sin was as offensive to God as it was. My focus was on the works and not the grace; that too, is deception. Sin's design was to blind me to the light of Christ and keep me away from God and His Word, and it was accomplishing this very effectively. The more I practiced sin, the deeper and deeper I sank into it, and the tighter and larger its roots grew in my heart.

When one is completely focused only on self—and I was living it—this selfish behavior is what I now call the inward "I" syndrome. You would know it as selfishness. My only focus was on me, myself, and I. In my life, there was no room for anyone else, especially God. I did what I wanted when I wanted to do it. It did not matter what it was, nor did I care about the consequences. If it felt good, I would be the first one in line to do it. I truly did not care if I offended or hurt anyone else because, deep down, I was full of hurt, anger, bitterness, hatred, and pain. I was living these out and hurting those closest to me.

Many times, when I hurt someone by my sinful behavior, I thought, *Good, how does it feel?* If anyone got hurt in the crossfire, they must have done something to cause my reaction. It was my world, and they revolved around it. I ruled my home with an iron fist. My children did not love me they feared me. I always thought they left the room when I got home to give me time, but the truth was they did not want to be around me, to live through another day of anger, vulgarity, yelling, with a condescending mindset and behavior. I didn't deserve the title of dad, believe that!

There was no light in me at all. I was darkness. I was freely living and walking all around in it. I was blind to the truth of God. How in the world could I live like this? The answer is this: I was dead in my trespasses and sin, and sin controlled my life. I habitually practiced it, and I loved the things of the world because it fed my desires and my sin—this entity, this beast growing within me. I was living in the world and loving it. The world was living through me, and this was my life. I could and would do anything!

BUT GOD ...

Throughout the book, you will find my comment, "BUT GOD." Here's why. Sixteen years ago, on the day ordained for me by God, Jesus stepped into my darkness! Once the light of Christ shone on those illusions, God's light revealed it was my sinful nature, all along.

For several months, work was progressing as what one would call normal. There was something happening which was well beyond the norm. I had constant interaction with several men in my workplace. I did not know it then, but they were Jesus's disciples. They were disciples working the harvest. Jesus made me their mission. For me, they were men interested in me. They wanted to know all of me — what I thought, believed, and how I lived. Our conversations were well beyond the mundane and far from scripted. I was blind to what was happening. I learned later God was moving in my life, and He desired for me to repent, turn from my evil ways, and follow Him.

I finished a full day at work and mentioned to one of my co-workers as I was leaving, "God is trying to talk to me!" He was one of several disciples of Jesus that God put into my life to lead me to Himself. My co-worker's eyes grew wide in amazement. He, like the other disciples were students at the Dallas Theological Seminary (DTS). They took God's calling as a disciple very seriously, and were intentional every step of *the way*. After this brief discussion, I headed to my car for my forty minute drive home.

I was a creature of habit, and I had a lot of them! When heading home, I would turn on the radio to listen for the traffic report, especially if it was severe weather. This was a clear, sunny fall evening, so weather was not a concern for traffic. The traffic report is always helpful, especially in Dallas, Texas. Delays are a psychological beating, because they make a commute twice as long if you get caught in them. I wanted to avoid any delays, as the drive was long enough without any traffic jams. But on this day, not only was my co-worker amazed, so was I, and I was driving in total silence.

My office was located in the North Dallas area. Anyone familiar with Dallas, Texas would know where Midway and Alpha Roads cross.

All who know the area know this is a busy intersection in both directions, especially at rush hour. I pulled to the red light on Alpha and stopped. Midway is a six-lane roadway, three in each direction. I was still pondering my own comment. Gazing at the light in total silence, I wondered, *Why would I say, "God is trying to talk to me?"* As my light turned green, I proceeded into the intersection.

Focused straight ahead, I pulled out and then caught a blur of a red object approaching from my left. I yanked the wheel to my right and stomped on the brake as hard as I could! I remember taking a large gasp of air. It happened in a split second, but it seemed to be in slow motion.

Tires screeched as the driver of the red car tried to stop. Both vehicles came to an abrupt stop in the middle of the intersection. I looked to my left into the face of the driver. His eyes and mouth were wide open, with a look of horror on his face. The front bumper of his car was so close to my driver's door I could not have slid my hand between the two vehicles. As I looked around the intersection, no other cars moved in any direction. It was as though everyone was frozen in time. They must have anticipated this horrific event. An accident was going to change the lives of two people—and all the people at the intersection for that matter if they kept their eyes open! BUT GOD ...

Once everything came to a stop, I put my vehicle into reverse and backed up to allow the red vehicle to pass. All traffic remained stopped, regardless of the color of the lights, and I was able to drive through the intersection. I drove the rest of the way home, only driving about five miles an hour as my mind raced. Only after the event did I realize what had happened. In the split seconds it occurs, there is no time to assess or test what to do. It was as though my heart was racing a thousand beats a minute! I was pondering all the different possibilities and you can believe; death was one of them.

Like the red car, another car appeared to my left. He drove alongside me, he too at five miles an hour, and he was trying to get my attention. He motioned for me to roll down my window, and as I did, he said, "You didn't see that guy? I was sitting next to you at the red light."

I muttered, "No, where did he come from?"

"He came from the middle lane. When you pulled out, that red car ran the red and I thought you were going to get killed!" His face told the story of what I was feeling. He looked horrified, and I must have looked to be in shock. Believe me, I was!

I was an auto liability claims manager. I handled death claims for those killed in auto accidents. I understood the finality of death, and its impact on one's family. Believe me, it was by God's grace and mercy I was going home rather than to the morgue. It was not my cat-like reaction, nor was it my great peripheral vision. It was God, and only Him!

Jesus chose to use something I was so good at, and remarkably familiar with. I learned, I did not have time, and I needed to repent. Life as I knew it could come to an end at any second. If this was the day God chose for me to die, I would be standing before Him. I would have been *locked in sin, with no time for repentance*. God would have held me accountable for it all, every evil thought, evil word, and evil deed. And my friend, there were millions of them. There would be no hope, no life, and no Advocate. It would have been judgment. Jesus's decision would have been eternal separation from Him. I would have been cast into outer darkness, into the flame of fire, with those who weep and gnash their teeth forever.

You see, there is no time—no time to confess all the sins I'd committed throughout my entire life. There were so many, I couldn't even count them all, even if I tried. I am certain you can relate when you've committed sins and have completely forgotten them. I am here to tell you, apart from Jesus's saving grace, you are accountable for every single one of them, whether you remember them or not. There was no time to quote Romans 10:9, a biblical truth that says, "that if you confess with your mouth Jesus as Lord, and believe in your heart that God raised Him from the dead, you will be saved." So, if you want to confess this truth, the time is now! Because a time may come, when the only time will be for a breath before the end of this life and the start of eternal separation from God in hell begins.

But God in His love and mercy for me gave me a chance to repent and repent I did. He gave me new life, and it was my first day of walking the His light. I began to live the life He intended for me. Jesus exposed my sin, which was consuming and controlling my life. If He did not step into my darkness, it was going to kill me. Jesus brought me into His light and saved me from the domain of darkness. I could not save myself from the bondage—I'll call it my Egypt—where sin had me shackled.

When Jesus saved me, He gave me a new heart, put a new spirit and His spirit in me. I was free from the bondage of sin. It no longer had power over me. I learned one of the greatest abilities given by the Spirit of God is the ability to say NO to sin. I could never say no before God saved me. There was no consideration for saying no when sin was consuming my life.

God gave me a fresh set of eyes to see. I could now see Him, see the depths of His love for me, and see grace, mercy, and truth. The works of His hands. The beauty of creation. His way, providence, promises, commandments, and warnings. I could see wherever I looked, *everything* is biblical. *This* ordained day, Jesus made me a new creature, PRAISE GOD!

A New Life Created in Me

This heart and spirit transplant caused me to begin *Walking, The Way*, as I started following Him and crucifying my flesh. Of course, this did not mean I was to hammer spikes into my hands and feet. What Jesus was and is calling me to do is to dispose of (crucify) the sin in my life. In doing so, it would be dead to me, confirming there is no life in it. Jesus gave me the chance to renew my mind through the purity of His living Word, so I began to saturate my mind with the Word of God, because my mind was cluttered with so many wicked thoughts. I found when I was meditating on God's truth and promises, there was no room for the images and sinful thoughts of my old self.

I was able to finally learn what true love is, and it was from God. I learned to love others like God loves me. I desire to love and please Him more than I want to please myself. Through His love, I learned of His forgiveness of me, giving me the ability to forgive others through the act of love. It created in me a burning desire to share the *Good News* of Jesus Christ, and the work He has begun and will complete in me. I disciple everywhere He leads me, as Jesus made me one of His disciples!

I am eternally grateful to Jesus for freeing me from the bondage and captivity of sin and making me a child of the only true God!

I've heard from so many *everything* is in the Bible. Well, I would say, I am in there too, more than once. And if the truth be known, you are also. When you read it, I pray you find yourself, like I did. I found myself in the book of Luke, in the parable of the two debtors. Jesus is talking about a woman, who was like me, having a life full of sin and unable to pay the debt. And, like her, I have had my debt paid by the blood of Jesus, praise God! Jesus says, "For this reason I say to you, her sins, which are many, have been forgiven, for she loved much; but he who is forgiven little, loves little" (Luke 7:47).

For what God has forgiven me, today, I love much! Thank You, Jesus!

You will find the more you read God's Word, the more you will reflect on His truths, and then you will begin to apply them in and through your life. On the last page of each segment of this book is a page titled Reflections. I thank Mark for his suggestion to add a reflections page to the book. It is placed there for *you* to jot down your inspiration and actions to take as God the Holy Spirit reveals His truths.

By the end of this book, I pray God reveals Himself to you as He has done to me! Confess the sin preventing you from being a disciple of Jesus, so that you too will do the will of the Father.

ABBA, I love you. I am so thankful for You choosing me for this mission at such a time as this. I ask You to touch the lives of every person who reads or listens to the words of this work You have ordained for me. Be glorified in the work of Your Spirit that is alive and working in me. Give them a fresh set of eyes to see You, and the wonderful work of Your hand. Make Your agape love alive in them. Free every captive from the bondage of sin, so they can live in the light of Your love and grace. Create a desire in them to read, study, meditate, and live out Your Word and truths every day for the rest of their time on earth. Create a clean heart in them oh God. Renew their mind as You have renewed mine. Make known to them they can find hope, and their only hope is in Jesus. And they, just like me, and the millions of others throughout the history of this world, will express the love, gratitude, and thankfulness to You for Your saving grace through faith. And they too will be one that begins their journey to the fullness of life You promise to everyone who believes in You. Demonstrate Your power through Your Spirit, and by the work of Your hand, they will become new disciples walking the way of Jesus. I ask for Your blessing on my mission and this work, and You will be glorified in it all. I ask all of these things in the mighty, loving, and powerful name of Your Son Jesus, amen.

I pray the God of Abraham, Isaac and Jacob; the great I AM, blesses *your* time and *your* life as *you* begin *Walking, The Way!*

LOVE ...

"If you love Me, you will keep My commandments." (John 14:15)

NEWFOUND LOVE

After reading the Preface, you might be surprised to know that, if you had asked me back then if I loved, I would have said, "Of course I do!" Love was what I defined it to be. Based on my heart and how I was living, I was so, so wrong. How could I love anyone else when deep down inside, I did not love myself? I truly did not know what true love was, nor did I expect God could love a wretch like me, especially since Jesus is awfully specific about expressions of love toward Him. He says in John 14:15, "If you love Me, you will keep My commandments." Well, before He saved me, I did not keep His commandments because I did not know what they were. How could I? I did not read His Word to know what they were. I guess if one looks at the Bible and says, "Sure you do. Jesus is talking about the Ten Commandments, just keep those." I will testify that I did not keep them, so I did not love Him.

Yet based on the hollowness of my religious beliefs, I was going to heaven because of my *religious works*, even though I was dead in my trespasses and sin, and God only allows the living to be with Him in eternity. My heart and life were full of sin, and He has forgiven the sin of those born of the Spirit who are in Christ. I was not in Christ, yet I was under the law of sin and death. I did not realize He was loving me all along. I was blind to it, and did not have any love for Him, but He still loved me.

Many people really do not have any idea of what God's love really is, what it means, and how it works. I know you have heard the word "love" used for such things as loving people, shoes, cars, restaurants, vacations, and jobs. It is easy to say, "I love you," and love everything about you, because it's one's own manufactured love, which is non-existent in relation to what God calls and describes as love.

It is a natural behavior to love your siblings, parents, and family members, right? This is the "normal" tendency, but only if you have the love of God in your heart, can you truly love them. If you don't, then you do not genuinely love them as God loves and defines how it must be lived out. When you read what God says love is and how He loves in 1 Corinthians 13:4-8a, and if you are not loving like He describes, then I would say, no, you are not loving others as He loves you and them.

Love is so versatile, adaptable, and resourceful, it can withstand the greatest evil or the mildest trouble. It can defuse a hostile condition and extinguish the flames of anger that seek revenge. It can be patient when all the circumstances scream for action. It can defuse pride, arrogance, and vanity. It can turn a narcissist into an externally focused creature. Love never considers gratifying itself or harming others. It has its way of softening the most rigid condition and possesses the purest passion for others. It's so strong it covered an uncountable amount of sin. And it can penetrate the hardest shell any human can possess. This was my way of explaining what God's love did to me, and now His love is flowing through me to others.

1 Corinthians 13:4-7 says, "Love is patient, love is kind *and* is not jealous; love does not brag *and* is not arrogant, does not act unbecomingly; it does not seek its own, is not provoked, does not take into account a wrong *suffered*, does not rejoice in unrighteousness, but rejoices with the truth; bears all things, believes all things, hopes all things, endures all things." God in His mercy demonstrated His unfailing love toward me by exposing my sin, rather than forever condemning me in it, and He allowed me the opportunity to repent of it. Once I repented, He put the power in me to turn away from sin. Know, in love, that Jesus will free you from the yoke of slavery of sin, and you will grow in understanding of God's love for you, and you will begin to love others like He does. This has occurred in my life only by the grace of God and, as a result, I

live in them and they in me. Now I do not take into account any wrongs suffered, as I continue to live spiritually in this fleshly existence.

Love Came Knocking

When love is not displayed, you may hear this question asked of you: "Do you love me?"

Would you be surprised hearing an answer like, "Of course I do!" Or are you used to giving or hearing the same answer? Why do you think the person is asking the question in the first place? Do you expect it's because you are not displaying the love they expected to receive, or the love you promised to give? Believe it or not, saying "Of course I do" is not answering the question. The "Of course I do" response is evasive and unresponsive to the question. This question seeks a response which provides reassurance and affirmation. Before Jesus saved me and made me into a new creature, the "of course I do," was my response. My love was based on the love I manufactured. And it became a natural response to say, "Of course I do!" In my mind, I was saying, *How dare you ask me if I love you! I know what love is, and it does what I am doing. So, if you do not see what I am doing, you're blind to my actions of love. You must be, to ask me, if I love you!*"

When this question is asked, what do you suppose they are seeing, hearing, and feeling from you? I know what my spouse was seeing, hearing, and feeling from me. She was witnessing a man who had no idea what love really was and was making it up all along the way. And under the surface, it was all about self-gratification.

I had a polluted mind and heart; thus, the words and actions of my love were polluted as well. This is the truth, whether you want to believe it, or admit it, or not. My manufactured love was contaminated, foul, and spoiled. I do not know how Bonnie was able to cope with the stench for so long—I began to realize, BUT GOD was applicable to my life! It was God all along who preserved my life and marriage.

He must have placed a rose of Himself under her nose to help her not get sick of me, so she would stay and not leave. Most importantly, He was preparing me to learn to love her like He loves her and me. I was in for a huge awakening because when Jesus stepped into my darkness, He obliterated all my notions and began to replace them with His truth about His love for me. If you really want to know, be prepared for their honest answer when you ask your spouse, "Do I love you like God loves you?" Ask God for strength when you hear, "No! Not like God loves me."

Shortly after being born again, I received my first paperback NAS Bible from a disciple whose name is Mitchell. Mitch was one of the disciples Jesus placed in my path. I came across 1 Corinthians 13, which is titled, "The Excellence of Love." As soon as I began to read it, God the Holy Spirit made it perfectly clear my thoughts of love needed to be completely changed. The more I read and meditated on "The Excellence of Love," the more I saw I needed the Holy Spirit's help, guidance, teaching, and power to live according to His Word. It took a while to comprehend the magnitude of God's love for me.

I learned and understood that it's not just the activity of sex creating love. God created love in us because "God is love" (1 John 4:8). And when God lives in you, you love! It is only when salvation comes into your life do you begin to understand the unadulterated agape love of God, and His love floods your entire being.

More Than Commonplace

God's love is so evident, yet sin obstructs the full understanding of God's love and how He loves us individually and personally, and not just collectively—so much so you see stories, poems, and songs written about love. Some parents have chosen names for their children meaning love. Psychologists say there is a love language lived out with expressions through gifts such as jewelry, flowers, and chocolates. And, by calling or being called "my sweetheart."

A chain store has the name love, an airport bears the name, and it is even a score in tennis. So, if love touches people, places, and things, it must be everywhere, yet the true meaning of love is not lived out the way God loves and intends for His love to be displayed by everyone, everywhere. The amazing thing is, one would expect to see the love of God in the body of Christ more than anywhere else and the body is all of Jesus's disciples.

Yet there are so many people who profess to be Christ-followers, which should make them disciples, through whom God's love does not seem to flow to others. There is no question the action or the appearance of love seems to be present in their "inner circle" of their personal relationships, but based on God's truth explained in His Word, it should, and must, flow everywhere to everyone!

Unbelievers view the Christian's existence and question how they could make such a claim about the only true God's love for them. The Christian's life as they see it does not fully reflect this important attribute of God's love for others. The lack of expressive true love for God and others creates a conflict in the minds of the unbelieving. They are using what they think love is as their guide. The person proclaiming to be a Christian is saying they are using the Bible as theirs. The unbeliever looks for similarities, but what they find in the proclaiming Christian is inconsistency. And thus, the word "hypocrisy" or "hypocrite" forms in their mind.

One expects the promise of spending eternity with God, if they desire to do so, to be a reality. Being deceived, they find themselves moving away from that promise. The devil, the ruler of this world, continues to blind the minds of the unbelieving! You can believe it or not. If God says it's true, and one rejects God's truth, know, this rejection of God's truth is a sign of spiritual blindness. As a result of the lack of authentic love relationships, Satan continues to deceive the unbelieving. It is a continuous deception to believe one can live according to one's own desires, thus they manufacture love to be what they *make it* to be.

The Light of the World has come, and it is Jesus Christ. The devil cannot stop the light of Christ in this world. His only opportunity is to darken humanity's understanding. You must believe that he does make it his business to do this. He knows who Jesus is, and by keeping *you* in the "dark," he wins, and you lose!

A darkened mind affects one's bias, which increases prejudices. It utilizes ignorance and selfishness to continue in error. The mind is blind to the gospel of Jesus, who is the image of the invisible God as the Bible says in Colossians 3:15. Jesus intends for His gospel to illuminate humanity's mind. And when illuminated, the truth of the only true God is made known to them. There is no gray area. You are either a believer in Jesus Christ or you are not. So, I'll ask you: Where are you standing? What do you believe? Are you illuminated, or are you in darkness?

This results in confirmation, from the unbeliever's perspective, and they respond by turning their backs on the Christian, when this lack of love directly reflects on God. Unbelievers hear the proclamation from the Christian, "I am an ambassador for Christ," yet the Christian's fleshly actions are speaking so loudly the unbelievers cannot hear a word the Christian is saying. Talk about hypocrisy! Can you now understand why the word "hypocrite" rolls so easily off their tongues in discussions about those who proclaim to be Christians?

If it is more than just commonplace, it should be evident in our thoughts, words, and deeds. We should not only be talking it; our lives should be unmistakable, and our walk should confirm it. Loving is a command. Moses, when speaking to the Israelites in Deuteronomy 6:5, made it clear as to how they were to love God. Jesus, in Matthew 22:37, restates what Moses was inspired to communicate. He commands how we are to love God: "You shall love the Lord your God with all your heart and with all your soul and with all your might." So I will ask: Do you love Him with all your heart, soul, and might? Expect if God said it, He expects His disciples to *live it* if we are going to claim we love Him.

Love is apparent in some places, and in and by some people. I would expect Jesus to say love has everything to do with our lives. Based on God the Father's testimony about His Son, it cost Jesus everything, as He freely displayed His love for us when He gave all His humanity for us to learn how to love.

Did you know there are over one thousand songs with "love" in the title? Why do you think this is? Is it because God made it so? If love is so important, then why so much focus and desire on accumulating so much stuff? Love is not part of the accumulation of material wealth. Do we acquire things so we can feel we have value, and are to be respected and admired for our stuff? If we have not accumulated all this stuff, are we to be disrespected or frowned upon since we do not seem to have the same worth as others, with all the stuff they have accumulated?

Is it for people to *know* who we are so we can have access to high places, the pleasures of life, and recognition for the accumulated success?

People can be defined in so many ways. Age group can define them, like millennials or baby-boomers, or gen Xers. Job classification, ethnicity, and even religion can define us. But very rarely is someone defined by how they love. Yet love is what Jesus says defines His disciples.

The fact is the only ones who genuinely love are those born of God. Here's the confirmation from the Bible, 1 John 4:7 says, "Beloved, let us love one another, for love is from God; and everyone who loves is born of God and knows God."

According to Jesus, love has everything to do with being His disciple so much so that love, truly confirms whose you really are.

LOVE DEFINES YOU

I love you enough to speak this truth from God's Word. There are only two types of people on this planet. This truth goes well beyond the place you live, how much income you have or do not have, nor where you attended college. It's not who you married, or even where you worship. It strikes right at the core of either you love, or you don't, and this echoes the mentioned of "Whose" you are.

Read 1 John 3:10, it says, "By this the children of God and the children of the devil are obvious." Here's the unadulterated truth, there are only two kinds of people walking on the face of this earth, children of God and children of the devil. It would be easy for one to say, only the "worst of humanity," like murderers are the children of the devil.

But, I must caution you, as that's a very shallow and foolish mindset to possess. You would be astonished if God revealed the children of the devil to you. I must alert you; you would not have to go too far to find them yourself ... believe that.

Based on how I was living before Jesus saved me, you could easily have said, "David, you are a child of the devil." You know the amazing thing? I would have cursed you out, attempting to convince you I wasn't. Imagine that? Can you relate?

The way we love, walk, talk, and live confirms and makes known whose we really are. Look behind you, and what do you see? You must be truthful with yourself and determine if you see the practice of righteousness. You must use God's word as the benchmark, if you do not really know and understand what righteousness looks like. You must also consider based on God's Word, whether you love your brother, or you don't. Then, look in the mirror and ask yourself, whose does God's word say that I am? *If* you find God's love flowing in and through your life, *then* you should be one who loves much, regardless! Know, if you don't, Jesus can deliver you from the bondage of sin and unbelief, which is the root cause of why you are not loving like God loves you!

A Love Inexhaustible

Jesus said, "By this all men will know that you are My disciples, if you have **love** for one another" (John 13:35). The amazing thing to consider is, it's not how much one knows the Bible; it is all about love. Love is first mentioned in Genesis 22:2, when God talks to Abraham about Isaac, the son "whom you **love**."[1] In 1 Kings 10:9, we read, "because the Lord **loved** Israel forever." Then, in Psalm 146:8, we read, "The Lord **loves** the righteous."

Wisdom speaks of love in Proverbs 8:17: "I **love** those who **love** me; And those who diligently seek me will find me." Solomon warns of the love of money in Ecclesiastes 5:10: "He who **loves** money will not be satisfied with money, nor he who **loves** abundance *with its* income. This too is vanity." The Lord describes the length of His love, which is everlasting: "The Lord appeared to him from afar saying, 'I have **loved** you with an everlasting **love**; Therefore, I have drawn you with **loving-kindness**'" (Jeremiah 31:3).

Jesus said how and who we should love, stating, in Matthew 5:44, "But I say to you, **love** your enemies and pray for those who persecute you." He tells us the greatest commandment: "You shall **love** the Lord your God with all your heart, and with all your soul, and with all your mind" (Matthew 22:37).

---

1   Emphasis of the word "love" and its derivatives has been added here and in the rest of the quotations in this section.

Jesus speaks to the depth of God's love in John 3:16: "For God so **loved** the world, that He gave His only begotten Son, that whoever believes in Him shall not perish, but have eternal life." Jesus also addresses the disciples' bonds with each other, which reflect His **love** in John 15:12: "This is My commandment, that you **love** one another, just as I have **loved** you."

We live in the security of Jesus's love, as described in Romans 8:35, which states, "Who will separate us from the **love** of Christ? Will tribulation, or distress, or persecution, or famine, or nakedness, or peril, or sword?" And, "nor height, nor depth, nor any other created thing, will be able to separate us from the **love** of God, which is in Christ Jesus our Lord" (Romans 8:39). "But the fruit of the Spirit is **love**" (Galatians 5:22).

Ephesians 5:25 describes how husbands should love their wives, "Husbands, **love** your wives, just as Christ also **loved** the church and gave Himself up for her." My favorite memory verse, Galatians 2:20, states, "I have been crucified with Christ; and it is no longer I who live, but Christ lives in me; and the *life* which I now live in the flesh I live by faith in the Son of God, who **loved** me and gave Himself up for me."

Think of Jesus, or any first responder, even those in military service who defend our country and are saving lives and who give their lives sacrificially. Jesus says in John 15:13, "Greater **love** has no one than this, that one lay down his life for his friends." Jesus went to the cross to pay the wages of sin. This is one of the greatest expressions of love, the cross!

It is on the cross Jesus gives His life as the perfect sacrifice to pay the debt we owe, which we cannot pay ourselves, although the unbelieving world does not recognize or understand the depth of Jesus's love for them. The more I grew in understanding of Jesus's atonement for my sin, the deeper my love and devotion was for Him!

We have a great high priest who can sympathize with us, and His name is Jesus. He understands how sin and its bondage opposes the love of God, because it is God's love flowing through us to others, and not our own.

Love and sin both proceed out of one's heart. Your muscular heart does its job, moving blood through your body. Many touch their chest when talking about their heart, but that is not where it's located. The heart I am referencing is in the core of your mind.

The blood flowing from your physical heart circulates through the brain. Thus, what consumes the heart—love or sin—flows from the heart and permeates the mind.

Therefore, a heart consumed with sin can only live out sin. It is a heart incapable of imitating God's unconditional love. God's Word confirms what proceeds out of a heart full of sin. It brings forth "evil thoughts, murders, adulteries, fornications, thefts, false witness, slanders" (Matthew 15:19). A heart full of God's love lives out God's love. It's as simple as that.

There must be the love of God in a new heart for love to exist the way God intends. Sin consumed my heart. It produced malice, hatred, bitterness, and outbursts of anger. I was envious, jealous, held grudges, and was cruel. Ask Bonnie. She would testify sin consumed my heart. These are true indicators of a heart of stone and not one of flesh given by God. There is no potential for an unregenerate heart to imitate God. An unregenerate heart cannot love nor forgive. Therefore, God calls it a "heart of stone" in Ezekiel 36:26. It is cold, rigid, and obstinate, incapable of loving God and others. The disciple knows forgiveness is one of the greatest expressions of love. This is how inexhaustible love really is and can be in the life of Jesus's disciples.

LOVE'S MELODY

There are many wonderful Christian songs about love, and these songs of worship and praise are a love language to God. I would expect that when God's people are singing to Him of all the wonderful works He's done in creation and their lives, it brings Him joy, happiness, and love.

However, more often than not when I am attending a service, I notice people who proclaim they love God with all their hearts, and should be in one accord with the body singing, praising, and worshiping the only true God, with their hands in their pockets, not singing, or sipping on their java while continually looking at their phones. I can understand if a person is in a trial that singing to and praising God during the trial may be difficult. But sipping java, standing tightlipped, and staring at your phone, has nothing to do with a trial. It makes me want to ask if they understand the wonder of Jesus's sacrifice for them. And if they do, and Jesus is the one leading worship, would their behavior be the same in His presence? If you are a coffee or tea sipper or addicted to your smart phone, you should consider what God is calling you to do as His disciple. Put them down and join in with the other disciples who love to sing to God and tell of His wonders, and 1 Chronicles 16:9 comes alive in you!

Just meditate on the fact Jesus Christ, our Lord and King, would leave His glory and majesty, and give His life for a condemned person like you and me. God's love is truly AMAZING!

Romans 5:6-8 says, "Christ died for the ungodly. For one will hardly die for a righteous man; though perhaps for a good man someone would dare even to die. But God demonstrates His own love toward us, in that while we were yet sinners, Christ died for us." May I echo, AMAZING LOVE! Jesus imitates the Father, and the disciple imitates Jesus. The world talks about items you cannot leave home without ... well, love *is* an action that you can only live eternally with it.

But what is love? Really, I mean really, what's love? The Bible clearly defines what love does and anyone with understanding can define what love is. You must ask yourself: Are these love *actions* by God's supernatural power evident in my life, or does my life reflect actions from a heart full of sin? Does the observer or the recipient see outbursts of anger, revenge, jealousy, bitterness, and hatred?

The Bible explains the love of God and how He loves. If we are to love like Jesus, as it says in Ephesians 5:1, "be imitators of God, as beloved children," then it would only make sense we would have to know what love should be, and what it looks like in action, in order to replicate it! When God gives you a new heart, His love is in it! This is the answer to the million dollar question! The new heart given by God, has His love in it! Now, it's His love that flows from your new heart to the lives of others. And when it does, you will find yourself singing at the top of your lungs to God for His saving power!

You know the amazing thing I've learned? I cannot carry a tune, but God loves my singing anyway, because I am making a joyful noise with all my heart to Him. Read Psalm 100. It's only five verses, but it speaks volumes of how we as disciples are to *respond* to the work of Jesus and the life and love He has bestowed on us.

A CALL TO LOVE

Let me share with you a wonderful opportunity I had to love as a disciple of Jesus along my journey on the path of life. It fits into the *wherever* we go and how we are called to love others, as we respond out of the love God has for us, and we have for Him. Some believe love takes effort when it is a way of life. Once the love of God is freely flowing into your life, it flows out just as freely as it comes in. God's love touches all you encounter, and it goes well beyond loving someone when something has happened. It requires one to tap into the well of love to either respond in a loving way toward someone unloving, or to grant forgiveness when a sin has been committed.

Remember, we must always look to Jesus for what He suffered; it was for the sin of the world. There is no sin greater than the sin of the world, regardless of sins committed against me or you! You must come to the reality of this fact! I expect there are saints saying, "But you were not murdered for Jesus's sake, were you?" I understand abuse, lying, infidelity, and addictions of all kinds, to name a few. Yes, they are egregious, but you cannot forgive. Jesus forgave those who killed Him! Other saints died, and you are living. Quit whining and start living! And the first step to living is recognizing your own sin against God. Stop focusing so much on what has happened to you!

God intended for love to be at the forefront of all we do, especially to our spouse and family, and when we are among the masses. There is a tendency to think work is about work, and love does not enter the workspace. When so engrossed in one's career, one can miss wonderful opportunities to speak and live out the love of God in another's life.

When one exercises, most view this as "personal time," and love does not enter into "personal space." For example, you see someone, but since your focus is on yourself and your workout goals, you pass them by, not knowing that a word of encouragement, or a prayer, could have been timely for their struggle or present trial. You are there, and so are they. Are you loving everyone, everywhere? *Love doesn't take time off and has no boundaries*!

Heck, it could be a warm greeting, saying a few encouraging words, a simple loving glance, or a nod of acknowledgement which could bring joy to them. They respond to your *act* of love, and God is glorified in these moments.

When at the supermarket, the attention is on the task at hand, and love doesn't make it on the list. Numerous times when at the supermarket, I wonder how many disciples there are. If I can tell by the expression of love, then I would say, it's discouraging to see there are only a few. Meaning, many people do not bring love with them, as it stays in the well with a label on it saying, "Open in the event of emergency." Until it is summoned for an immediate need, it stays dormant and inactive.

I am certain this was not how Jesus loved when He walked among the masses. Do you have something special, like an heirloom used by grandma or papa, passed on to you? You have it but only to put it away in a box, never to use again. Yes, I understand the significance of safe-keeping. But was this the only reason they gave it to you? Did you ever ask? I would imagine it would be pleasing to the one who gave it to you for you to use it. In doing so, it would bring them into remembrance. This may be one of the reasons they gave it to you in the first place. They used it all the time! And when we remember, it brings about joy, stories, and conversations. God is no different. He has given us His love to share. God gets the glory when our conversations lead to and are about Him. It brings joy to all three—God, you, and the person involved in the conversation.

God's purpose for love is for us to also encourage and edify one another. God says in Hebrews 10:24, "and let us consider how to stimulate one another to love and good deeds." We are to be mindful of every opportunity where the Spirit of God will lead us to hearts prepared to receive His Word, truth, and love. When we do, it creates an excitement that leads to motivating the hearer to respond to God's call to love and the good works He has ordained for our lives and theirs. We must have our eyes, ears, and hearts opened and be ready to follow and respond to the promptings of God the Holy Spirit.

One day, Bonnie and I had just finished lunch and were coming out of a restaurant. One parking space over sat a young couple in their minivan. The windows were painted with giant white letters: "JUST MARRIED!" They were sitting in their vehicle and looking at their wedding photos. The parking spot next to my vehicle was open, so I could look right into their vehicle, and they looked up and saw me looking at them with a smile.

There must be something said about intentional eye contact. It seems that most of the time, when *intentional* eye contact occurs, each person peering into the eyes of the other, engagement should not be far behind. It only seemed natural to congratulate this newlywed couple. I guess I did have the choice to just get into my car and drive away. I did not know this young couple, nor did we attend their wedding. Regardless, I was compelled to greet them, and the engagement began. This is the power of the Holy Spirit at work in my life. One would think my mission was to go to the young couple to congratulate them on their recent wedding, or just say "congrats," and get in my car. But then, this would make me the generator of the action. No, I began to walk toward them. I had no motive in mind. The Holy Spirit moved me. It is God moving in us!

I approached their vehicle, since their window was down, and stated, "Congratulations and welcome to a unique group of people—married people!" I believe being married—one man and one woman—is a gift from God, and unique these days, since it appears the marriage rate is fifty percent or so, and the divorce rate is reaching seventy percent. So being married, and for a long time *is* a blessing from God!

They both immediately smiled. Anyone who understands the love of God could see this new love beginning to mold and take form. This was a Psalm 139:16 moment, as

> Your eyes have seen my unformed substance;
> And in Your Book were all written
> The days that were ordained for me, When as yet there was not one of them.
>
> Psalm 139:16

their vehicle had not been there when Bonnie and I entered the restaurant. I never saw them drive in and park. They could have just parked and came in to eat, and no engagement would have occurred. So why would God desire for us to meet? Have you experienced these moments and just let them slip by? What do you think would happen if you engaged? One never knows the blessings and works God has ordained for us— that is until we begin to walk in them!

However, they were there when we exited, and it was as though I was drawn to their vehicle. To confirm, this was the first time, and the last, I would encounter and engage with them. As of the writing of this book, I have yet to see them again, BUT GOD ... This moment must have been one of those days and moments written down in the book ordained for us, and for them.

After I congratulated them, they were excited to share photos of this special moment in their lives. They were a handsome couple, and the photos were well done. The photos did two things. First, they were a great reminder of our wedding and of God restoring our marriage! Second, they provided an opportunity to encourage and impart wisdom, as their marriage was a week old, and ours, years. I inquired if their marriage was centered around Jesus. Their eyes and smiles gleamed, and immediately they both responded in unison: "Oh, yes, sir!"

I replied, "PRAISE GOD!" If we are to live out the Word of God in our lives, it should be flowing out of us as richly as it dwells within us.

One of my memory verses is Colossians 3:16-17. It says, "Let the word of Christ richly dwell within you, with all wisdom teaching and admonishing one another with psalms *and* hymns *and* spiritual songs, singing with thankfulness in your hearts to God. Whatever you do in word or deed, do all in the name of the Lord Jesus, giving thanks through Him to God the Father."

I love to disciple those contemplating marriage, those who are married, and those who are married and struggling. I love the response I get when I tell them their love and marriage could be sweeter than they could ever think or imagine. When I make this comment they always seem to be interested; after all, this is a new way of life for them, and it may be a spark needed for others. This newly married couple were no different. We told them that we had been married for over thirty-eight years, and they both said simultaneously, "wow, CONGRATULATIONS!"

My response as I looked at Bonnie was, "BUT GOD," and she smiled and nodded in agreement.

I asked them if they loved each other, and their response was, "Yes, sir, of course!"

"Well," I said, "don't." Immediately they had questionable looks on their faces, as though this genuinely nice guy just turned into a block-head, since I mentioned do not try to love your wife, nor should the wife try to love her husband.

We tried marriage with our own manufactured love and almost destroyed it! Our experiences from childhood made up our love. We both came from parents whose marriages were not centered on Jesus and they had lots of shattered dreams. We took the good and bad of each and then melded it together to set our own standards, conditions and expectations. We made what love was to be to us, and for me, it was a poor example. But it was all I had to go by. I must tell you; it was far from what God said love is, what it's supposed to do, and how it's lived out.

Love constructed by humanity will fail, and the failure rate is extremely high. Actions confirm or refute true love. My expressions of love were driven by my ulterior motives.

Deep inside, I was an angry man. Profanity was a regularity in my speech toward Bonnie. But when I brought flowers or jewelry as a gift, those were loving actions toward her, right? The reality? Intimacy was my motive, not love. I had a heart of stone. How could I love? I needed pleasure and she was the means to accomplish my desires. Regardless of how I treated her, if I gave her something, then I loved her. When I did, I expected—and at times demanded—she love me in return.

When she did not respond to my love actions, I assumed she didn't love me like she said she did. Is this the love God is saying we should have toward others, and them toward us? Are love actions only based on what someone does or gives? Gifts are not the only true indicator of love. On the outside, all would say, "Oh, how loving." Yet God, looking at my heart, says, "Oh, how selfish and evil!"

Scripture says God is love (1 John 4:8). "The Excellencies of Love" are described in 1 Corinthians 13. In a manufactured love—love is what I think it should be, and I set the standards. The truth be known, God is the standard, not me! I damaged my marriage for sure! If God had not rescued us, we would have destroyed our marriage, ourselves, and everything built upon it, our children included. Many spouses do not even consider the magnitude of hurt and pain they cause their children when selfishness and sin consume their life, marriage, and all the relationships they have acquired.

How ridiculous to say do not love your spouse? Well, you see, what happens when you try to love your spouse using your own version of love is you immediately set expectations and standards for the love you give. And it is human nature to believe in reciprocity—whatever is given, something is expected in return. When those expectations and standards are not met, *disappointment* immediately sets in like mud, and you begin to trudge around in your marriage. Have you ever felt like someone has added fifty pounds of caked mud to your Florsheims?

Now here are two people, confessing before God and witnesses they love each other, only to find it is not as deep or sincere as initially thought. Don't! God tells us how to love in Deuteronomy 6:5 and Matthew 22:37. The main points of both passages are, we are to love God with all our heart, soul, mind, and strength. May I ask you, if you are to love God with all your heart, how do you have any love for your spouse? Simply put, you don't.

This is the way we are to love. We love God with all our heart, mind, soul, and strength *through* our spouse, and her *through* you, and the residue of God's love will be more than enough for you both. They looked at each other and smiled. Their smile brought joy to my heart as they understood it would be God's love, and His love never fails!

Before departing, I suggested they print off the passage 1 Corinthians 13:4-8a and put in on the refrigerator. They smiled again. I asked, "Why the smiles?"

They said, "this passage was a part of our marriage vows."

"PRAISE GOD!" I responded. Believe me, it is a great passage to memorize and meditate on, as it is a constant reminder of the love of God, how He loves you, and how we are to love others.

It is on our refrigerator today, and has been referenced, reviewed, and serves as a *constant* reminder for me, Bonnie, and our family! It is centrally located, which in our home is the fridge. Place it on your fridge to serve as a *constant* reminder for you and everyone who sees it, to love others with God's love!

New Creature

Before the Lord saved me, I was oblivious to the love of God and the love Bonnie had for me. We have been married for thirty-nine years, praise God! It would have been easy for me to say that those thirty-nine years were full of love. Unfortunately, they were not. Salvation for me came only sixteen years ago, and if you were doing the math, this is twenty-three years of an unregenerate life, attempting to be a husband and father. I was loving with a self-manufactured love with standards and expectations because I never knew of God's love for me.

New life occurs when God the Holy Spirit regenerates you to new life, and truly life begins in Christ. This is one of God's amazing works, read 2 Corinthians 5:17. It says, "Therefore if anyone is in Christ, *he is* a new creature; the old things passed away; behold, new things have come." How could anyone who does not know or understand the love of God, love like God? The answer is, you couldn't, and you don't.

The only way the love of God becomes visible to those who are interacting with a person saved by the grace of God is by witnessing God's love, characteristics, and attributes in their thoughts, words, and deeds. However, one would have to know of God's love to recognize it and confirm its presence. One could easily deceive themselves and others by the good things they have done and place those things into the "love" category.

This is how one deceives themselves into thinking that they are loving another by giving diamonds, flowers, dinners, and trips. These actions, regardless of the condition of the heart means I love her, right? NO, it doesn't. These good actions are signs of love according to the world. If I did not love her, I wouldn't have done it, right? NO, wrong. I did it because it was the "thing" to do, as my expression of my manu-factured love.

Ask them if you are confident enough and capable of hearing the truth. Would they honestly tell you or withhold the truth in fear of your vengeance, which would be displayed on your face, words, and actions toward them once you found out the truth? Could you handle it? Would you even care enough to want to change the way you love them? Could you change with your own power? I will tell you, you could try, but over time, you will end up right where you started. Ask your spouse ... they will surely tell you! Your behavior changed for a while, but it is "the same ol' you!"

When God's love is not at the center of the relationship and, those actions are completed, numerous expectations and standards are set. When they are not met or exceeded to your satisfaction, disappoint-ment is not far behind for both of you. I know. We lived it.

Only through my new life in Christ and learning of the love God has for me could I see the immense flaws in my idea of love and language. What good is date night on Friday if Monday through Thursday I am not loving her like Christ loves the church! I should love my spouse like Jesus loves me. Are you loving your spouse like Jesus loves you? Again, it may look good and be a loving act to those watching, but what is really happening behind the closed doors of your home, car, work, and on the telephone out of view of the watching world? Would intimacy really be intimate and loving, or is it also just an act of manufactured love? It all looks good on the outside, but inwardly it's full of dead men's bones. It means living a life of hypocrisy, which looks like love on the outside, but on the inside is a heart full of pollution and defilement. In other words, a heart full of selfishness, pride, evil thoughts, greed, and a plethora of other sins.

Many people perform religious rituals. They believe these rituals make them right before God. They also believe these rituals will save them. They go to church on Sunday, because this is what Christians do, only to find God's displeasure in how they are living. They find that

God did not complete His work of salvation and sanctification in them. Their religious actions have been and are futile.

Joined in Love

A marital relationship must have Jesus at the center, bottom, top, front, rear, both sides, and on the inside and out. We must be enveloped in His love. He must be our focus, and our marriage must be built on the love of God for it to survive through trials, flourish, and be as God intended for it to be. This is the only way it will reflect God and be as vibrant as His intimate relationship with His bride, the church. Marriage is a divine institution, a union, designed by God, of two separate people (man and woman), wherein they become one flesh. The bond created in marriage is the highest spiritual bond known to humanity.

There is a difference between the bond between children and parent, as children are the seed of man and the egg of woman. They are pieces of each other, no doubt, and it is proven in their DNA. In children, you can see the transferring of genes and traits from each parent. This is obvious in the physical characteristics of build, eyes, and hair. Look at a set of twins; they are the same, but also vastly different.

In the bonds of marriage ordained by God, God joins together the spirits of a man and a woman. The two become one flesh. Each has their own self, fused together by the power of God. No mixture of the genes and traits. Thus, two separate sets of DNA. Each created being has its own spirit, with no DNA, yet with one flesh. This is an amazing miracle of God in humanity! God creates a supernatural union where the man and woman become a part of each other. In other words, they become infused into each other. The love of God interlocks and is the binding of these two individual creatures in heart, mind, body, and spirit. It makes total sense why the husband is to love His wife the way God intended, because their marriage is a reflection of Himself and the love present in the Trinity. There is a spiritual union bound together in love, and there is no room for selfishness or pride. It is the same principle of total surrender to each other which is present in the Trinity. When Jesus made me a new creature, I was able to examine *my* actions and how I lived as a husband before He saved me. God's love was not at the core of my marriage, or any of my other relationships, for that matter. When I was saved, God gave me a new heart and spirit. He placed His Spirit in me, creating this new creature. I was able to look at my "old man (self)," and the image I saw was very disappointing. I remember asking God, "What did I look like before You saved me?" And what came to my mind was the ugliest ogre I've ever seen. And in His loving voice, He said, "My children do not look like this."

Although I had religion and a self-manufactured love, there was no relationship with Jesus at all, nor was there any love for God and others. My life was *all* self-serving, and the root of sin was continually active and planted very deep in my "old-man's" heart. I remember saying to Bonnie, "There is no such thing as 'unconditional' love in life or marriage."

Marriage is a give and *take* relationship! And I was the taker. I only gave what I deemed her to have. I would expect had she been aware of all of me, she would not have wanted it, or desired to be bound to it for the rest of her life. I was blind, could not see, and did not know it. Not only was I spiritually blind and dumb, but I was dead too.

When the devil blinds you, you are under his influence and power. Believe it or not, you are worshiping him. You are a slave, living in darkness and believing false doctrines and error because you do not know God's truth. You can be deceived so much, and you believe anything, even to the extent of good being evil and evil being good. You may find yourself seeking pleasure through a sexual encounter because pleasure is good and does make one feel good. But, biblically, it is really sin, because sex outside of marriage is fornication if you're not married, and adultery, if you are. Yet one can be so deceived to believe this sex is good when, in fact, the act of sex outside of marriage is evil, and you are living under the influence of the devil.

Why would someone want to have sex outside of marriage? The world would tell you; it's our human nature to seek sex for pleasure. I disagree. It is our sinful nature and we are called to abstain from sex outside of marriage because it is a sin against self, the other person and God. God intended sex for one purpose, to make a human being in His likeness possessing a soul and spirit. It is to be consummated in the bond of marriage. The world will tell you to have sex with anyone and everyone you meet, and if it is good and feels good, do it! Look closely at the media, and, tell me what you see. You cannot see a show or a commercial without the inference of some sexual connotation, be it infidelity, fornication, or homosexuality.

Only after God illuminates your darkness with His marvelous light can you believe and see you were blind. How does one know what's missing if you are blind? You can't! You continue to go about your life, bumping and stumbling around, living by your sense of what you think is the right thing for you to do for yourself, and there is no consideration for others at all. If things do not go your way, everyone has hell to pay. Sound familiar? Do you see it and hear it ... hell? Why would one use the association to hell unless they were *already* living it?

Through the power of the Holy Spirit, I now understand why it is necessary for God the Holy Spirit to renew the mind. Scripture says, in Romans 12:2, "And do not be conformed to this world, but be transformed by the renewing of your mind, so that you may prove what the will of God is, that which is good and acceptable and perfect." I was conformed to the world, living out Satan's deception daily over the course of several years. I was held in captivity by the devil's schemes, plots, and plans.

My mind and heart were distorted and polluted, full of sinful thoughts, bitterness, hatred, and anger. The mind of an unregenerate person, such as I was then, can only manufacture love and create their own definition of it. There is no consideration for others if the truth be known.

You must be completely truthful with yourself and look at your relationships. But remember, when living in deception, you can be deceived to believe those relationships are good, when they are evil.

It's also a challenge to be completely truthful with and about yourself. If one has a distorted or polluted view of self and life, being the seed of Adam, then love—what God defines love as, how it should be, and how it is to be lived out in our daily lives toward God and all who we encounter—would naturally be nonexistent. The fall of man was so consequential, even if one does not have a distorted or polluted view of their self and their life, they still fall under the curse God placed on Adam and Eve, animals, plants, and the ground (Genesis 3:14–19). His judgment is eternal separation. Therefore, in this separation, God's love will not naturally flow through the life of an unsaved person as it would for those who call upon the name of the Lord, trusting in Him for their salvation, and are saved. It is only by the power of God one can live out God's love flowing through them toward God and everyone they meet! Amen?

If anyone asked me before I was saved if I loved Bonnie, my response would have been, "Of course." But Bonnie was saying something totally different. Her perspective was, "Your actions are speaking so loud, I cannot hear a word you're saying." In other words, "You say you love me, but the way you treat, speak, yell, and act toward me and the children is not loving at all."

Saying "I love you" was commonplace for me, yet how I was living and treating her was in direct conflict to what "I love you" really should have meant. In my spiritual blindness, I did not understand what she was really communicating, because, in my perspective (and one's perspective is reality), I was just me. Take it or leave it! I would have checked the box as one who has a loving heart. Hmmm ..., based on my growing in understanding of God's Word, NOT! In fact, this was extremely far from the truth compared to the description of what God says love is and does. My behavior was neither loving nor biblical. How could it be? I was dead, and dead things do not live out the truth of God's Word and works. This is the truth.

Guilty or Free to Go

God's love attributes are evident in His disciples' lives every day, with everybody, everywhere the Spirit leads them. What if the world was going to judge you as a disciple of Jesus? Some who claim to be Christian say they possess and demonstrate God's love attributes. Would the world see you in contempt of the world's practices or in conformity to them? If the sentence was death for the evidence of loving like God, would you be released or condemned? Remember, they would be able to see and hear testimony of what truly is revealed in your heart and lived out daily. I would imagine most would quickly say, "I would be condemned," and freely walk to the gallows for execution. But would you? Would you, if they brought to the witness stand your spouse, children, neighbors, co-workers, employees of establishments, and random people you do not know? Would you be surprised or relieved when they released you and did not condemn you, as you so easily proclaim you are a lover of people as God loves people?

But I must ask you: Have you considered what Jesus would say? He is the One you will be compared to, and you should know, He's the standard, model, and judge. Eternity—either life or death—rests on *His* decision. The love of God must be an *intrinsic* characteristic of your new-self, created in Jesus. It must be in the fabric of your spirituality, which leads to obedient and effective discipleship and living out His command— "Go and make disciples!"

You no longer must try to make love what it should be with your spouse, family, and others, because God's love flows through you to them. Believe me, it is a beautiful phenomenon to live and love like God does. I must testify, Bonnie is not drawn to me because of the changes in my attitude, speech, behavior, and quieter tone. This is the same for my daughters, they are responding to me out of love, and no longer in fear. My life is so much richer for the relationships we all now have that's grounded in the love of God. They all are drawn to Jesus, and now His Spirit is living in me, and He's the One who is irresistible! And *if* Jesus's Spirit is living in me, I am living out His love attributes, and they are flowing through me to others; *then* guilty I would be.

The disciple continually lives a life of love, and this love is for the world, just like God's Word said He loves the world. There is a difference between being a friend of the world and loving the world. If you are a friend to the world, you will see devotion to self, materialism, egotism, pride, lusting, philosophies, and striving continuously for more wealth and the accumulation of possessions. You will find yourself seeking more and more wealth, materialism, prominence, and power, which is the sin of covetousness. These acts, along with the acceptance and practice of sinful living, confirm where your treasure really lies.

The disciple neither loves the world nor the things of it but loves the people and desires to impart the gospel to those who love and are a friend of the world. In 1 John 2:15-16, "Do not love the world nor the things in the world. If anyone loves the world, the love of the Father is not in him. For all that is in the world, the lust of the flesh and the lust of the eyes and the boastful pride of life, is not from the Father, but is from the world." The happiness and pleasures gained are in the things of the world and not in and of God. James 4:4 says, "whoever wishes to be a friend of the world makes himself an enemy of God." If the world sees in you all its worldly attributes then, rest assured, "you are free to go."

To love the people of the world is to communicate the love the only true God of the Bible has for them. We outwardly live out and express our love to God and confirm His love is flowing through us when we preach the gospel of Jesus Christ. Through love, we appeal to God to save them just like He saved us from the attraction and clutches of sin and the captivity of the devil. We pray God will give them a new heart, His Spirit, and He will make them a new creature in Christ. We express the need for repentance, and God will reconcile them to Himself. We know a life full of sin is a sign of spiritual blindness, and we implore God to remove this blindness so they can see His deity, love, wonders, power, beauty, magnificence, radiance, and glory.

In the early days of my salvation, I often wondered why Jesus chose the initial disciples and every disciple since. It must be because His disciples would love people like He loves people. As Jesus's disciple, you can love with His love richly flowing in you and freely through you to others. The world then knows and can identify the true disciples of Jesus by how they love. If one displays no evidence of true love for God and others, then one is not Jesus's disciple. His disciples demonstrate love and patience, consider others more important than themselves, ask and offer forgiveness, and bear, believe, hope, and endure all things. The love of God never fails, and His love flowing through you will never fail, either. You can believe that!

For the first time in my life, there was no need to *try* to love Bonnie, my daughters (Danielle, Lindsey, and Angela), and others. It became a natural characteristic of my life. I began to freely and willingly serve and please Bonnie more than I wanted to please myself. I understood Bonnie was my helper given to me by God, and she was there to help me grow spiritually. No longer did I desire to assert my authority as her husband. I learned I must live with her in an understanding way. That means that when there are disagreements, my way and opinion are no longer the only ones I go by. Her thoughts, ideas, and opinions have value as well, because God has equipped her to be my helper, and help she must!

She could provide valuable input, and I was all ears to hear. She was watching out for my blind spots, and I was willing to listen and heed her advice. We began to live with a genuine perspective of growing in one flesh as God intended. As we continue to live in the flesh, there will be times when we could hurt each other. But we both know and understand our sin against a holy God is far greater than any sin we could commit against each other. I have memorized "The Excellence of Love," and when Bonnie does hurt me, I say to myself, "Love does not take into account a wrong suffered." I still may be hurt, but I am able to freely forgive, which does surely help with the healing. I know that Bonnie would echo my comment. I know, Jesus will not take into account a wrong He suffers by me, and I must imitate Him. This gives me the ability to immediately and freely forgive anybody.

It did take time for her to heal, trust, and see my faithfulness to God and her. There was a lot of time she had to endure my sinfulness, as well as many wounds and some of those were very deep. But God gave me the patience to wait for His work of healing in her heart. My life change was authentic and not a deceiving act of wickedness. She began to witness it was Jesus's Spirit now living in me, and it was truly His work being carried out. Thank You, Jesus! Prayer, reading of God's Word, studying, serving at church and others, pleasure, fun, excitement, happiness, and joy in our marriage became as constant as the sunrise.

We are loving God through each other, and the residue of His love is more than enough for us! I must testify it is true God can restore what the locusts have eaten (Joel 2:25a)! We are a testimony to God's work in a marriage when you fix your eyes on Him and love Him with all your heart!

Love Renewed

It was easy to say I love you, and I had said it so many times by rote before being saved it really had no significant meaning since my actions toward Bonnie and my daughters said something totally different than the words spewing from my mouth. I cannot remember when it started, but we have a family practice to ensure that whenever we part, be it personally or on the telephone, we say, "Love you." And it means so much more because it is purposeful versus just a blurb. Now there is true love for each other. I do not remember who was the first to institute it, but since it is my book, I'll claim it! I hope this made you smile. I do know one thing for certain it is now God's love flowing through me to all of them!

A Prayer for You:

ABBA, I love You and thank You for this day! This is the day the Lord has made, let us rejoice and be glad in it. I thank You for loving me so much, You would send Your Son to die in my place. I know in my heart I was not deserving or entitled to Your love. Yet, You loved me. And when I meditate on it, the thought of Your love for me brings tears to my eyes and heart. I cannot even fathom the magnitude of Your love. I truly see Your amazing grace and marvel at it every day, especially when I see Your will, work, and plans being carried out in my life.

Lord, I pray this section encourages those who desire to know and feel Your agape love for them. I pray You draw them to Jesus so that they will find life in Him. As they look to Jesus, I pray the Holy Spirit will empower them to know Your love for them. They will begin to love themselves, and others as You love them. I know I could never love until You saved me and gave me new heart which possessed Your love and life. Now I am living a life full of love, for You, family, others, and myself. Thank You, Jesus!

This has been a wonderful segment to journey through, as it has continuously reminded me of what my life was like before You saved me. Your love and forgiveness freed me from bitterness, hatred, and anger. These deeply rooted sins consumed my heart. I know, without You, nothing is possible, and by You, all things are possible.

The emphasis You place on love in Your Word is very apparent. I pray You open the eyes and hearts of those reading this book, by the power of God the Holy Spirit to see Your truth in Your Word. I pray You give them the ability to see and hear You. I thank You for giving me the ability to love others and communicate to them, knowing in my heart, soul, mind, and spirit how You love me and have given me the task to speak the truth in love. I thank You for the Holy Spirit and His power, teaching, reproof, correction, and training. This is truly Your amazing grace.

I love You with all my heart, all my soul, all my mind, and all my strength. Touch the lives of all of those who read this book and use it as an instrument to save the life of another so they can learn of Your unfailing love. I ask and pray in Jesus's name, AMEN!

Reflections

THE BIBLE—THE WORD OF GOD

"For the word of God is living and active and sharper than any two-edged sword [...] and able to judge the thoughts and intentions of the heart."
(Hebrews 4:12)

TRUTH OR FICTION?

Unbelievers say stories and fables make up the Bible. They question the Bible's validity and call it fiction. Only with the work of God the Holy Spirit could anyone comprehend what the Bible says and how it applies. They learn of the Lord, the God of Abraham, the God of Isaac, and the God of Jacob (Israel). It is He who provides eyes to see, ears to hear, and understanding.

Unbelievers also claim God does not "speak" through His Word to them. Yet God speaks to Jesus's disciples, and His speech is the disciples' daily bread. Unbelievers cannot understand the truths in it, and they do not know that the author of the Bible is God, the great I AM, Himself. The unbeliever's perspective about those stories is true, believe it or not. There is a story about creation, found in Genesis 1, a story about the creation of man and woman in, Genesis 2, and a story about the fall of man in, Genesis 3. And the stories go on and on and on!

God communicates to humanity about our own depravity. He shows His marvelous works and provides us a context in which we can understand. God communicates how and why this happened. The ruler of this world, Satan, has blinded the minds of the unbelieving. They remain in darkness, prevented from comprehending Jesus's deity and majesty. Jesus brings light to the unbelievers' spiritual darkness and transfers them from the domain of darkness into the kingdom of

God the Father's beloved Son, Jesus Christ. Satan continues to blind as many unbelievers as he can, preventing them from seeing and living out God's work of salvation, the salvation He performs in the lives of His chosen people.

These blinded unbelievers cannot see the wonderful work of the Bible and how the Lord God utilized man to write out what was on the Lord God's heart. The Lord God wanted to communicate how sin entered the world, the consequence of unbelief, and how sin through deception resulted in the fall of man. The Lord God wants humanity to know of His great love for us. He desires to rescue and save us from sin. He is holy, just, and righteous. To die in the sin of unbelief in Jesus Christ results in God's wrath and eternal separation from Him.

How did this happen? Adam and Eve's sin was so severe, it destroyed God's perfect relationship with humanity. When it did, evil had its reign in man and upon the earth. Every person born after Adam and Eve carries this sin. God knew the extent of the captivity and damage sin can have in one's life and in the world. You see it today, and it is more than the heinous acts of people. It is pride, jealousy, hatred, immorality, selfishness, deception, dissension, addictions of all types, and strife. Believe me, there is more, so much more, and you know there is, because you see it every day, everywhere, and in everyone.

You may turn a blind eye to it or put it in the "smh" category. For those non-texters, this means "shaking my head." Yet the action by most is the same: nothing! Sin continues to reign on this earth. You cannot deny sin is at the core of this darkness, and it is destroying everything in its path. Look at the lives of those controlled by sin. You see destruction all around them. When sin is in control within one's heart, it will attempt to destroy one's life and everything associated with it, even one's relationship with God.

Most judge people on their behavior and what they say. And when they do, they place them in the good or evil category. To prove this fact, read Genesis 3:5. This was Satan's promise to Eve. She would gain insight, but it was really deception. The sin was disobedience to God. When she disobeyed God's command, it says, "For God knows that in the day you eat from it your eyes will be opened, and you will be like

God, knowing good and evil." The lie was that she was going to be "like God." But she would be totally unlike God because God is faithful. She, being disobedient by following the promptings of the devil, was unfaithful. Can you see how deceptive sin can be?

There's only one way to escape sin's clutches and the destruction it causes. It is by God's grace and through His Son, Jesus Christ! There is no other way to remove your spiritual blindness. We all need spiritual eyesight to see the love God has for each one of us! He desires for us to enjoy and live out an intimate personal relationship with Him. It will be from now and forever.

Consider comparing something quite common in our everyday lives: reading the book and seeing the movie. Some books make good movies. What is your choice when given the option to read the book or see the movie? You have the same choice: live your life by how man says to live or live according to God's Word. Well, most people would agree that unless you are an avid reader, reading takes time and work. Or you can see the movie in a few hours, letting your eyes and ears do all the work. I've heard many people state, "The book was better than the movie." And why do they say that? Is it because of how the mind creates images, while the movie does all the creating and imagining for you?

Some books read as fiction, and others are true stories. Yet there is the tendency to believe the writer because of their reputation. So what the person (humanity) says is true and believed without any hesitation. It says volumes about one's belief system to know events and people mentioned in the Bible did exist. Historical facts prove this point. Yet so many still do not believe it is true, because they do not know the Author. Sometimes it takes time to process information before taking action. Other times, the action comes long after the reading of it. Some books can be so deep, complex, or cerebral the average reader puts it down and it becomes a dust collector, never to be touched again.

All books—depending on the topic, depth, or simplicity—cause one to think and take action— that is, if one recognizes the *need* to do so. Some books make the reader look at themselves and recognize trends or behaviors. Consider the so-called self-help books, which inspire and motivate the reader. These suggested changes are to make them into a "better person."

If man has produced ways to make a "better person," it only makes perfect sense God would and could, since He is the Creator! Know this: God's intention (plan) since creation was for humanity to be and live like Jesus. This quality of life will change the way we love and live. Man claims that the suggested actions will get you proven results, moving toward a *better* you! God says to live a life according to His Word and truths, imitate His Son, and live a life that is full now and forever!

Movies tend to be real, even though they can be fiction. The mind cannot differentiate between fiction and reality. Why do you think virtual games are so successful? You lock into it, and the images create a "reality" in your mind and come to life. But the truth is, it is only an illusion. But real, nonetheless. If not, why does one act the way they do? Consider this perspective about watching. Those who walked with Jesus saw His works. They could have said—and if they did not say it, they surely were thinking it— "These are amazing works to witness!" It had to be they followed Him everywhere He went. How many people do you know who have seen a movie sequel several times? Why? Then you hear them exclaim, see it, it is an amazing movie! My friend, this perspective and Jesus's work then and now are the same thing! God is still delivering, healing, changing lives, and making disciples!

Those who saw Jesus's works then are like Bonnie today. She, like they, have the same comment two thousand years later: "It is an amazing work of God to witness!" Without her reading, understanding, and believing God's Word, how would she know the work of God? How would she know if His work was real and true in anyone's life? There was one sure point—she saw the work of the devil in me, and it was real and true! You must believe that!

Now, this would make comparison of the two men, my old and new self, quite easy. She was totally in her right to be cautious to believe the testimony of my life change really did happen. She needed to know for sure what God said His work would look like, and if His work was evident in me. Based on her own perspective and experiences, she was probably thinking—oh, he's trying to change so our life together could be better. He's made so many promises in the past and is a manipulator. But they were all lies. Out of all the things he could say, life change was not one I would expect, as leopards do not change their spots! He'll get tired of putting on the show, and when the other shoe drops, I am outta here! I'll wait, and he'll revert to the same guy he was before he made such a claim, *Jesus saved me and changed my life.* I will tell you, that mindset was over sixteen years ago. She finally realized, THERE WAS NO OTHER SHOE! Praise God!

She did find out that Philippians 2:13 was alive in my life. That passage says, "for it is God who is at work in you, both to will and to work for His good pleasure." If God did not make known to her His works through His Word, the Bible, she would not recognize them in me, *nor* in herself. Here's another BUT GOD! God had to save us both. Things that make ya go, Hmmm…

Books, regardless of topic, create a mode of thinking. *Walking, The Way* is no different. It is written for you to stop and think about what your life looks like and how you are living. What are you professing? Do you have an intimate relationship with God? Is your relationship consistent with what God said your life should have? Does your life imitate Jesus's? Do you love others like He loves? Is your life consumed with your own needs, wants, and desires? Are you practicing sin?

That has seemed to be the case in the lives of the unbelieving. They may have read parts of or the entire Bible. They see no evidence of God's work, which is a consequence of unbelief. They put it down, never to pick it up again—that is until God saves them. This, my friend, is the aim of the devil: to keep you from the truth of God so that you can end up in the same pit as him. It would be the same thinking as many criminals have: I'm going to take as many as I can with me when I go. *Reading God's Word makes you THINK!*

I suspect that if God wanted to go cerebral with the writing of the Bible, no one would understand Him at all! If we cannot understand all of God's attributes with our finite minds, how could we understand His writing if He wanted to write the Bible on His intellectual level? The Bible is written in such a way that *all* can understand once He provides understanding of it. God even blesses the reader and the hearer for reading the book of Revelation. However, if you read it very closely, God has a condition: the reader and hearer must "heed" the things written in it. Revelation 1:3 says, "Blessed is he who reads and those who hear the words of the prophecy and heed the things which are written in it; for the time is near." If we are to heed, we are to take notice, pay attention, give regard to, and observe what God says is true and the consequences for unbelief.

I can only speak for myself. Over the course of forty-seven years of my unbelieving life, when I was dead in my trespasses and sin, I did read some of God's Word from time to time, but none of it made an impact on my life; this was the consequence of unbelief for me before Jesus saved me. The evidence was proven by how I was living and practicing sin, and my treatment of others. I only picked it up when God made me a new creature in Christ, and now I can't put it down, nor do I go a day without reading and meditating on it, as it is the source of my daily bread. One of my favorite passages is Psalm 1:2, which says, "But his delight is in the law of the LORD, and in His law he meditates day and night." The more I read and meditate on it; the more God the Holy Spirit illuminates my mind and provides me with more understanding of it. The more I read, the more God's Word influences my thoughts, words, and deeds.

What do you suppose the mechanism is for this action to occur in the mind? All I know is, this is an action performed in the mind with instruction from the heart. This is exactly why God warns us to watch over our hearts, because it is the heart compelling the mind to act. What fills the heart is what soaks the mind. It will either be righteous or unrighteous living; there is no gray area. If righteousness and the Word of God are lived out and flourish in the life of the disciple and others, God's truths come alive in one's life! If unrighteousness floods and saturates the heart, then the unrighteous acts of lust, pride, selfishness, and immorality of all kinds are lived out as judgment through the mind and its members.

This is what authors ask the reader to do, and God is no different. He desires for us to read His Word, and we are to consider everything contained in it. You must consider your actions will define where you stand regarding your belief and your eternity. The Bible reveals how our life on earth should be lived out. The only way to know of it is to read it, in order to see and understand it and *live it*.

How can you believe, it if you do not know what to look for? God still has the heavens and oceans full of undocumented works He performed throughout the history of humanity. Here are two primary subjects in the Bible you should always look for: the workings of God, and the person Jesus Christ. Know this—whatever Jesus says is true, and we can claim all His promises. But I must tell you, pay close attention to His commands, and His warnings too. We must have faith in the works He did, does, and will do, if we are to live in accordance to His Word.

When I read the Bible initially, it was interesting how my mind envisioned the lives of those mentioned. These were ordinary people who were flawed and deficient, angry, liars, adulterers, selfish, weak, murderers, inadequate and despondent just like me. And God used them to accomplish extraordinary things. These were extraordinary acts of righteousness, courage, faith, belief, strength, sacrifice, trust, repentance, obedience, and prayer, and throughout it all, it was about love—theirs for God and His for them. The more I read and grew in spiritual understanding by the power of God the Holy Spirit, the more my attention began to move from the people and events onto what was really happening.

It's God and His work in the lives of His people who loved and had faith in Him alone, and He responded in love and faithfulness to them.

God says His Word is a lamp to our feet and a light to our path. God knows this is a dark world, and we need the light of Jesus Christ to live, work, and walk through it faithfully. If humanity needs a compass to find their way in the light of day because they are directionless, then how important does the compass become to the possessor of it? How much more priceless is the Word of God to the possessor of it because it will take its power, light and truths for you to find your way? The light of Jesus truly illuminates darkness. Knowing this makes me wonder why there are so many who proclaim to be "Christians"—which would make them Jesus's disciple—yet they do not read His Word continually, or at all. The Bible tells of those who proclaimed to be a disciple of

Jesus, and when trials came, or Jesus called for complete surrender, they walked away. Could this be a sign of spiritual ignorance (darkness), or just plain ol' pride causing them to refuse to read, study and meditate on Jesus's words? The real deception? You do not need God and can make it on your own. The truth, you are walking your own way and not following the Good Shepherd. If not following Him, you'll surely end up in a different place than Him.

Consider this: Jesus, who is one with the Father, walked on this earth over two thousand years ago. Do you believe? His desire was the same then as it is now. He watched the initial disciples marvel at the works of God the Father, and He watches today as we marvel at the works of God. He loved us so much He wanted His works to be recorded so we could have His truths, just as they saw and heard. We can read and imagine as the Holy Spirit brings those truths to life! I pray God the Holy Spirit will inspire you to read and live by the Word of God. Remember what Jesus said in Matthew 4:4, "But He answered and said, '"It is written, "MAN SHALL NOT LIVE ON BREAD ALONE, BUT ON EVERY WORD THAT PROCEEDS OUT OF THE MOUTH OF GOD."" How can one live by every word if they do not even read one of them? I will testify that you can't. I expect all who proclaim to be His disciple will be held accountable by Jesus, and I anticipate that no one's excuse, will excuse their disobedience to His communicated and recorded commands. And living by the Word of God *is* one of them!

Safe or Sword?

Before salvation, I was one of the biggest hypocrites claiming to be a Christian. Why? Here's one reason, and believe me there was a plethora of others. I had nine different copies of several different translations of the Bible in my possession. You could find them in the drawer, in boxes, on bookshelves, and on the coffee table, although I never read it, studied it, or followed any instructions in it. However, it gave the impression of my religiosity and we were a "Christian home", right? —Again, sin's deception.

The only time I opened the Bible on the coffee table was to place some important items in it to ensure they were safe. I once put some

Texas Ranger baseball tickets in there, so I could find them when it was time for the game. I even stored important documents in there. It looked like a file folder full of stuff as opposed to what it was really full of—God's Word, truths, and promises. It seemed to be the safe for my stuff because no one else touched it, either. I was a poor example of what a father should have been as a disciple for my family.

This was my life with all I lived through, and I was stuck with and in it, because I didn't know of anything different. I was deceived to believe this was the hand I was dealt, then play it out I must. That perspective, too, is deception. This would be a sign of self-deception, one of the worse kinds. It's not the hand I was dealt; it will be God being glorified in the saving and transformation of my life!

Everyone plays with the same deck, but some have never turned the cards over to see what is written on the back. Close examination would reveal and expose "sin," a well-disguised word, in a subliminal message. But it is only subliminal to you, everyone else who knows, sees it for what it is! You keep playing with sin and you will win. And by win, I mean you will fully live it out. This really leads one down the path of destruction. I was so focused on the face card, I could not see how I was living was about spiritual life or death, leading to eternal separation from God. And I have said time after time, "another card!"

How could I discern what a new life would be? I was so focused on myself—needs, wants, desires, and being all I knew—it occupied my heart and mind. Did I give the impression I was okay on the outside? Yes. But not on the inside. Did I have fun? Yeah, at times, but it did not last. I was never satisfied with anything and never felt fulfillment.

I had a big ol' gaping void right in the middle of my existence. It did not matter what I did, I couldn't fill it. I was a product of my own continuous destructive practice of sin. By the time you attempt to correct it, the foundation has already begun to decay, and the structure is about to collapse. Why do you think that without the power of God so many marriages end in divorce? The damage done is uncorrectable. The judgment of my sin was being lived out in unrighteous living and sinful habits, through my heart, mind, eyes, ears, hands, and feet. When I was lusting, which was the sin in my heart, then the adulterous thoughts entered my mind, and my eyes and feet acted on the sin consuming my heart and flooded my mind. The consequence? My marriage was on the brink of destruction.

I never considered why I had so many copies of the Bible. I had some religion, so if you are religious, you should have a Bible, right? Where was I on the religious scale, with nine of them? I must have been religious, right? Can you see the deceptiveness of sin?

I cannot even remember if I bought them all or some were given to me, but I must have thought the Bible had some magical power. It was only after salvation did I learn of the transforming power of God's Word; the decisiveness and truth of what God is saying *to me*! If you were to see it from a spiritual perspective, it was really God in His mercy surrounding me with His Word. I did not see it then, but it was His lifeline to me. Yet I wanted to continue to tread water in the dark among the sharks, even though His Word was all around me on the surface. What a fool I was to think I could swim out of my darkness when I had lost my bearings and could not see the light at all.

It would take the work of God Himself to reach into the darkness of my *Serengeti* and pull me into His light. Sin is like a lion; it's a predator, looking to devour its prey. It approaches very silently, and when it has its grasp in you, you know it, and death is imminent. Sin will shred you to pieces, just like a lion, when it tears its prey apart. God had to write His Word on the tablet of my heart. This was truly the precursor of what He was going to do in my life. I could then say yes, but also, no. I had no idea of the wonderful works God can do in the life of a person.

The Word of God is more than just a paper weight, or table dressing for appearances, or an accessory to carry. God provided it to make Himself known and to illuminate our minds to sin's corruption, which destroys everything in its path, and I was in it. Know this: if sin can damage one's relationship with God, it can ravage anything, and it will, if you answer its crafty call.

I never seriously considered the power of God's Word and the impact it would have on my life until I began to read it, and the Holy Spirit provided me with understanding of it. It was just a Bible, just words on a page. I do not even remember if I ever called it what it is—the Word of God. God calls His Word "the Sword of the Spirit." It is so sharp it was able to righteously judge my actions, words, deeds, beliefs, theories, opinions, and every evil intention of my heart.

I was spiritually dead and would not have been able to comprehend what God was saying, ever. Not until He saved me. I was spiritually blind, and the truth be known, being spiritually dead, I had no desire to read it anyway. The Bible would have made absolutely clear the full extent of my depravity and, the consequences of it. It would reveal my *only* solution was the Author and Perfecter of my faith, Jesus Christ!

A New Heart and a Renewed Mind

God's Word has the power to renew your mind. I know, I am a recipient of its power! Romans 12:2 says, "And do not be conformed to this world, but be transformed by the renewing of your mind, so that you may prove what the will of God is, that which is good and acceptable and perfect." The heart is at the core of our mind, and they are separate yet inseparable.

If the heart is the core of the mind, then what flows from the heart floods the mind. *If* the heart is corrupt, *then* you should expect corruption. God gave me a new heart. My old heart was corrupt—full of perversion, immorality, distortion, and dishonesty. It was entangled with anger, hatred, bitterness, pride, greed, selfishness, rebellion, and the continuous practice of sin.

What flows from my new heart into my mind is love, a desire to love God more than myself and anything, or anyone else. The Holy Spirit created a hunger for His Word. I found myself loving and serving others. I wanted to be obedient and pleasing to God. My new heart was of flesh, not cold and hard as stone. It influenced my mind to stop pursuing sin, which is opposed to God, and to start living a life conformed to the image of His Son. Thank You, Jesus!

Unless Jesus delivered me from the bondage of sin, it was going to control my mind, and eventually kill me. God in His mercy created a new creature, enabling me to finally change. He enlightened my mind to recognize my sin, the root and cause of it. I could see the damage and destruction it was causing to me and all those around me.

How would one know they are in bondage unless they are free? I needed to saturate my mind with His Word, it was my only *cure* against my addiction to pornography. The constant focus on the Word was the only hope I had to crush my addictions, which were really sin, and their grasp and power in and over my mind.

God gives us a new heart, but we keep the same mind! Therefore, my mind must be renewed to accept and live out these newfound truths of God through my eyes, ears, hands, and feet; and begin to understand everything God says is genuinely good. It changed my evil perception, which was just the opposite, believe that! It was the goodness of God's love flowing from my new heart to Him and others.

God the Holy Spirit created the ability in me to focus on the wonders of His word and work: His love, forgiveness, grace, blessing, protection, and provision. He has given His life for me so I could be free to finally live in and for Him!

Sin is truly death, and life can only be found in Jesus Christ. We may think we can overcome the sin in our life by our own power, but we are being deceived and fooling ourselves. I needed to focus on God and His Word, to not focus on sin at all! This was the only way not to focus on it at *all*! You want to live free? Start focusing on what God says and read Philippians 4:8. You will begin to focus on what God does and not on the sin entangling you!

God's Word reproves the unruly by identifying the hidden or disguised sinful behavior in one's thoughts, words, and deeds. How would one know they are unruly—until they begin living an orderly life? To be unruly is to be disobedient not only to others, but especially to God. How would one know they are disobedient, until they learn obedience? How would one know rebellion, until they learn submission? There are more people seeking freedom from bondage than we could ever imagine. So, how would one know they are in bondage? I hope you said, "not until they are free!"

God and His Word destroyed all the strongholds in my life which prevented me from knowing Him. Strongholds are anything or anyone opposed to the knowledge and works of the only true God. You will encounter these barriers in people, philosophy, traditions, religions, and all the world systems. All are empty deception, schemes of the devil designed to blind the mind to the light and person of Jesus Christ.

Many say the devil does not exist, yet God's Word confirms he does. *If* you believe the lie the works of the devil do not exist, you are continuing to live in this deception, *then* he can continue to blind your mind to the truth. See how sin can be so deceptive, and how the illusion is so believable? And you won't be alone, so it must be true, right?

The devil's work is crafty, duplicitous, and clever. How else could he disguise himself? If you saw him and what he can do in you, you would surely not trust or believe his lies, would you? But the truth is, if God does not complete His mighty work in you, you will! There are only three ways to live: God's, the devil's, or your own. Two of the three, lead you away from God!

If, God does not do His mighty work in you; then, you will surely do what the devil and you think you should do to satisfy your needs, wants, and desires. The devil wins, and YOU LOSE it all!

Look around you. Unbelief is everywhere. God in His infinite wisdom knows we have neither the ability to defeat sin in our lives, nor the capability to defend ourselves from the devil's schemes. The devil creates spiritual battles, attempting to tear down the body of Christ, His church, and to thwart the work of Jesus's disciples in spreading the gospel and being and making disciples from those who were like me, living and worshiping him.

If you recognize the signs of unbelief in your life, repent and ask God to give you a new heart. He can save you from sin's captivity. Experience a renewed mind and begin to love, trust, and have faith in Jesus Christ alone. One more saved life *means* one less life lost.

Captive or Free?

We consider our country a place of freedom, as we can go most anywhere we choose compared to some parts of the world where oppression and confinement are rampant. Yet we are slaves, held in bondage by sin. Sin and its craftiness are prevalent. And because of its cunningness, it's becoming commonplace and it is widely acceptable behavior.

Examine the world with spiritual eyesight, comparing what you see in God's Word to what is happening. Can you see the difference between how God says we are to live, and how our culture today is really living? Can you see greed, pride, power, and selfishness, which amount to idolatry? How about sexual immorality, such as fornication, homosexuality, rape, adultery, and the ease of accessibility to pornography? And then there is jealousy, envy, drunkenness, anger, strife, and dissention. Do you see them, or do you turn a blind eye to it all?

Sin has an undeniable stronghold in the fabric of our culture, attempting to commandeer as much ground as it is allowed. The same happens in people. When one allows sin to become a stronghold in one's life, it wreaks havoc, creates confusion, and causes chaos as it attempts to destroy anything in its path. Ask Bonnie—she will testify to this truth. I was captivated by it, and slowly but surely, if God had not stepped into my darkness, we would have lived its destruction. All I can say is, BUT GOD!

If a disciple of Jesus abandons their duty, responsibility, and obedience to go and make disciples, this disobedience allows sin and deception to continue to flourish, spreading like wildfire. If freely allowed to continue, sin will eventually destroy everything, from the inside out, to the point of non-existence.

Sin's occupation in humanity can become so great and cause so much harm to Jesus's disciples and unbelievers alike, it cries aloud to God for His justice and vengeance. Jesus is a righteous judge and can execute His judgment at any time He deems fit. Rest assured, you are seeing glimpses of it today. Sin has been so rampant in humanity, from the fall of man, it caused God to bring judgment upon the whole earth with a flood.

Two cities were pulverized with sulfur and fire into extinction, leaving no evidence of their existence. Some of the Israelites, held captive by sin, were in the wilderness, and twenty-three thousand fell in one day, while serpents and the destroyer destroyed others. You can find God's warning in Paul's letter to the church in Corinth in 1 Corinthians 10:1–14, titled, "Avoid Israel's Mistakes." As faithful disciples of Jesus, we must do as He commands: "Go therefore and make disciples of all the nations" (Matthew 28:19). And the use of God's Word is our strongest and most reliable offensive weapon. We are called to be *purposeful* in seeking and ministering, thus making disciples to the lost, people like you read about in the preface. Engage, because avoidance, is disobedience to your calling.

As disciples of Jesus, we must stand firm in our faith! We must live out faithfully God's command, mentioned in 1 Corinthians 16:13–14, which says, "Be on the alert, stand firm in the faith, act like men, be strong. Let all that you do be done in love." We must be aware of the deception active amidst us, as it was when Paul wrote his letter to the church in Corinth. Paul warned them of their need to be on watch and not be lulled into complacency, but to keep their footing in defense of the gospel. The same applies to us. We must not sleepwalk. Instead, we must be resilient and fixed on the truth of who Jesus is and what He has done to free the captives held in the bondage and darkness of sin like me.

If you do not fully understand your duty as Jesus's disciple, then I suspect your sword, shield, and helmet are over there somewhere. Our mission is to love with the gospel, donning the armor of God from head to toe, with our sword and shield tightly gripped, pressing onward to the upward call of God in Christ Jesus.

If the disciples God placed in my life took the perspective of there was no hope for me and left me to my sin, then they would not have been doing the will of the Father. Their disobedience to their calling would be addressed by the judge, Him. But they didn't! They responded in love for God and the lost, and God was glorified. They demonstrated obedience to the promptings of the Holy Spirit and lived out the gospel. They preached the truth in love, the Word of God. What is preventing you from being obedient to Jesus's command to make disciples by preaching the gospel with your sword (Word of God) in hand?

You know it, as you see it everywhere you look. We cannot free ourselves. It takes the power of God through Jesus Christ to bring about freedom—and *once* free, *always* free. Look at your life. What is holding you captive? You must be honest with yourself. If you are living a life of deception, then trust those who are telling you! If you cannot move freely about spiritually, you are in captivity! Look to Jesus. He is the only One who can break *every* chain. John 8:36 validates this truth: "So if the Son makes you free, you will be free indeed." If you want to finally live in spiritual freedom, then look to Jesus (Hebrews 12:2)!

Real Time

It is the Word of God. Meditate on this for a moment ...

God through love, provided His living Word for us to have written on our hearts and minds forever. We all read books. Some we keep, but most are either placed on the shelf, in boxes, or discarded. I imagine, someday so will this one. Our minds are the same. Some information is retained for immediate reference, while most is compressed into memory, or some even forgotten. God's spoken Word in written form is for us to read, reread, and refer to all the days of our life, because it is the *living* Word of God.

Jesus's disciples know that when they read, study, and meditate on God's Word, it will not matter the circumstance, event, trial, or season of life. God's Word applies perfectly to everything you are living through in your walk, and His Word never gets old. God is amazing. His Word is in real time, because time as we know it does not apply to Him!

Many people have a family member, grandparent, parent, sibling, teacher, coach, friend, mentor, and/or other disciple who has spoken biblically or provided sound wisdom, causing them to stop what they were doing or saying *and think*. This could be the time for you! *Think*. These disciple's words influenced them to change the way they were perceiving, walking, or living. The disciple's words were so profound when implanted, that when the moment arrived, those words fit, result-ing in the need for *immediate* reflection.

Because of the impact on our lives, whenever we encounter a cir-cumstance, event, or trial, those spoken words come flowing back, causing us again to give attention and *stop and think*. They always relate and cause us to take action, as complacency is not an option. These are words of love, prayer, encouragement, admonishment, inspiration, comfort, rebuke, experience, knowledge, and wisdom which impact us for our own good, and they serve as an oasis, providing refreshment as we journey along the various terrains of life, and could be very parched.

God's Word is no different. We must look to God when we encounter any circumstance, event, or trial. Since God's Word is in real time, it has real-time solutions and wisdom, and it provides understanding and clarity for all our questions. God provides His answer to what we are facing and how we are to live through it. Many want to go to humanity first, which makes me always ask, "Why go to the leaf or the limb when you can go to the root?" I honestly believe that if Jesus wanted us to go somewhere else for what He could provide, He would have told us. I believe that's true!

Jesus says in Matthew 11:28, "**Come to Me**, all who are weary and heavy-laden, and *I will* give you rest" (emphasis added). Why do you think He wants us to come to Him? First, it is God who puts the thoughts in the minds of His creation! He has the power in real time to hear and address everything we, as His disciples, encounter. In Him, "are hidden all the treasures of wisdom and knowledge," (Colossians 2:3).

So if He has *all*, then why go to someone who has so much *less;* not to mention their troubles, which could be more than yours? Why would you expect someone to give you rest in your circumstance, event, or trial, when they may not be at rest themselves? Besides, you are not aware of the sin they could be struggling with or what's consuming their heart. The only advice they should give is just like every disciple before you: GO TO JESUS! Anything short of this, be very, very, cautious.

Jesus is the perfecter of our faith, and the Father has placed all things into Jesus's hands. We must do the same and go to Him, as He is able to do more than we can *ever ask or think*! Read Ephesians 3:20; it confirms this truth: "Now to Him who is able to do far more abundantly beyond all that we ask or think, according to the power that works within us." In other words, God has an infinite comprehensiveness and richness of His love, grace, mercy, peace, comfort, and wisdom, just to name a very few.

Whatever you are in need of, all you must do is follow His command to "Come to Me!" It does not matter how many times we go to draw, there will always be enough to satisfy. It will never be old, will always be fresh, and will apply perfectly to our circumstance, event, or trial in real time! The only point to make here is our time is not His time. We must be cognizant; *all* things happen in God's timing and not our own! Are you willing to wait for Him after you have placed "it" at His feet? When the Spirit of God is living in you, and you see, have witnessed, or are living proof of His work, then you know God is faithful to respond in our time of need in real time. Do you believe?

Boot Camp

Let's look at spiritual growth from a military perspective. When soldiers enlist, they cannot go to battle and skip boot camp, regardless of their physical prowess, mental toughness, or sheer athletic ability. When you become a disciple of Jesus, you are entrusted with the most precious gift you could ever carry, The Word of God.

Ask any soldier who has successfully made it through. In discussing various aspects of military life with Chris (I call him CD, a disciple that's a soldier), I learned of a saying among those who did it: "The quickest way out of it is to **FINISH** it!" That's biblical. Paul talks about *finishing* in his letter to Timothy. You must believe what 2 Timothy 4:7 says, "I have fought the good fight, I have *finished* the course, I have kept the faith" (emphasis added). The soldier is expected to finish and to finish well. God awaits the arrival of His soldiers as they *finish* their mission work as His disciple.

It requires all of yourself for carrying the treasure, and know, it will take all of yourself on the battlefield too. As a disciple of Jesus, you are required by Him to deny yourself for the advancement of the gospel. Luke 9:23 says, "And He was saying to *them* all, 'If anyone wishes to come after Me, he must deny himself, and take up his cross daily and follow Me.'" We are called to live a life of self-denial as His disciple. We learn through God's truth how to endure the hardships of life, just like the soldier learns to endure the hardships of war.

Paul completed the work God had given him with a good conscience. He faced the struggles of spiritual warfare head-on! Just like the soldiers in boot camp, who face the challenges and struggles head-on as they prepare for war. We must be trained in God's Word as our minds are being renewed to help us break the habits of sin. Like the soldier's mind and body are conditioned to function in the capacity of effectiveness, we too are trained in the capacity for spiritual effectiveness.

As with the military, all do not perform the same jobs. They may go through basic training for the "basics," but there is more, so much more to the complexities of it all! CD and I also talked about the demands, sacrifices, relationships, bonding, trust, and immediate and long-lasting effects war can have on your life. It impacts you and those around you differently. The significance of genuine unity is displayed by numerous people from different walks of life coming together to form a solid cohesive unit.

There is a high level of trust flowing freely between each of them; after all, they are responsible and accountable for each other's lives. This aspect of military life is demanding and requires sacrifice. Boot camp must be grueling; physically and mentally because the battles within the war are that! How else could they survive, accomplish the mission, and protect the freedoms so many take advantage of and for granted?

Along with the training is the armor. We see it today in war as equipment: helmet, flak jacket, knife, boots, pack, ammo, etc. Sound familiar? Helmet, breastplate, shield, girdle, shoes, and sword? *If* they need armor to fight the battles within the war, *then* disciples *need* the armor of God to fight the schemes of the devil. God knows we need it, so He commands us to "put on the full armor of God." God addresses our need for His armor, and if you are working as a disciple, you *will* need it! Again, if you do not read His Word, you won't know what it is, and why you will need it! God's armor is battle-tested by Him, and it will fit each disciple perfectly. Wearing the armor of God should provide confidence to follow and live out His Word and faithfully follow the promptings of the Holy Spirit.

So what does this boot camp look like for a disciple of Jesus? I can only speak from my own perspective. It begins with repentance. You learn the truth of the only true God, Jesus Christ and the Holy Spirit. Once you learn the truth you begin to see the error (sin) in your life. You identify the lies you have been living and destroy their stronghold on you. You begin to live by the truth. God now entrusts you to grow in the knowledge of His word and handle it with the utmost care (2 Timothy 1:14). Then you live out your mission of discipleship by teaching others and always being ready to make a defense for the hope that's within you—with the gospel!

I must say, it is difficult to be like Jesus, but it is not impossible. He would not be the standard if we could not attain it! God is gracious and patient, as He knows it will take time for us to break the old habits of sin, and for this new way of living to take shape. There is heart change, which creates the action of the renewing of the mind.

But, my friend, it takes grace, love, faith, obedience, trust, and surrender of my entire life for and to Him! I could only accomplish this way of life through the working and power of the Holy Spirit. He is the drill instructor, if you will, and teaches by providing the means to understand so we can complete the work ordained by God for His disciples.

At first, it is unfamiliar, as I saw myself with a fresh set of eyes. I was not this strong-willed person. I was weak and had no self-control, which was totally opposite to what I thought of myself. At my moment of salvation, on the day ordained for me, Jesus made it evident to me the enormity of my sin. He required me to begin to learn how to die to selfishness and evil desires. No longer could my needs, wants, and desires control what I do and when I do it. It was no longer all about me. It was all about *Him*!

I needed direction. I was lost and had no bearings. The only way out of this captivity and bondage was in and through Jesus. At salvation, God the Holy Spirit created a desire in me to want to change. The truth is, I was tired of living this way, but I did not know how to change. Did I read all kinds of self-help books? Yes. Did they work? No. What I needed was a heart and life change! I needed to read, study, and meditate on God's Word and truths and how they applied to my life for my mind to understand what change would look like and be. God was calling me into an intimate relationship with Him, to be His disciple, and do the will of the Father. I refused to walk by and do nothing but stare!

I took action, learning who Jesus really is, and what He's done to bring salvation to me! This led to a freedom I could not fully understand initially, but there was a freedom from the captivity of sin. The more I grew in my training, the more it became evident I was free to finally live. How could I have communicated the promises of God if I did not read His Word to know what they are? I couldn't, nor could I have lived them out. I would say just because you put on a uniform does not make you a soldier, and a part of His army.

Know this: 2 Timothy 3:16-17 says, "All Scripture is inspired by God and profitable for teaching, for reproof, for correction, for training in righteousness; so that the man of God may be adequate, equipped for every good work." This is the most effective training one could ever undertake, believe me! I pray you consider putting on the armor of God as one of His warriors and get into the fight!

Ephesians 6:11-13 gives you the description of how God will equip you to fight in the spiritual battle. He's calling you to duty, to seek those who are lost, and if you are willing, there's room on the front line for you! I love sharing this passage with my military brothers, it's 2 Timothy 2:4, "No soldier in active service entangles himself in the affairs of everyday life, so that he may please the one who enlisted him as a soldier."

If one possesses the mindset "I'll just remain silent," and that person professes to be a disciple of Jesus, they are deceiving themselves. A faithful disciple that's donning the armor of God possesses a life and works of disciple making, it's that plain and simple. Deficiency with use and experience with the sword of the Spirit confirms the lack of equipping. Then expect fear, avoidance, and complacency to set in. Jesus expects His disciples to *move* in response and defense of the gospel. The idleness of a disciple reflects a posture of hoping the enemy will pass by or pay no attention, as they attempt to blend into the foliage. A subtle reminder: the foliage is the world. This could be a very disastrous posture to take if you are a disciple of Jesus because the consequence of disobedience is discipline. Consider this: inactivity, laziness, apathy, or immobility in following Jesus's command to make disciples is truly disobedience, and in the military, AWOL. If you need a definition of AWOL, Absent WithOut Leave. Thus, you are absent from completing your assigned task as a disciple. You are not following His commands, and it confirms your only concern is for yourself. And you are AWOL!

Any disciple who walks and lives in solitude is easy prey for the enemy. But if they are sowing, teaching, and preaching the gospel, they become moving targets and are harder to hit. When in a group, a member of a community of faith, there is coverage from all sides for your spiritual protection. If one attempts it alone, they have no one. But a community has someone at the front, leading. There is one on each side, watching. And one protecting their rear as they trudge through the trial. As disciples of Jesus, we are active, on the move, with disciples in company. Like the drill instructor makes soldiers, disciples of Jesus make disciples and are accountable to Jesus for their lives, like the drill instructor is accountable to their commander.

There is truly a war going on all around us, and in us as well. Galatians 5:17 confirms this inward spiritual battle: "For the flesh sets its desire against the Spirit, and the Spirit against the flesh; for these are in opposition to one another, so that you may not do the things that you please." I learned that the more I walk in the Spirit, the less my flesh can control me, and I do not live out those sinful desires. Take a moment to look around you with spiritual eyesight. There are casualties everywhere! Will you just keep walking by and do nothing, or will you put on your armor and respond to His call to arms?

The truth, it's intense, an inward and outward war for your soul. It determines whether your soul spends eternity in heaven or hell. So I will ask, are you going to surrender to the enemy and remain in captivity and be paraded around in chains, or FIGHT?

Last Resort, or First Option?

If we are paying close attention and believe what God says in His Word, we know that there is spiritual warfare and it has been going on from the fall of man. Everyone will face battles along their path of life. Battles are within the war, and the most frequent battle raging is one's own sin. It may be easier to blame the devil or others for your sinful nature, but if you are, you're missing the key point: "your" sinful nature. You may be one who claims ignorance or outwardly denies the practice of it, but when faced with God's truths, you will realize you could easily be overtaken if you are not spiritually trained and prepared.

Salvation and damnation are not a game. At stake are your soul and spirit. This war is about eternal life in the presence of God, or eternal death, separated from Him forever. What will determine your eternity is whether you believe in Jesus Christ and know He is the only way to eternal life, and if you do the will of the Father.

The disciple's faithful devotion to serve God comes from love, adoration, and gratitude to Him for what He has done for them. God the Holy Spirit creates a desire in the disciple, and they acquire the ability to read and study His Word, enabling the disciple to grow in the knowledge of God and become a useful vessel to spread the gospel. God the Holy Spirit, through the use of the Bible, provides this knowledge, understanding, and wisdom on the how and what for the battle plans being executed every day in our spiritual warfare as we faithfully carry out Jesus's mission to *"Go and make disciples."*

The dangers and pitfalls of sin and its clutches lead to hopelessness, misery, despair, and anguish, and they can be very destructive to all relationships. It doesn't matter if those relationships are founded in love and on Christ; sin can damage them. It takes the love of God to mend, heal, and repair them, and it's only by the love of God that they can be restored! I know. We are a living example of the saving power of God that mended, healed, repaired, and restored! BUT GOD!

If there are demonic forces mentioned in the Word of God, before and after Jesus's time on earth, you can expect they are present today. If present today, expect either fight, or to surrender and be held captive and become Satan's slave. We must be on guard every day. As a soldier in Jesus's army of disciples, we must be strong in the Lord and the strength of His might and not our own. If we attempt to fight in our own strength, we will be overpowered, as we are vulnerable to deception, traps, and plots, especially if we live apart from God and His truths. Satan's aim is to deceive as many as possible. You can see in the world today that, so many are being deceived to believe there is life apart from God. The enemy desires to fight against the truth of God and continues to attempt to prevent God's kingdom plan of redemption through deception. The devil uses one's lust, pleasure, pride, and a plethora of other sins to distract and hold one captive in the bondage of sin.

The Lord desires for us to read His Word each day, as it provides daily food, sustenance, and nourishment for our spirit, heart, and mind. The daily reading of His Word would be the same as with the first disciples, who spent each day walking and listening to the teaching of their rabbi. There is so much to learn and grow in the knowledge of God for ourselves, others, enemies, and the world.

Jesus said in Matthew 4:4 that, we are to live by every word spoken by God, and the Bible is His *every word*. The Word of God washes away the soot impeding understanding; it is the key mechanism to renewing your mind, thus providing the ability to live out His truth in your daily life. It empowers all disciples to be obedient to their calling. What an amazing promise from God. Read 1 Peter 2:9, it says, "But you are A CHOSEN RACE, A royal PRIESTHOOD, A HOLY NATION, A PEOPLE FOR *God's* OWN POSSESSION, so that you may proclaim the excellencies of Him who has called you out of darkness into His marvelous light;"

If you are a student of the Word of God, you can relate to this statement. Colossians is one of my favorite books! But then again, so is Philippians, but then, so is Ephesians, and Proverbs, Psalms, John, Joshua, Matthew … well, the whole Bible! It would depend on the season of life; as mentioned, God's Word is in *real time*!

The Bible is all about Jesus and His loving words to His people. His disciples sow the seed, and "the seed is the Word of God" (Luke 8:11). Finally, some have said the "middle" of the Bible is Psalm 118:8, which says, "It is better to take refuge in the LORD than to trust in man." Maybe they meant, the "nucleus." What great advice from God, "take refuge in Me!" The Bible has 31,102 verses. So, the "middle" is Psalm 103:1—2, it says, "Bless the Lord, o my soul, and all that is within me, bless His holy name. Bless the Lord, o my soul, and forget none of His benefits;" So you see, it is really *all* about *Him* and not you!

Therefore, God calls us to devotion and reliance on His Word and, His omnipotence, omniscience, and omnipresence. We must fully trust in His sovereign will, unlimited wisdom, forever abounding love, grace, mercy, and power. We walk in faith, trusting in His faithfulness, knowing He is righteous and just and is a rewarder of those who seek

Him. I hope and pray you strongly consider being sharpened by His Word, daily.

If God is going to be your *last resort*, He must be the *first option*! Many times, people scurry about from pillar to post, person to person, seeking either someone to take their side in a dispute, or looking for answers as to the whys of life. Then when they run out of somebodies, they either give up or they come to their senses and turn to God as their last resort.

Just imagine how much better you would be if you **look to God** *as your* **first option** *versus your last resort.*

A Prayer for You:

ABBA, I love You. We have come to the end of another segment of this book. Your Word causes me to focus on the importance of it for living. Learning of You and Your words, it brings to mind how deficient I was with Your truth in my heart and mind. As a result, I was living out the judgment of my sinfulness through my heart, mind, and members. You call us to live out Your Words and way in our lives. When we do, we can see the work of Your Spirit being carried out which causes us to treasure You even more. I am humbled by Your grace and faithfulness to Your Word. I pray this segment will be a useful instrument for You, God the Holy Spirit, and will cause those You are drawing to Jesus to assist them by motivating, convicting, and encouraging Your disciples, and all of those You are preparing to become one. I pray this book is a spark to their hearts and it creates a desire to know who You are, and they will begin to faithfully read, study, and meditate on Your Word daily!

Lord, I ask, that if any of Your disciples are complacent or stagnant in doing Your will and work, You will inspire them to respond in faith to complete the work ordained for them by You! I pray to You, God the Holy Spirit, to stir their hearts and encourage them to look to You as You rekindle the flame that was burning in them when they first heard of *it*. I ask You to make them useful vessels in Your kingdom plan of redemption, as it seems the world is continuing to attempt to suppress Your name.

I know each day You give us instruction on the work that is to be done. I ask You to move mightily in the lives of the mentors, and the mature in Christ, to continue to press on as faithful servants. You are our source of the life we possess in Jesus. Create in them a burning desire to proclaim Your gospel as You wrote it on their hearts on the day of salvation. Make known to them Your promises are true, and the joy they receive from You when they do Your will oh loving Father.

Lord, I pray and ask You to encourage them to walk in a manner worthy of the Lord, and to live a life pleasing to You in all respects. Because of Your work, they will bear fruit in every good work. And by Your Spirit, increase in the knowledge of God. I pray You strengthen them with all power, according to Your glorious might. They will obtain steadfastness and patience with all they encounter. Because of the reality of Your work, they will display the gratitude and joyfully give thanks to the Father. Because they now know the truth of who You are, they will forever know, it was You who qualified us to share in the inheritance of all saints in light. It was You, is You, and will always be You who rescue us from the domain of darkness. And because of Your unfailing love, transferred us into the kingdom of Your beloved Son. It is only through Jesus we have redemption, and the forgiveness of our sins.

May You be glorified in the life of Your disciples. May they live out Colossians 1:28–29: "We proclaim Him, admonishing every man and teaching every man with all wisdom, so that we might present every man complete in Christ. For this purpose also I labor, striving according to His power, which mightily works within me!"

I know in my heart, because You said You do, that Your eyes move to and fro throughout the earth that You would strongly support all of those whose hearts are completely Yours. I pray Your eyes would stop on us. I ask all of this in Jesus's name, AMEN!

Reflections

FAITH...

—

*"if you have **faith** the size of a mustard seed ..." (Matthew 17:20)*

MISPERCEIVED

Faith has been controversial for centuries. Some do not know what, or whom, they should have faith in. Many think faith in themselves and their abilities is enough for them to endure, live, and survive. Some believe faith is derived from religious teachings. Those who are disciples of Jesus Christ believe their faith comes from God. And this is what causes the controversy. As you can see, though these are only a few of the numerous opinions, there must be an absolute answer to how each of us acquire faith, how it works, and how it is applied in our lives. Because if we do not have an absolute answer, we don't know who is right, or who to believe and follow. Based on God's Word, man is flawed. To be frank, God says man is evil. Jesus confirmed this biblical truth in Matthew 7:11, where He says, "if you then, being evil, know how to give good gifts to your children, how much more will your Father who is in heaven give what is good to those who ask Him!" So, I ask you, whose opinion, man's or God's? You choose!

It doesn't even make sense to address the perspective of faith in self. I can only speak for myself. You may have a different opinion about yourself, but I once had faith in myself, and it was one of the worse decisions I ever made. Before I was saved and before God removed my spiritual blindness to see I was lost and dead in my trespasses and sin, I had what I would call a *common* faith. I trusted when I put the key into the ignition that the car would start, the water would flow from the tap, and the light would come on when I flipped the switch. It was far from the spiritual faith God provides. I was living a kinda "self-motivating" faith, so to speak, and my slogan was, "If it is to be, it is up to me." What a blockhead! I never kept one promise I made to myself, and there were failures and broken promises everywhere. I was living a continuously sinful life, and as a result, I was a blind guide, spiritually dead, and did not know it. Now I know faith in self is futile. If we honestly looked at ourselves and our decisions, actions, and words we speak, should anyone else put their faith in us? Wisely, they shouldn't. The truth be known, we would fail them again, time after time.

When one looks at the perspective of religious teachings that are *designed* to bring one to, or *create* faith, these teachings, if not based on biblical truths, can be very deceptive. Once these false teachings become deeply rooted, conflicts create opposition. One's understanding could just be mere confusion about faith because it has not been defined what faith really is since there are so many different perspectives on the face of this earth.

What must a person do to get the truth about faith? There is only one reliable source withstanding the test of time, and it's the living Word of God, the source of man's wisdom. All others fall short. Let's look to what God says about where we get it and how it should work in our lives, because it is a vital gift to our spiritual growth.

The subject of faith has led to wars between nations. It creates conflict between family members and between groups of people all around the world. Some people passionately debate faith, while others converse about it. Some ignore it while others, wanting to go deeper to find answers, complete comprehensive studies and write books to define it for the rest of the masses who are seeking to know more and to know the truth to provide more understanding.

These studies range from faith in God to what faith should look like, to faith and religion, the different types of faith healings, true saving faith, and faith in action in ordinary living. The common consensus is that there are two key elements in the foundation of one's faith: it involves the mind, because it requires one to believe something, and it involves trust, for what one believes is true.

Based on the Word of God, there is but one faith, and this faith is in the only true God in the Bible. This faith depends on one's belief and definition of what they perceive faith really is. It may be easier to establish if someone loves or not, compared to determining if one has a spiritual faith. The real challenge is if one's faith resembles God's definition and expectation of faith without referring to His word as the guide.

People can even recognize a person's behaviors and when they are slipping back into old patterns of conduct, versus if one is living out one's faith. Surely, one could recognize the presence of a grudge being held, and if one is a friend, or foe. But, when it comes to faith and spirituality, this topic strikes at the core of existence and belief for everyone. If you could see the hearts of humanity, you would see that *everyone* wants to know if what they believe is true, and if the nature of their faith will lead them to eternal life. Some believe there's an eternal existence, while God's Word states there will be an existence, and it will be either in God's presence or not.

So the subject of faith raises all kinds of questions, discussions, examinations, disputes, and controversies. At times, these discussions can lead to horrific acts of violence because of one's deep-seated roots of belief. It doesn't matter if it is right or wrong, if it is right to them, and if you oppose, you're an enemy and the conflict has now been created, as someone has to be right. And if they're not in agreement, they fight until the opposition is destroyed.

Many associate faith with religion. I've heard people ask others, "What is your faith?" Their answers are interesting, as most associate their faith with a religious denomination like Methodist, Baptist, Presbyterian, Catholic, Jewish, Islamic, Christian, Lutheran, Orthodox, Buddhist, Hindu, or non-denominational, to name a few.

One must come to the clear understanding regarding faith and religion, as they are two different things entirely. Religion is said to be man, through his works, *striving* to "reach up" and attempting to "earn" his way to God. God seeing these religious works, as good, allows man into His presence—that is, if his good works surpass the bad. Only then God will accept him. Faith is trusting God will do the work of salvation in man's life that God promised He would do. Faith in God is an expectation and belief of what God says will happen; and in believing, one believes even though this faith is not seen, God's work is carried out in their life now and forever. The difference is man doing the work, versus God. This is a significant difference between religion and faith. To confirm it from my perspective, here's the difference.

When I was living as a Catholic, I lived as though the sacraments I completed guaranteed my religious works would be acceptable to God. Heaven was going to be my destiny, and the self-motivated actions performed so that others would see my "Christian" works, would confirm my "Christian-ness." God would see them as "good," because they outweighed the bad I did, although I denied the frequency and extremity, He would allow me into His presence.

Today, my faith totally rests in and on the work of God. I knew how I was living, and that I was deceiving myself to believe I could practice sin, and spend eternity in God's presence. I knew the day Jesus stepped into my darkness, and I knew the very moment I could not save myself, and every bit of my self-righteousness was a filthy rag compared to Jesus. All the "religious work" was really done in vain because pride and selfishness were the motive behind everything I did. It takes Jesus to peel away the deception so one can really see how God sees.

So now I have faith God will do the works He said He would do through Jesus in me, as I live out His works in and through my life. Like Lazarus, I did not come out of my darkness, my grave, until Jesus called my name.

I no longer must work to prove my faith in God; my works prove my faith of God living in me!

So the works of God cause me to believe God will perform all He has promised to me in Jesus. God's love inspires and leads me, and it gives my soul possession of the inheritance in the completed work of Jesus. This gives sustenance to my soul, and I no longer live for the works; I live *because of* the work, enabling me to believe. This work of God causes me to exercise my faith and I am filled with unspeakable joy. Jesus's Spirit dwells in my spirit by spiritual faith, and my soul is filled with the richness, completeness, fullness, fruitfulness, and the finished work of God through Jesus Christ. The reality is, I experience the abundant reality and living with this hope; it becomes the object of my faith.

Those of faith in the only true God believe that God, through love, coming to earth, became a man, giving His life as a substitute for me, because of sin. He came "to seek and to save that which was lost," as it says in Luke 19:10. That my friend, is you and me.

There are numerous perspectives and beliefs of what true life change is, and thus the conflict. For the many who do not have faith or believe in Jesus, who is the only begotten Son of God, become their adversary. And isn't the devil identified as the "adversary" to the disciples of Jesus? Can you see the connection? The result, persecution in the early days of the church; and dissension, wars, imprisonment, and massacres today.

Faith Must Be Exercised

Believe it or not, there are signs of faith actively working in the ease of everyday life. We may not think about it as faith, or realize we use it, but we use faith regularly. Simply put, we exercise *common* faith when sitting in a chair, expecting the support of it as soon as we plop into it. We freely drink water from the tap or fountain, expecting it to be clean because it is clear and odorless. Food prepared and eaten in a restaurant is safe and clean because a sign says employees wash their hands before returning to work. We switch on a light and expect illumination. We insert the key into the ignition, or depress the fob, and the car starts. We use faith daily. Do you want to know why? Because God has given each a measure of faith and it is being used by you, daily.

Here's the proof that answers the question, "Where does it come from and how much do I have?" Romans 12:3c says, "… as God has allotted to each a measure of faith." Measure is an allotment, ration, portion, or amount. In other words, God gives an amount of faith to each human being, individually. God, in His infinite wisdom, provides for each person an allotted portion of faith.

I've researched the Bible everywhere, and nowhere could I find what the measured amount of faith is for each of us. It makes me wonder, though, if the measure is the same for all. I want to say no, but then again it could be, and most do not exercise it. Then again, you see some with great faith, so what is given? Does it grow like the mustard seed? It must, because there are passages in the Bible confirming faith either "grows," as mentioned in 2 Corinthians 10:15, or is "greatly enlarged" (2 Thessalonians 1:3).

Also I couldn't find where the faith God provides is doled out by Him over the course of one's life, thus creating the "growing" aspect. If it was, it would be confirmed in His Word, and it is not in there anywhere. So, the answer is no, it is not doled out. Is it just a sprinkle, since Jesus mentions one should have faith the size of a mustard seed, and it is tiny? Then it is possible it could be just a sprinkle and how we exercise it causes it to grow.

I could, I suspect, since everything is biblical, expect that exercising faith would be the same as with the body and the mind. An unexercised body results in limited strength and little endurance. An unexercised mind results in loss of function. I know for a fact that when I injured my cervical spine from a weightlifting injury, I realized how important exercise is to the muscles, as my left triceps atrophied because of the lack of exercise.

Could faith be the same? I would say, yes, faith is the same. I have lived it out personally, and you will see how God works when we believe and live with complete faith in Him. Since we know it can grow, does it also atrophy from lack of exercise? Could you be missing out on the wonders and works of God because you fail to exercise your spiritual faith? There is no need to exercise your common faith, because you use it every day! It is this spiritual faith we receive from God which must be continuously displayed and lived out. This is an important message for all who proclaim to be Jesus's disciple. Are you exercising your faith in God, or are you just going through the motions, the same as you are doing with your common faith?

You may not recognize that your faith has really begun to atrophy, but then again, this may be one of the reasons you are not seeing the power of God working in your life through your faith in Him! So you keep asking, "Why is God not moving?" But the real question is, "Do you really have faith in Him, so that He will move?" As a result of this gift of spiritual faith, as we move, it confirms our faith and what we believe, and when we move, so does God! This is one reason unbelievers in Jesus Christ will be without excuse of the knowledge of the workings of God— because they have faith, but refuse to believe in Jesus, and God has made faith and His Son evident to every one of us. For those proclaiming that they are disciples of Jesus, the absence of God moving in their lives should cause them to stop and question themselves. Do they truly have the saving work of Jesus in their life, or are they proclaiming that they do, and are not really saved. Does the lack of evidence mean that they are just exercising common faith?

Faith Can Make You Well

Three times, with three different people, each with a different infirmity Jesus healed and carried their infirmity away. With all three, Jesus said the words *go*, *faith*, and *well*. He told them to *go* because they all came to Him. The first message is we must go to Jesus, as He is the source for all healing. It may not be the healing we think it should be, but it will be healing, nonetheless.

I remember when my fellow disciple Keith was having open heart surgery, and his physician said, "I do the work, but God does the healing." That is true for our physical, mental, and spiritual healing. *God does the healing.* It is amazing how when your body gets a wound, whether a paper cut or open heart surgery, the body begins to heal almost immediately with the healing properties placed in us by God. I have learned that we have those same healing properties for the mind as well. If we could come to an understanding, and quit picking the scab off those emotional wounds, they would heal just like the ones to the body. In other words, you can receive healing from Jesus for the sins you committed and those committed against you.

Will there be a scar? Yes. Does it hurt anymore? No. Is the scar a reminder of the event? Yes. Can I move on? Yes, because I believe Jesus can heal anything and anybody, but it takes *faith* in Him. Remember, we do not see things or think of things the way God sees and thinks of them. He is God and we are not. But we can and must go to Him with hope and anticipation of His healing, and it must be without a scintilla of doubt.

True faith in God is demonstrated in our going to Him first in all aspects of our life. It confirms our faith, hope, trust, and belief in Jesus. Have you ever found yourself standing there, peering at all of those around you, wondering, *Who can help me in my dilemma?* There seems to be no one who can give you the healing or remedy you seek, nor can they give you the answers to your questions. Yet you keep seeking *someone* versus finding *the One* you need who will heal you. This great Physician's name is Jesus Christ!

As a result of those people coming to Jesus, He did make them *well.* He restored not only the physical malady in their lives, but also their spiritual condition. Like so many today, it may not have been the total physical healing they wished, yet there was healing in accordance to what God wanted the healing to be. We must learn to live with the will of God in mind for everyone's life. It is not our will, but His will be done.

Jesus left us the example in the Garden of Gethsemane, where He says, in Matthew 26:39, "And He went a little beyond them, and fell on His face and prayed, saying, 'My Father, if it is possible, let this cup pass from Me; yet not as I will, but as You will.'" Many times, we look at the physical, and desire to see healing of the physical as a true sign of God's healing power. As a faithful followers (disciples) of Jesus, we must be careful that our desire is not greater than the desire for the will of the Father to be carried out in and through our lives and the lives of others.

You must know that the spiritual healing is so much more important. This physical body is decaying and will die, yet for selfish reasons, we want to keep it. The only good use for it is the lodging of the Trinity! You know the amazing thing? All believers in Jesus Christ will get a heavenly body because our earthly one is not fit for such a wonderful place. Our body came to life on this earth; it will remain here. Besides, why would God want a body born in sin, captivated by it, flawed, and full of scars? He wouldn't, or He would let us keep it, believe me it's true!

God desires for us to possess a heavenly body, just like His own. He knows how wonderful it is, and John knew it, too. He says in 1 John 3:2, "Beloved, now we are children of God, and it has not appeared as yet what we will be. We know that when He appears, we will be like Him, because we will see Him just as He is." Let go of this physical element of life and begin to live in the spirit. This is where we have full access to God! God's Word says, in John 4:24, "God is spirit, and those who worship Him must worship in spirit and truth." This does not refer to going to church where your singing is your worship! Your worship is your life, how you love, walk, talk, and live as a devoted disciple of Jesus.

God's Work Develops Faith

With so many different views, beliefs, and opinions about faith, we must have one supreme answer, an absolute authority, possessing a well-defined explanation, confirming truth, and ruling out error. You only have two choices: either believe man, who is flawed, or God, who is perfect. Man is influenced by various things, and sin and Satan cannot be ruled out. Therefore, trust only in God's guidance, wisdom, and goodness for any answer to the truth. The same applies here. If you desire to know if what I am saying is true, ask Jesus! There are numerous examples to provide understanding of what faith really is, so those who *desire* to have it, receive it!

Jesus said, "you of little faith." Many times, Jesus was speaking to His disciples, men who were chosen by God and following Him. Hmmm, what does this say about the rest of us? We all start out the same as possessors of little faith. And this spiritual gift of faith is to be active, exercised, growing, and pleasing to God. I suspect today is no different than when Jesus said it. We are those with little faith. Could this mean the examples of faith were the same then as they are now? Yes, it is the same then as it is now. God is the same, and so is everything else. Same sin and same salvation.

How can we remove doubt and speculation, and obtain a faith which removes uncertainties, and replaces them with assurance and conviction? It takes the strength of God through the power of the Holy Spirit. You cannot do it in your own strength. You need the work of the Holy Spirit to respond for you to possess a faith consistent with Jesus's. Jesus's disciples grow in understanding through this spiritual gift of faith. When we receive the gift of faith from the only true God, our life as a disciple reflects the same faith in the Father as Jesus does. This is pleasing to the Father as the works of the Son are being carried out in humanity—His disciples. You!

The Word of God addresses faith. There's a whole chapter on faith, in the book of Hebrews, Chapter 11. Many call this chapter the "Hall of Faith" or the "Heroes of Faith!" Here you will find names of people, and some even nameless, living out acts of faith in the only true God in the Bible. They may be nameless to us, but God knows who they are! Hebrews 11 addresses God's faithfulness and what He accomplishes through His people. There are those who gain approval. All gain understanding and respond in reverence. They obey the commands of God. They look beyond what is seen and trust in God's promises. *They step out in faith.* They all understand that God created the earth and it is not their home. They desire to honor and are faithful to God alone.

There was testing, and those tests reveal the trueness and depth of their faith in God to themselves. Through their trials, they develop confidence and a willingness to endure to honor God. They walk away from sin, and freely leave the things of this world. They look to God and live in accordance with His Word, commands, statutes, ordinances, and commandments. They see and live the wonders and works of the Holy Spirit. The mysteries of God are revealed to them, and God is not ashamed to be called their God.

It is God who's at work in, for, and through them, and that's biblical! This is where Philippians 2:13 would be echoed—God is working. He was the same then as He is now! Hebrews 11 is a faith model for all disciples, a faith displayed in men and women who are of the same nature as you and me. If we live as they lived, we should respond as they responded.

If God is not moving, you must be stationary and not moving in faith. If you are not responding to God in faith, I would hope you have a desire to ask Him why? I have said to so many that when you ask God, you better have a pencil and paper ready to write down *all* He reveals to you. May I give you some advice? If you do it, you are demonstrating faith He's alive, is listening, and will respond. If you think I am foolish, then do not grab the pencil and paper, and this will confirm the inscriptions in the volumes of "the books" about you and your faith. I pray He will reveal Himself, and what you need to do. When He does, respond and do what He says, in *faith*!

FAITH TRIGGERS MOVEMENT

I see one action everyone in Hebrews 11 had in common, and *everyone* did it! I hope you've seen it or see it, as this action is also required of *you*, if you say you believe in the only true God. There is a trust and confidence—in other words, faith. God responds in faithfulness to do what He promises, and that's biblical. Hebrews 10:23 says, "Let us hold fast the confession of our hope without wavering, for He who promised is faithful." Whether you know this promise, or it is the first time you've heard of it, our lives must be lived out as we believe it!

May I say, God continues to amaze me, and I hope you can say the same! Here's the evidence … I was in the editing phase of the book. I was looking for an example to communicate to you how those in Hebrews 11 lived and responded by faith to God. After all, they are called the heroes, and it's human nature to want to imitate your heroes which is why there are dangers and pitfalls of mimicking those who are unbelievers. Although those mentioned and unmentioned are just human, they did respond to God's calling, and in doing so, God completed some amazing works in and through them! And, my fellow disciples, He is the same and will do the same today in you! But that too takes *faith*!

As expected, God provided me with a live example, me. I was at our workout facility on the stationary bike when a disciple came over and got on the bike right next to me. I must tell you; I broke my ankle over thirty years ago, and it required surgery and screws to repair it. As the body decays, the condition of my ankle deteriorates right along with it. At times, it seems to be accelerating at a faster pace. There's tendonitis, inflammation, and extremely limited motion. The stationary bike is always my last resort because the movement causes my ankle to ache the rest of the day, and sometimes even days later.

I normally use the elliptical machine, but on this day, they were full! I had a decision to make either go home or ride the bike and deal with the pain. I suppose I could have just decided to go home, but I didn't. I did not realize at the time the decision to ride was God giving me the opportunity to decide how badly I wanted the answer to my question about how those mentioned throughout the Bible moved in faith. God was going to accomplish two objectives with me: the example I so desired to communicate to you, and a need to encourage a disciple. May I say again, God, You are amazing! I did not realize until it was done that it was a Psalm 139:16 moment for both of us. Do you see isolated moments with people as ordained moments in time? They *are* your Psalm 139:16 moments. I pray that this passage and biblical truth gives you a fresh perspective so that you begin to approach those ordained moments with confidence and *faith*!

As we were pedaling along, we covered several topics ending up on faith. Imagine that! He stated, "Right now, it is like looking at four doors, and asking God which door I should go through, as I do not know what could be on the other side of the door I choose."

My response was, "No! That's not how faith works!" Remember, I was the one looking for the answer about how those in Hebrews 11 responded. Yes, there I was responding to how faith works. God is incredible! I must tell you, before proceeding, we must be attentive to the words coming out of our mouths, because it is God's Word in action. Romans 2:21 says, "you, therefore, who teach another, do you not teach yourself?" I guess the answer with the inspiration of the Holy Spirit, was the answer for him and me as well. Amazing!

Most want God to tell them what to do, or where to go. Faith is walking toward the doors, believing God will lead you to the door He wants you to enter! It requires *stepping out* in faith, *trusting God will be faithful*. We step out, believing and trusting our loving heavenly Father will lead us where He wants us to go! If you are not moving spiritually, this should tell you something about your faith! Are you moving, or standing like the stationary bike, moving but going nowhere?

Take time to read about the life of each one mentioned in Hebrews 11; it will bless your life! A challenge for you, as you read the Word of

God, can you find those not mentioned in the chapter but performing great acts of faith, somewhere else in the Bible? Here are a few
examples which God made evident to me: Abram, a worshiper of idols
before God called Him (you know Him as Abraham), believed and left
his country, family and all he knew, trusting God as he "went forth!"
Abel "brought!" Enoch "walked!" Noah "did!" Moses "responded!"
Rahab "acted!" David "accepted!" Samuel "answered!" Daniel "prayed!"
And Joseph "fled!"

Do you see it? They all *moved*! They *moved* in faith, as they all knew
He who promises is *faithful*! All of them, every single one of them in
the whole Bible! God works out His faithfulness in His people who
move in faith! PRAISE GOD! Do you stand there and just look at the
doors, or do you start "*moving*" and trust God in faith as He leads you to
where He wants you to go?

There were many days I sat
at the table with blank pages in
front of me, contemplating what
I was going to write. Seeking
the Holy Spirit in prayer, I
asked in faith for His guidance
so I could write down what He
inspired me to communicate to
you. In *faith*, I picked up the
pencil and "*moved*," awaiting

The evidence of the Spirit's work

His inspiration and instruction. You see, I hoped with true conviction
that He would respond! And the evidence is the contents of this book.
Every day requires prayer to God the Holy Spirit, as He is the source of
power, instruction, and teaching.

The only true God has provided us Hebrews 11 to give examples of
faith in Him. With so many distractions and deceptions from the truth
throughout history, and when living in an evil world, what should one
believe? Due to so many of these distractions and deceptions, many
manufacture their own beliefs, attempting to become spiritual people.
Or, they believe and follow *any* person who is influential and convincing. This, my friend, is extremely and eternally dangerous. This is exactly

why God intervened and testified about what faith in Him should be and look like when lived out. You can find all the examples you need in God's Word. It was true then and it is true now, but it takes *faith* in and from God to believe!

Crying Out Is Moving

I would like to circle back to the three people mentioned earlier in the section *"Faith Can Make You Well."* Of the three people, there was a man with leprosy, a woman with a hemorrhage, and a man who was born blind. The one I would like to point out is the man with blindness, named Bartimaeus. Both he and his father were blind. Can you imagine the disappointment for a dad to know his son has the same infirmity and will live his whole life in physical darkness? Can you see the parallel? Could it be the same as an unbelieving father and husband, attempting to lead an unbelieving child and spouse? It would be, that is unless God intervenes ...

The mercy of God is revealed to those who are born of those spiritually blind and have no means to learn the truth of God from their own family. This must tug at the mercy cord of God's loving heart. Can you see how it breaks God's heart when children are raised in a home of the unbelieving who are spiritually dead? Can you see why, through faith, being a disciple is so important in our culture today? But I must say, it is no more important than it always has been.

Bartimaeus, because of his faith in the only true God, and God's faithfulness to His own promises, *moved* by crying out with all his heart to God. He lifted his voice to God because he trusted in what he knew was true. And the promise he trusted in was that when the Messiah comes, the eyes of the blind will be opened. Bartimaeus knew he was blind, and God knew it too. Was there more than one blind person during the time Jesus walked? Yes. Did all of those who were blind receive their sight? God's Word says in Matthew 21:14, "And *the* blind and the lame came to Him in the temple, and He healed them." So, not only the blind, but the lame as well. PRAISE GOD!

Could we interpret this as meaning that only the physically blind would see? Yes, we could, but then it would be a limited view of God's work. There are many more who are spiritually blind than physical. God will respond the same to the physical blindness as He did with Bartimaeus and all the others. For those who cry out due to their spiritual blindness, God in His mercy will hear the cry and respond in love providing sight to see Him. And when you trust in the promises of God, Jesus Christ came to save the lost—the spiritually blind are the lost—then you know He came to save you and me, but it will take faith to believe. When you do, know this: He can and will heal you!

Well, I am certain that Bartimaeus heard the buzz of the crowd. Based on his crying out, I would suspect that he was not right next to the road. He may have started there because he was a beggar, but as the crowds grew, he was moved back. In other words, it doesn't matter how far you are from the path, how many people are in front of you, or the buzz of the crowd, Jesus's ear is inclined to hear the cry and He will respond just like He did for Bartimaeus.

This is a Psalm 139:16 moment for Bartimaeus. Psalm 139:16 moments are happening every day, everywhere. I was one and so was Bonnie, and you can be one too! Just like it is for the millions of others, God has ordained the day of salvation to save each one of those who believe in His Son, Jesus Christ. I said previously that I was in God's Word when I was talking about the woman. Well, I am in here again. But for the mercy of God, He would open the blind eyes of this sinner saved by the grace of God.

In our desperation for release from the bondage of sin, others may discourage us because of their lack of faith in God. Know this: Satan can and will use other unbelievers in Jesus, who are really servants of Satan, to attempt to keep you deceived, to keep you in desperation or hopelessness. They will suggest everything except God the Father and Jesus. And every disciple of Jesus will point you away from yourself and unto Him. You can believe that! But we must trust and take refuge in God and not listen to or be influenced by men when the things coming out of their mouth are not biblical. But you must know what is biblical, or you could be easily deceived by a blind guide. And to know what is biblical is to know God's Word because it is the love God has for those in need of healing, and His Word will confirm this truth as well. But you must be a reader of it to know what His promises are to those who desire to be free from the clutches and pitfalls of sin and its deceptions.

You can be a vessel God uses to lead them to Himself. Jesus stopped and called Bartimaeus to Himself. What a blessing. God calls, and the Father draws you to Jesus. This is the work Jesus says of the Father in John 6:44, "No one can come to Me unless the Father who sent Me draws him; and I will raise him up on the last day." See, even the Father is "*moving.*" *Drawing is moving,* and He is *moving* you out of spiritual blindness into the light of Jesus so you can see the truth of who He is. Are you listening for the voice of God? He could be calling you! Do you feel your spirit *moving,* as the Father is *drawing* you to Jesus?

There are times in our lives when all we can do is cry out. Even in the crying out, we *move,* versus just sitting there, doing nothing, murmuring and complaining. Or, we have this superficial hope God would move in our direction, and perform His mighty work in us, when we truly do not believe He will.

Did Jesus know Bartimaeus existed? Yes, He knew; He's God! Could Jesus have walked in the direction of Bartimaeus? Yes, He could have. But what was in Bartimaeus' heart making him respond the way he did? He knew the truth of the Word of God, and he trusted in His promises. The Spirit of God was working. This was confirmed by what Bartimaeus said: "Jesus, Son of David, have mercy on me!" God's ear is attentive to the cry of those who need the mercy of God to come into their lives. If you are one of them, then *cry out* to Him! He will respond to the poor in spirit.

Bartimaeus did not just sit by whining and complaining God was passing by and did nothing for him. He *moved,* and without sight to see Jesus, and with so many in his path, he could not have reached out and touched Him. One could expect with the selfishness of others that no one would have made a path for him to get to Jesus. Most seem only to be concerned about themselves. While others' way of life is so sporadic, there is a great need for discipleship everywhere. So Bartimaeus cried out to God, who has ears to hear those who cry out to Him. Jesus will respond to you—that is if you cry out to Him! You must know and believe this! If you desire to read the blessing of Bartimaeus' life, you can find it in Mark 10:46–52.

These passages are great testimonies to God's miraculous works and saving grace through faith. Can you see the similarity today? There are outcasts in our society everywhere—those who are oppressed and suffering from physical illnesses, or are spiritually blind. God, in His mercy, is saving people every day. Some may say times have changed. Times may have changed, but sin remains, and so does God's amazing grace given through faith in Him. Do you have faith in the only true God? If not, then *cry out!*

If He Said It Would, It Will

Yes, these are aspects of faith, the assurance of what I expect will happen. The three people mentioned above expected if they could get to Jesus, something miraculous would happen. It did! They were sight, healing, and cleanliness. The same applies today: life change will happen when you get to Jesus. There is something separating those three and the others mentioned in Hebrews 11 from the masses today and throughout history. It is their assurance of things hoped for. They honestly believed something miraculous could happen. I know, it happened to me, and it could happen to you! The first step in *moving* is to believe that what God said He would do, He WILL do! He said in Romans 10:13, "for 'Whoever will call on the name of the Lord will be saved.'" And the whoever is anyone; it does not matter where you've been, what you have done or haven't done. *Our God is here to save!*

Jesus broke the chains of bondage and sin and made me free. He gave me the spiritual gift of faith in Him. I began to love Him, my wife, daughters, and others with the love of God. I began to understand how I was to be as a husband. I became the father my children deserved versus the one they had been stuck with. I became an honorable employee, working with integrity, as a testimony to God's work in my life. It demonstrated my belief and love for Him. When Jesus made me His disciple, I began the work of discipling. I freely and lovingly proclaim the power of God. And most importantly, I have an intimate relationship with the only true God through His Son, Jesus Christ.

But so many do not know what Jesus looks like, especially if they have not read the Bible to get a *perfect* picture of Him. However, the reality is so many who proclaim to be Jesus's disciples are not representing the *Christlikeness* which draws people to Him through them. They are just going through the motions so they can go to heaven based on their claim to be Christian. The reality, if the truth be known, they really don't want to go to hell, more than wanted to live in eternity with God. It is utterly amazing when God does move in the heart of a person and it's a divine appointment! True discipleship is not soliciting to add to the kingdom of God; it's God adding to His number day by day those who are being saved! When one has a soliciting mindset, they are doing for self, if the truth be known. When God is using you as His vessel, then it's God as always, doing the work!

When Jesus was walking on the earth, the Bible says the "crowds" followed Him because they saw the works of God and the love He had for them. Are you mixed into the crowd and feel unnoticeable? Are you walking alone down the path of life, just expecting when you arrive at the narrow gate you will have automatic admission because intellectually you know the truth of who Jesus is, but your deeds are void of the Spirit's work and power? They, like us, could not see all the workings of Jesus, but they hoped, and their actions confirmed faith was working. Just like in the above examples, the belief for the expected outcome was real and true, so they *moved*!

God's Word addresses faith's meaning, origin, allotment, nature, works, and resulting actions. May I say that it takes faith to believe everything written in Hebrews chapter 11, and the entire Word of God, for that matter. Yes, it takes faith to believe in the only true God, Jesus Christ whom He has sent, and every word written in the Bible. You have seen what Jesus said in Matthew 4:4. Or, you dismissed it, and turned the page without consideration for it. So, if you did, now go read it, highlight it, and make it a memory verse.

In the life of the disciple of Jesus Christ, the Spirit of God creates a desire for the daily bread from God just like He did for those in the wilderness after He delivered them from bondage. You need daily nourishment for spiritual strength, for your spiritual wellbeing and journey in this dark and evil world. Where else can you get the strength to persevere, endure, work, and survive? God's Word serves as bread, food for our heart, mind, and soul. John 1:1, it says, "In the beginning was the Word," and Jesus is the Word. It is through Him, by the power of the Holy Spirit, that we receive nourishment from His Word, HIM! Jesus said that He Himself is the bread of life, so it only makes sense that if we do not have His physical body like the initial disciples, then we have His Spirit and His words to keep us from being famished throughout this demanding journey of life on this earth.

Sound familiar? You were delivered from bondage, are on a journey to the promised eternal life, while in the world, and you need daily food, just like the Israelites were in need of manna. See the parallel? The Bread of Life is to minister to us as we live out our ordained life as disciples, and this life requires faith to do the work needed to bring the gospel to the lost! Faith in God will require you to step out, and to step out, is to move! If you have not already, know stepping out is the first move of faith, and your movement will take you well beyond whatever you may have felt you could accomplish under your own power and ability.

I will tell you; you will go farther than you could ever think or imagine you could. Faith in God is an incredible gift! It allows you to accomplish work beyond your own expectations and experiences. The next time you read the Bible, look for the "conditional" clauses of God. You may have seen a few of them along the way. I expect the Spirit was prepping you for now, because there are a few hundred of them. Here are a few of them to give you hope. Jeremiah 15:19a states, "Therefore, thus says the Lord, '*If* you return, *then* I will restore you,'"[2] We read in 1 Kings 3:14, "*If* you walk in My ways, keeping My statutes and commandments, as your father David walked, *then* I will prolong your days."

Proverbs 24:14: "Know *that* wisdom is thus for your soul; *If* you find *it, then* there will be a future, And your hope will not be cut off."

---

2 Emphasis added to "if" and "then" in each of the following verses.

1 Corinthians 15:14:	"and *if* Christ has not been raised, *then* our preaching is vain, your faith also is vain."
Galatians 3:29:	"And *if* you belong to Christ, *then* you are Abraham's descendants, heirs according to promise."
Galatians 4:7:	"Therefore you are no longer a slave, but a son; and *if* a son, *then* an heir through God."

Remember, *if* God says it will happen, *then* it will, because God is faithful to keep His promises.

If They Are Asking, You Must Have the Answer

There have been numerous discussions about faith, and normally they raise various questions: What is faith? How does faith apply in my life? Do I have faith? How can I acquire this faith from God? What or whom should I have faith in? Should I have faith in myself? Are all faiths the same? What makes one's faith different than others? Are faith and religion the same thing? What is saving faith? How does blind faith work? There could be hundreds of different ones, and some the same but asked in different ways. The commonality is that they desire to know.

Unbelievers ask good questions. Jesus expects His disciples to respond to their questions as He responded—in love. Jesus answered the questions in His time with a question or an answer. Both can get to the root of the question—that is if they are willing to answer the question.

Jesus knows the spiritual blindness of the unbeliever. They are hurting and misdirected. Every unbeliever in Jesus on the face of this earth needs to hear the gospel. You were or are one. I was one, too. Everyone needs rescuing from the bondage and captivity of sin. And when you live in spiritual blindness, you're separated from God. Spiritual darkness and blindness keep unbelievers from seeing the light of Jesus Christ. If they are asking you these questions, they have a real desire to understand this new life. They are seeking to know the truth about the only true God.

There can be a myriad of answers for the above-mentioned questions. One's answer always depends on what or whom the person asking has their faith in. But the only accurate answer from a disciple of Jesus is faith in the only true God of the Bible. It should cause great concern when anyone has faith resulting from religion or their hope in anyone or anything other than the only true God and His Son, Jesus Christ. The truth be known—they are really living a life of hopelessness.

The gospel is the entire Bible because it all points to Jesus. Yes, the gospel message is about sin, depravity, repentance, grace, and salvation. But the gospel is also about the inquirer. What do they believe? How long have they been asking those questions and of whom? What were some of the answers they received? Did the answers answer their questions? How are they living and why do they want to change? If we disciple the "whole" man, we demonstrate Christlikeness, as Jesus displayed His love for the people, which included their souls. When it is life on life, love for your neighbor, the gospel is being lived out more than it is talked about. Remember as a disciple of Jesus, you are commissioned to answer those questions. You are to answer not only with our minds and mouths, but with our lives as well.

Believe or Be Deceived

It is hoped this segment on faith causes you to pause ... to reflect on what you perceive as your faith, especially as to what and/or whom is the focus of your faith. Take time to read, study, and meditate on Hebrews 11 called, "The Triumphs of Faith." "By Faith" is mentioned twenty-seven times in this chapter. The first mention of faith in God's Word occurs in Genesis 32:10, where Jacob is talking with the Lord, and expresses his unworthiness for the lovingkindness and faithfulness God has shown to him. The final mention of faith occurs in Revelation 22:6, where the apostle John is communicating that the words of Jesus are "faithful and true." Faith is mentioned over three hundred times in the Bible.

One of my memory verses is 2 Corinthians 5:7, "We walk by faith, not by sight." The disciple of Jesus believes by faith that one day we will be at home with the Lord. Second Corinthians 5:8 says, "we are of good courage, I say, and prefer rather to be absent from the body and

> We walk by faith, not by sight.
> 2 Corinthians 5:7

to be at home with the Lord." I know by faith that Jesus is sitting at the right hand of God the Father, and we live with the conviction of dwelling with God forever. Even with burdens and tragedies of life, and the presence of sin, there is an assurance my tent on this planet is only temporary, and there is a dwelling place in eternity prepared for each disciple of Jesus who does the will of the Father. Read John 14:2-3 for a wonderful promise Jesus makes to all His disciples. He has prepared a place in eternity so we can dwell with Him forever! Thank You, Jesus.

Hebrews 11:1 says, "Now faith is the assurance of things hoped for, the conviction of things not seen." Spiritual faith flourishes on the certainty, "the assurance," of things hoped for in Him. Even though the disciples cannot see all God has planned, they do see the workings of His divine mighty right Hand and Spirit in, on, and through their lives. The disciple walks in faith, sharing the *Good News*, the gospel of Jesus Christ with all whom they encounter. The disciple does not know where the seed will land, or which heart is prepared to receive it. In other words, we cannot see God's actual fingerprints, but we believe through faith, as Abraham believed God; it is the workings of His Spirit. God the Holy Spirit's work empowers the disciple through faith. What He said has happened, is happening, and will happen, as written in His Word! It is by the Spirit's work, truth, and teachings we believe and have faith!

Faith is not something we can make up ourselves. We do not receive it from our parents, as with genes or traditions. It is not passed down from generation to generation. Faith is not acquired from our efforts to work and study. We cannot earn it, nor are we entitled to it. It is freely given by God, just like His grace. Because of this, the disciple learns through faith to worship God in spirit and truth. Our lives are an imitation of the lives of the initial disciples, and those who follow us, theirs will imitate ours. Is your faith worth replicating? Faith enables the disciple to understand the creation of the heavens and the earth, and that it was God who created them, as Genesis 1:1 tells us. He spoke it into existence, and no matter how hard a man tries, his efforts will be in vain, as no man born of the seed of Adam, will ever become God.

Faith creates the ability to become steadfast in your theology and doctrine, the same as concrete when it solidifies, and becomes immoveable. The disciple of Jesus Christ becomes immoveable when facing the trials of life, or the many shifts and waves of false doctrines, teachings, and philosophical mumbo jumbo created by Satan as he attempts to attack and invade the truth of God. These falsehoods are designed to distract and deceive all who do not have faith in Jesus Christ … yet. It is an evil effort to distort and an attempt to rob, steal, and destroy what God is accomplishing in and through His disciples. God's divine plan is for disciples to make disciples by sowing the gospel to the lost, which brings His redemptive plan for humanity into fruition.

Faith and Works

Faith has been debated for centuries whether between two disciples of Jesus (Paul and James), leaders from different religions, old and young, wealthy and poor, men and women, parents and children, theologians, and the common man.

People are deceived by the concept of being nice to nice people—doing good works to confirm themselves as religious or spiritual people, or believing that the good they do, from their perspective, outweighs any of the bad or sin in their lives. Thus, they have *earned* the "right" to enter eternal life.

There are many who believe the works they do make them right with God. God, seeing those works, and seeing them as a "good" person, will grant them eternal life. This is where deception impacts a person more than they could ever imagine. Works are important, but it is the motive that differentiates the work of God and man. Humanity's flawed understanding of the gospel occurs when one believes one's works alone are good enough. This confirms that they do not have a true understanding of the gospel at all! They do not realize *their* need for the work of God in their lives.

They do not accept that they are accountable to God, and they lack understanding of the wages of sin. These works neither diminish or remove sin, or its consequences. Those works are fruitless and create a false sense of security of one's eternal life. This may be one of several reasons for the many discussions and debates about faith, and the need for works as one's justification for eternal life.

James and Paul address faith from two different perspectives, yet similar. James says works prove your faith, and Paul says faith comes by grace. James was saying the same thing as Paul! My faith generates the works I do.

For a better understanding of Paul's perspective, read Ephesians 2:10: "For we are His workmanship, created in Christ Jesus for good works, which God prepared beforehand so that we would walk in them." The works we do, prepared by God, are a result of our faith in Him! James says, "For just as the body without *the* spirit is dead, so also faith without works is dead" (James 2:26). James confirm that our faith must be more than mere profession. James was Jesus's brother. I am certain they had conversations as youngsters. James saw and knew what the works of God were. He must have marveled at the fact God was His brother! James lived the works of God himself. He knew there was more to his salvation and eternal life than the claim to be an heir by relationship.

We must see that salvation is more than just religious association. The works of God through man confirm one's faith. There must not be any desire of the heart to be noticed or recognized by others, or for self-gratification. There must be *evidence* of work in making disciples. One's faith is useless or in other words, dead without evidence of the Spirit of God working as the disciple is making disciples. There is no gray area here with God, either. Your faith is alive and working making disciples, or it is useless and dead in just thinking your safe. By safe, your only interest is saving yourself.

Paul says in Ephesians 2:8–9, "For by grace you have been saved through faith; and that not of yourselves, *it is* the gift of God; not as a result of works, so that no one may boast." Paul says that we are saved by grace through faith, and God gives both grace and faith. He does it all! Without the work of the only true God, there is no faith in Him. God's Word confirms this truth in Philippians 1:6: "*For I am* confident of this very thing, that He who began a good work in you will perfect it until the day of Christ Jesus." Thank You, Jesus! The disciple's gratitude for God's work, created new in Christ, the faithfulness of His promises is seen as good. The disciple responds with a heart of gratitude, love, and worship! We understand that without the grace of God and being made alive, we are dead in our trespasses and sin. You can read what Paul says to the church in Ephesus in Ephesians 2:1, and the church in Colossae in Colossians 2:13. The harsh truth is that those spiritually dead are eternally separated from the only true God forever.

James and Paul are both saying the same thing: faith equals work. I believe if Paul were asked about his work, he would testify that this "new man" received a new heart, the Spirit of God, and was saved from spiritual blindness and sin on the Damascus road. The works he completed, such as, starting new churches, discipling new believers, mentoring, writing letters, defending his hope in Jesus, preaching the gospel, and giving his life for the gospel resulted from God's work in and through the Spirit by his faith! Exactly what James was saying: "I will show you my faith by my works" (James 2:18)! This confirms the spiritual gift of faith in the disciple, proclaiming, **faith** *alone*, in **Christ** *alone*!

Faith Comes by Hearing

We know faith comes from God, so how does one get this spiritual gift of faith? This could be the real underlying question when someone asks about faith. The questions they ask disciples may not be as significant as *why* they are asking. It may be some Christlike characteristic they see in the disciple, or it could be the Spirit prompting and preparing the heart (soil) to hear the gospel. We must turn to the most reliable source of truth, God's Word, to confirm how one receives this wonderful gift of spiritual faith. The answer can be found in Romans 10:17: "So faith *comes* from hearing, and hearing by the Word of Christ."

Faith comes from Jesus through the power of the Holy Spirit. The Word of God is the spark or catalyst, and the disciple is how Jesus brings the gospel to the ears of the hearer, just like He did when He was walking, talking, and teaching. This is Jesus's command in action, to hear. Thus, He bestows upon the nonbeliever the ability to hear His Words being spoken to them directly and personally by Him.

Jesus first chooses His disciples, and then He prepares them to preach the gospel. God opens the heart and ears of the hearer to receive

His Word. It is not the words proceeding from the mouth of the disciple causing the conversion—it is the hearing of the Word of God and then His Spirit convicts, leading the sinner to repentance, and conversion occurs.

This was evident in Acts 2, "The Day of Pentecost," when the disciples spoke the Word of God to each hearer in the language with which they would be most familiar. It is an impossibility that the disciples knew each person in attendance, as the scripture says they were "from every nation under heaven" Acts 2:5 says. How could they have known them all? They were from various regions, provinces, and countries. It would have been impossible to have known their birth languages. However, Jesus said, in Mark 10:27, "With people it is impossible, but not with God; for all things are possible with God."

From the observer's perspective, you would have to ask, "How could it be possible each person heard what the disciples were saying in their own birth language?" Being travelers, they had to know different languages to communicate and conduct business.

Others were saying that the disciples must be full of sweet wine. The inability to hear and understand, could be a sign of being spiritually deaf. Because if God had chosen them to hear the gospel, the gospel is what they would have heard. And the ones who did hear were amazed. The gospel brings amazement to the life of the hearer. When you hear the gospel, you can only say, BUT GOD, and my friend, this is when your spiritual faith comes alive!

It is the voice of Jesus by the power of the Holy Spirit that commands the ears and heart to open, thus receiving the truth of God. Jesus says in John 10:27, "My sheep hear My voice, and I know them, and they follow Me." Jesus commands hearing to the spiritually deaf. His command to hear can be found in Matthew 13:9, where He says, "He who has ears, let him hear." Jesus doesn't say "You should listen to what I am saying." He says, "let him hear." I would imagine no one was standing around with their hands over someone else's ears attempting to prevent them from hearing! No, it is a command just like it was for Lazarus: "Lazarus, come forth" (John 11:43). In other words, for those who have been chosen, their ears are opened to hear what I AM is saying! It is by Jesus's authority the ears are spiritually opened to hear His voice, praise God!

The Bible tells another story of God working in the heart of a person; her name was Lydia. Scripture says she was "a worshiper of God, and was listening, and the Lord opened her heart to respond to the things spoken by Paul" (Acts 16:14). Lydia's conversion is written in the Word of God and has been referenced for centuries as proof of God's work. And here, some two thousand years later, it is referenced again in this book. Amazing! Even though our names are not recorded in the Word of God, the disciple has assurance, through Jesus Christ, they will be the recipient of the white stone, with a new name, and our name is written in the Book of Life! Praise God! Philippians 4:3b says, "...whose names are in the book of life."

Is, Was, and Will Always Be God

This would explain why the disciples through faith, preaches the *Good News*, the gospel, wherever they go! Some would believe it is their testimony, but Scripture says, in 1 John 5:11, "And the testimony is this, that God has given us eternal life, and this life is in His Son." This is the testimony of the disciple of Jesus Christ through faith.

> For in it the righteousness of God is revealed from **faith** to **faith**; as it is written, But the righteous man shall live by faith."
>
> Romans 1:17, bold emphasis added.

It is the gospel, the Word of God! The gospel will come out of the mouth of the disciple. Romans 1:16–17 is one of my favorite memory verses, and if you are a disciple of Jesus Christ, it should be one of yours as well! It says, "For I am not ashamed of the gospel, for it is the power of God for salvation to everyone who believes, to the Jew first and also to the Greek. For in it *the* righteousness of God is revealed from faith to faith; as it is written, 'But the righteous *man* shall live by faith.'"

Only the Spirit of God knows the hearts, the good soil, prepared and ready to receive His Word! It is vitally important that the disciples, through faith, not only preach the gospel wherever they go, but also prays for the hearer, that God would bestow the Holy Spirit on them (Acts 8:15). John 15:26 says, "When the Helper comes, whom I will send to you from the Father, *that is* the Spirit of truth who proceeds from the Father, He will testify about Me."

Faith is following Father God with a trusting heart

God will perform all He has promised to us in Jesus Christ. God's Spirit dwells in the disciple by faith, and one's faith is filled with the fullness of God to the measure He desires. It was God's plan for the Father, Jesus, and the Spirit to abide in the life of the disciple, which occurs by faith! The new spirit gets filled with joy, knowing an eternal relationship has been created with God through Jesus Christ. God's love and goodness begin to flow through the life of the new convert, who becomes the next disciple in line to make disciples. The disciple begins to exercise Christlike actions in their new-found faith.

When God saved me in October of 2003, a short time later I was inspired to create a sticker to display an outward sign of my new-found faith! It's what faith means to me! When Jesus abides in the disciple, faith in God is activated and takes root. You come to know the only true God and believe *He is*, apart from those who wonder or speculate if there is a God, and if His Son is Jesus Christ. Faith is beyond the realism of something you can see since the mind evaluates the solidity of existence of what is real by what it can see. Faith brings us to accept those things that cannot be seen. In short, since God cannot be seen, it takes faith to confirm He is alive, and that the gospel is the truth!

Faith guides the belief mechanism to recognize and appreciate the attributes of God, such as God is Spirit, infinite, unchanging, wisdom, power, good, love, mercy, holy, true, just, eternal, omnipotent, omniscient, and omnipresent! These attributes are only known to those who have faith in Him. This knowledge creates a desire to read and study His Word and to live life in accordance with it, creating an authentic and fervent love for God and the desire to please Him. God's people living by faith has been evident throughout the history of the world.

Most importantly, God! It was God and will *always be* God who's at work in the lives of His people! God in His sovereignty will continue to bestow the spiritual gift of faith on His disciples who, by faith, engage the power of God the Holy Spirit, *believe*, and *move!* They will as Hebrews 11 says, "conquer kingdoms, shut the mouth of lions, and perform acts of righteousness." And it was then, it will be now—they will have faith by the power of God the Holy Spirit. By the Spirit, they treasure, clench, and carry the Word of God within their hearts, equipped to share the *Good News* of Jesus Christ (2 Tim 3:16–17)! They follow in Jesus's footsteps and live out through faith "The Great Commission," given in Matthew 28:18–20.

As we reach this point, I will ask you: "what is your faith?" I hope your response will be different than when you answered that question in the past. I hope you see that denomination is knotted to religion and faith is wrought in God. When you respond with your faith fused to God it becomes the "trigger" for a spiritual conversation. Just like Jesus asking a question in response could be acceptable. Because you are really trying to help them see and know the truth of the only true God. This kind of approach allows for better understanding of the "root" of one's belief. *If,* the root is exposed, *then,* a meaningful spiritual discussion could be obtained, leading you both to seeing the work of the Spirit accomplished in and through your life and theirs. Have faith through the power of the Holy Spirit, the gospel is not far behind! Amen?

Please know, a faith filled life is pleasing to God. As you read and cogitate on the following, would your answers line up with what God sees as a life faithful to Him? Am I ... *repenting* of my sinfulness—*seeking* forgiveness from God and others—*loving* God with all my heart—*demonstrating* God's love through me toward others—*surrendering* to Jesus and

A faith that shines in the darkness

His commands—*living* by every word proceeding from the mouth of God—*proving* Jesus is Lord of my life—*treasuring* Him above all things—*walking* by the Spirit—*making* disciples— Know, God expects you to *step out* and *move* in faith?

Are you someone who wondered if God is real and does exist? This may be the time in your life, your season, that you find out ... BUT, it takes **FAITH**, and then *MOVE*!

My encouragement to you: *you will be exactly where God wants you to be, when He wants you to be there, even if it's upside down against that wall over there!* DO you **BELIEVE** and have *FAITH?*

A Prayer for You:

ABBA, I love You and thank You for today. This may be the segment of all segments because of the emphasis You place on faith. It's apparent You expect all who believe in You must have an unwavering faith. The faith You give is true with the assurance of things hoped for, and all our hope is in Jesus. When we hope in Him, we will never be disappointed. I lift up every reader to You today in faith, knowing You can do a mighty work in them, as You have done in me. Give them the faith to believe in You. Ignite the faith in those who are not living by the faith You have given them as You desire them to live as Your faithful disciple. I know how my life has changed from the faith You have given me in You. I know in my heart that it is by faith I have been saved through Your grace. Thank You for this saving faith, my new life, which only happened in and through the life and work of Jesus.

ABBA, You know all things, and You know who it will be reading this work. Through faith I pray it will be Your voice through the words on these pages bringing the truth of what You have said to Your disciples then and now. I ask You to demonstrate Your faithfulness; open their ears and hearts and bring life to those who are spiritually dead. Give them the ability to have the spiritual faith to believe. You can do all things, and nothing is impossible for You. You promise, that if we ask anything in Jesus's name, You will do it. Therefore, today, I claim this wonderful promise that You will bring hope to the hopeless, strength to the weak, life to the dead, belief to those living in unbelief, and true spiritual faith to the unfaithful. Send forth Your Spirit today into their lives as their eyes are reading these words. I ask all this in faith and the finished work of Jesus, amen.

Reflections

GOD THE HOLY SPIRIT...

———

"But the Helper, the Holy Spirit, whom the Father will send in My name, He will teach you all things..." (John 14:26)

JESUS IS THE STANDARD

There is no question, Jesus is at the center and focus of His disciple's life, as He should be, since God's Word clearly commands that we will be conformed to the image of His Son. You can find this truth in Romans 8:29. To imitate, one must *constantly*, with purpose, observe to replicate accurately, authentically and repeatedly. With the depth of His words and richness, wisdom, power, knowledge, mercy, grace, forgiveness, and love, it takes more than a few times to get it right; it takes years, if granted, to live out the image of Jesus in your own life.

In other words, once you become a new creature in Christ, you gain the capacity for Jesus's characteristics to become alive and begin to work—the amazing change of being controlled by sin to being in unity with God. Christ's characteristics are as natural in us as breathing; you do not consciously think about breathing, but it happens. Jesus's characteristics become the same in His disciples; you do them without thinking. Loving and serving Jesus by reading, studying, and meditating on His Word may be one of the wisest endeavors you undertake. Studying and imitating *the way* He loves, shows faithfulness, walks, talks, serves, worships, prays, obeys, sacrifices, and lives out the truth are actions the Holy Spirit uses in us to glorify the Father. He is "the way, and the truth, and the life" (John 14:6).

Jesus is the perfect example, and you should be so thankful for His life and sacrifice. What a wonderful thought and blessing, for God foreknew and predestined us to be conformed to the image of Jesus (Romans 8:29). It *was God, is God and will always be God* doing the work, making us like Him (Philippians 1:6). The disciple is commanded to be obedient to God's Word and live out Hebrews 12:2, "fixing our eyes on Jesus ..." There is no question that the deeper the disciple grows in understanding of God's Word, the clearer it becomes that the ability to keep or fix your eyes can only happen by the *power* of God the Holy Spirit! Without His *power* enabling us to fix our eyes on Jesus, we would look at something else—it's in our fallen nature.

The Possessor of the Power

In our Christian culture today, there is a person who does not seem to get the adoration He is so deserving of *all* the work He performs in every disciple. First, you must know and believe, He is God. As God, He *helps, seals, guards, counsels, grants salvation, guides, intercedes, regenerates, baptizes, convicts, provides power, reveals, indwells, advocates, sanctifies, comforts, witnesses, inspires, testifies, gives gifts, and teaches.* This person is God the Holy Spirit! Biblically, without God the Holy Spirit living and working in you, you are not saved and incapable of possessing the evidence of His work and entering the kingdom of God.

Jesus knows His disciples yearn for total dependence on Him, as He is our God, Master, Rabbi, Teacher, Mentor, Lord, Christ, and Savior! Jesus and the Spirit walked with the first disciples and knew their hearts because He had chosen them. John 15:16 confirms this truth. He knew their needs and they desired to be with Him. After all, He is God. I desired to walk with God, and I hope you do as well! God has given me the opportunity to walk with Him, and I must say that this has been the most exciting and amazing time in my whole life, including the sixteen years of being saved!

Psalm 37:4 is a promise I have claimed, and it is true in my life by the work of God the Holy Spirit. It says, "Delight yourself in the Lord; and He will give you the desires of your heart." Believe me, it is wonderful to be saved and free from the bondage of sin. But walking with God, man, I am inspired and exhilarated! He has set me on fire to do the will of the Father.

I wonder what Enoch thought and felt as he walked with God for three hundred years (Genesis 5:22)! Imagine walking with God for three hundred years. The intimacy, conversations, inspiration, growth, challenges, and blessings he received from God for three hundred years! God was so pleased with His relationship with Enoch, Enoch never died. Hebrews 11:5 says, "... GOD TOOK HIM UP;" With the writing of *Walking, The Way*, I have been walking with God for two years now, and all I can say is, BUT GOD!

As His disciples, we should live in confidence of Jesus's promise He would never leave, fail, or forsake His own (Deuteronomy 31:6; Hebrews 13:5). What an incredible promise to believe, know, and have faith in. Regardless, God will *always* be in us! Jesus knows the realm we live in and our hearts. It would be impossible for us to tarry, be faithful, stay on task, and overcome temptation, trials, weakness, death and conquer them all—without the Helper! God the Holy Spirit sustains, teaches, provides direction, enlightens, intercedes, and provides the *power* needed to press on. God the Holy Spirit is the power, we see and find Him leading, sending, filling, walking, and living. The following passages confirm this truth of how the Spirit works in and through the disciples of Jesus:[3]

"But I say, walk by the Spirit, and you will not carry out the desire of the flesh."

Galatians 5:16

Led:

Matthew 4:1
"Then Jesus was *led up by the Spirit* into the wilderness to be tempted by the devil."

Romans 8:14
"For all who are being *led by the Spirit* of God, these are sons of God."

Galatians 5:18
"But if you are *led by the Spirit*, you are not under the Law."

---

3   Emphasis added bold and initialize

Filled:

Acts 9:17

"So Ananias departed and entered the house, and after laying his hands on him said, "'Brother Saul, the Lord Jesus, who appeared to you on the road by which you were coming, has sent me so that you may regain your sight and be *filled with the Holy Spirit*.'"

Walk:

Galatians 5:16

"But I say, *walk by the Spirit*, and you will not carry out the desire of the flesh."

Live:

Galatians 5:25

"If we *live by the Spirit*, let us also walk by the Spirit."

Sent:

Acts 13:4

"So, being *sent out by the Holy Spirit*, they went down to Seleucia and from there they sailed to Cyprus."

This is where you can find the promise you are the recipient of the power from the Holy Spirit. Two things happen: the power of God puts the Spirit in you, and the power becomes available to you as the Spirit leads you. Jesus said in Acts 1:8a, "you will receive power when the Holy Spirit has come upon you."

I hope you really grasp this point: it doesn't matter if you are the smartest, most intellectual, or run—of—the—mill person. It will not rest on your "persuasive words of wisdom, but in demonstration of the Spirit and of power" (1 Corinthians 2:4). What is this power for, and how does the Spirit utilize it in the disciple? No one can accomplish making disciples and doing the will of the Father without the power of God the Holy Spirit. It was only by the power of the Holy Spirit that the initial disciples became witnesses of Jesus "in Jerusalem, and in all of Judea and Samaria, and even to the remotest part of the earth" (Acts 1:8). This is why there are disciples today. It is by the power of the Holy Spirit.

Living by the Spirit is the way of life for the disciple. The Holy Spirit is the power source for living a godly life. It is by His power and direction the disciple gets their bearings for how to live in accordance to God's Word. The disciple relinquishes control, in humility, surrendering their life to God the Holy Spirit. Living by the Spirit allows the disciple to live a life of freedom, freedom from a work-based religiosity to a faith-based Spirit-filled life. There is no gray area here, either. It is pride or humility, control or surrender, bondage or freedom. You can either attempt to control yourself or give up control to God and live a life of freedom from yourself and the sin that so easily entangles.

This regenerated life, directed by the Holy Spirit, lives out all Jesus intended for our living, worshiping, and doing the will of the Father. Galatians 5:1 reminds us we are free, no longer subject to slavery's yoke. One morning at the workout facility, Matt introduced himself and said, "I like your energy!" Believe me, I look forward to having a discussion with him some day, as I have learned that all things are in God's timing. I anticipate Matt and I will have some dialogue. What I suppose has happened is, Matt has been watching me. I am inspired to speak to several different men in the mornings before, during, and after my workout. Yes, I guess I could be so focused on myself and my goals that I could just ignore all the souls around me. But not! I am interested in where God the Holy Spirit is leading me, and you know, there have been some wonderful opportunities lived out because my eyes, ears, and heart are open to the Spirit's promptings. Some of our conversations were spiritual, and some just greetings, as the power of the Holy Spirit is working in me, PRAISE GOD!

Remember, being like Jesus becomes as natural as breathing! Yes, it is energy all right. What Matt was saying is, the same power is in you, and it is evident. Thank You, Jesus! One of my favorite passages is Colossians 1:28-29; you have seen it in my prayer for you. You see, it is the POWER of God the Holy Spirit working actively in me!

Without the Holy Spirit's power working in my life after salvation, I would have been trapped in the past, unable to break free from sin's rule and living out all the desires of my flesh. They both held me captive and in bondage for years. The Holy Spirit's *power* gives me the ability to look to Jesus continuously, and to read, study, and meditate on God's Word. So now, I reach forward toward the upward call of God in Jesus. It is by His power and work, giving me the ability to focus on others and not on myself. I now possess the ability to love God, others, and myself as Jesus loves the Father and others.

The Third Person

Scripture says that in the beginning, the Spirit of God was moving over the surface of the waters. The Spirit was moving from the beginning. Genesis 1:2 says, "The earth was formless and void, and darkness was over the surface of the deep, and the Spirit of God was moving over the surface of the waters." God the Holy Spirit was actively involved in creation. The Spirit *moves*. Although the Word of God mentions the Spirit of God, in fact, the Spirit of God is God the Holy Spirit. He is a divine Person of the Trinity. A Person who is co-equal, infinite, constant companion, holy, omnipresent, omniscient, and omnipotent.

He's a real Person with real characteristics, personality, and emotions. He loves and has a mind, emotions, and hurts; He experiences joy, can be disappointed, experiences happiness and sadness, moves, celebrates, hears, speaks, grieves, is quenched, and possesses His own thoughts and will. Hebrews 2:4 confirms the gifts we receive are provided by God the Holy Spirit, "according to His own will."

God says, "no one can say, 'Jesus is Lord,' except by the Holy Spirit" (1 Corinthians 12:3). Why is this statement by God so especially important for Jesus's disciples to understand? The short answer is that God told us there would be false prophets and teachers in this world. One must be incredibly careful to discern between truth and error.

Expect deception from false prophets and teachers. They can be so convincing, if one is deficient in the truths of the only true God and Jesus Christ, they will be tricked. False professors and teachers use prestige, reputation, status, manipulation, and influence. Their words sound like truth to mislead and deceive. These are powerful delusions of the truth, but these are error when compared to the truth of God's Word. These false professors and teachers are instruments of Satan. Matthew 24:24 says, "For false Christs and false prophets will arise and will show great signs and wonders, so as to mislead, if possible, even the elect."

But for the power of God the Holy Spirit, those in whom God places His Spirit in are not deceived. God gives His discernment and under-standing to distinguish between truth and empty deception. Praise God! This deception is dangerous. Consider your loved ones. What is their exposure? We must be very watchful and heed Jesus's warnings. We must scrutinize everything preached! Compare it to God's Word, especially if you are not familiar with certain passages. And if it is error, you now must decide if you are going to believe what God says or man. Are you going to trust God or follow man because of his reputation, influence, or a large mass of people are following them? There is no gray area here, either. Know, the unbelieving are already misled. Therefore, it is only a true confession of faith in saying Jesus is Lord. This only happens by the power of God the Holy Spirit. Jesus's disciples live by what He commands, and Jesus is Lord of their life.

All disciples are given the Spirit of God to perform the work needed to edify and benefit the body of Christ, the church (1 Corinthians 12:7). God the Holy Spirit provides gifts to God's chosen people, as He wills, in the form of faith, wisdom, knowledge, healing, miracles, prophecy, distinguishing of spirits, and various kinds of tongues and interpretations (1 Corinthians 12:6–11). These gifts are carried out in acts of service, teaching, exhortation, mercy, administration, and giving.

I would like to share how God the Holy Spirit's power works in us. You may be able to relate, confirming the Spirit's power and work in you. You are meeting with someone—it may be as you are discipling, or just having dialogue with a person—and the discussion leads to a spiri-tual conversation. There comes a need to mention a passage or several passages of scripture so applicable to the discussion. You really desire to share with them for this circumstance, event or trial. However, for the life of you, you cannot seem to bring the verse to mind. Yet, at the appropriate time, God the Holy Spirit quickens your mind, and brings it to remembrance for you to share.

Here's a major benefit of reading, studying, and meditating on God's Word. God the Holy Spirit inspires memorization and He uses those memorized passages in your life and in the lives of others. I remember when I first started memorizing passages. God wanted me to know and keep His promises, like Proverbs 3:5–6; "Trust in the Lord with all your heart and do not lean on your own understanding. In all your ways acknowledge Him, and He will make your paths straight." Ezekiel 36:26–27, you'll see it! Isaiah 41:10, and 2 Corinthians 5:17 are the first three I memorized. More times than not, those passages are exactly what is needed to be said and most importantly heard. Have you ever experienced this work by God the Holy Spirit? Then I would hope you are saying with me, "God the Holy Spirit, You are AMAZING!" This, along with so many actions performed by Him, makes me wonder how this work could be completed if the Helper was not working. I would say it is impossible. God the Holy Spirit is constantly working, seven days a week, twenty-four hours a day. God, in His great wisdom and foreknowledge, knows *all* disciples need the Helper to function effectively and to do the will of the Father.

The Bible says, "the Spirit searches all things, even the depths of God" (1 Corinthians 2:10). The Holy Spirit knows the innermost thoughts of God, and He responds. The Spirit of God lives in the disciple, as stated in Ezekiel 36:26–27. God puts a new spirit in us and His Spirit. One sure fact of life transformation in the disciple is the indwelling Spirit of God.

The Spirit of God knows the thoughts of God. The Spirit *moves* causing the disciple to *move*. It could be said this way: with God, no asking is required! God only needs to think it, and action occurs. When God is thinking of you and wants you to move, *you move!* Have you ever considered the thought of the only true God thinking about you? Meditate on this: God is thinking about you personally, and He desires you to be like Jesus in someone's life. He knows when and where you will carry out His message to inspire a fellow disciple, pray, encourage, and share the gospel to a heart prepared to receive it.

This may be a simplistic way of seeing the thoughts of God working in the life of His disciples. Stick out your hand in front of you. As you look at your fingers and want them to wiggle, you cause them to move by specifically thinking, right? You made them move by just thinking about it. The same is as with God. He thinks it, and the Spirit of God, knowing His thoughts, moves. This could provide an explanation as to why you move when you had no intention of moving or going, yet you did.

Here are some examples of the Spirit of God moving when you least expected Him to move you.

> Most habitually go the same way to work. This day, you take a different route to work. When you do, you meet ...

> You normally go to lunch about the same time every day, yet you go at a different time, and this happens ...

> You typically sit in the same place at church, but you sit over there, and meet a person who is in need of prayer ...

Hence, you moved when you did not even intend to. You see, God thinks it, and the Spirit and you *move* in unison. Why? The Spirit of God is living in you, and you are the vessel God uses to touch the lives of humanity.

I know when you look back on your life you can see the thoughts of God being carried out in you and in the lives of others. Take some time today to reflect deeply on this. The fact, the only true God has you on His mind, in His thoughts, for you to accomplish His will in someone else's life and yours is truly *amazing*! Do you agree? Just think of all the work ordained for you as a disciple of Jesus moving by the thoughts of God and the power of the Holy Spirit.

It is reassuring to know Jesus's request of the Father and promise to us is to have the Spirit of God living in His disciples forever! John 14:16 confirms, "I will ask the Father, and He will give you another Helper, that He may be with you forever." He will perform the same function and purpose, providing the disciple the ability to carry out the work ordained by God, forever.

Walk, do not run. Scripture commands us to walk by the Spirit. It is especially important to walk by the Spirit, so as not to carry out the desires of the flesh. When I read Galatians 5:16, it gave me a tremendous amount of hope and confidence. You read my struggles in the preface. I needed help and guidance to walk by the Spirit and crucify the sin in my life. Many times before I tried ... believe I did. But I failed because I was so weak as I was living in the flesh. Knowing the potential always exists to sin because of the flesh, the Holy Spirit gives me the ability to see and acknowledge that there is no life in sin, only death. I can act in response to the Spirit's influence in my life. Do I have choices? Yes, I do. But out of love, I desire to remain faithful to God in response to His love for me. I found over the years that I have become more aware of my sin, and take immediate action to avoid it. But when I do sin, I know God's love for me far outweighs the pleasures of sin, and I repent of my sinfulness. I know He is a forgiving God, and I make a conscious effort to sin less and less and to live a life pleasing to Him, more and more.

There's an enormous difference between walking by the Spirit and carrying out the desires of the flesh. This really illuminated my mind. When I saw the deeds of the flesh, and these deeds were so prevalent in my life, it brought joy and gratitude, knowing I was free from sin's captivity by Jesus's deliverance.

After salvation, I learned from Galatians 5:24, I must crucify these deeds daily for it, sin, to lose its power over me. First Corinthians 15:31 calls for me to die daily. I must not feed the desires of my flesh: pride, selfishness, greed, power, and lusting of all kinds. It could be easy to deny the presence of sin, but it requires you by the power of the Holy Spirit to truthfully analyze yourself. Know any sin in your life is not pleasing to God and must be crucified. It was my sin holding Jesus on the cross, and by His stripes, I was healed. Thank You, Jesus!

Consider this: there's a ship in troubled waters, needing to lighten the load. The weight of the cargo is preventing the control of the vessel. The decision is to jettison the cargo to sail on. It is fully freeing to lose the baggage, captivity, and weight of sin. It is only with the power of new life that sin loses its power over you. Just to be clear, read Galatians

5:19–21, as it lists the "deeds of the flesh" (Galatians 5:19). Deeds are actions. The actions of the flesh are "immorality, impurity, sensuality, idolatry, sorcery, enmities, strife, jealousy, outbursts of anger, disputes, dissensions, factions, envying, drunkenness, carousing, and things like these"(Galatians 5:19–20). We are called to identify them, confess, repent, and seek forgiveness from God for them. God is faithful to forgive and cleanse us when we confess our sin to Him. First John 1:9 confirms this truth. One of the most wonderful things to know is that in this intimate relationship with God, I have direct access to Him. He knows; therefore, I cannot hide, so in love I confess, and He is faithful to forgive and cleanse me.

It is by the Spirit's work we feel conviction for our sin. If not, we would freely continue practicing the sin and remain rebellious and an enmity to God. We have a great High Priest who is merciful and will sympathize with us. Hebrews 4:15–16 is a marvelous passage telling who He is, and with the work of the Spirit of God, we have the ability and confidence to approach Him. This would be living by the Spirit, step by step and day by day in obedience, trusting fully in the Spirit of God who will lead us through the challenges of everyday life and the internal battle with sin.

When we set our minds on the Spirit, it is "life and peace," as opposed to setting our mind on the flesh, which is "death" (Romans 8:6). When the disciple grows in understanding, they become more aware of the need for God the Holy Spirit to direct and assist with their ability to "walk by Him." To walk by Him means we move with and by His power, rather than attempting to move by our own. When we actively respond to His inspiration, guidance, and promptings, we can successfully fight and conquer sin and our lust of the flesh, eyes, and the boastful pride of life.

God the Holy Spirit makes known to us the will of God. He leads us and we follow Him faithfully and respond in obedience. Walking is a controlled action ... slow, precise, and intentional. It is an ever-pressing forward pace with one goal in mind: "the upward call of God in Christ Jesus," Philippians 3:14. It is walking with a firm footing of faith on the way leading to the narrow gate. This is the only way to find the narrow gate, as the Spirit of God knows *the Way.*

Jesus said *the Way* is narrow. If narrow, it requires paying close attention to where you are walking. Psalm 119:105 says, "Your word is a lamp to my feet and a light to my path." The disciple walks in this world which is full of darkness and sin. God's light is the same as the light-giving pillar of fire mentioned in Exodus 13:21 as the Lord went before the Israelites. God the Holy Spirit keeps the lamp burning to light the path. The disciple lives according to the light of Christ, which guides the disciple's feet on the path, claiming God's promises all along *the Way.*

Just think how walking with God could be. Could it be the same experience mentioned by the disciples on the road to Emmaus in Luke 24:13–35? I will testify to you, it will be, and you will be enlightened just like them. Jesus confirms today, as He did the day, He walked with them, that He has risen. Before salvation, our lives are joyless, full of despair and disappointment, which is if you are willing to admit it. Our happiness is fleeting and temporary. We are blind, desperate, worried, impulsive, anxious, impatient, filled with hopelessness, and unable to recognize Jesus, even if He were standing right in front of us. Just like the two on the road to Emmaus.

Unless God opens our eyes to see Him, just as He opened the disciples' eyes as it says in Luke 24:32, we would continually walk right by Him. When God in His mercy provides grace and faith, and puts His Spirit in His disciples, we come to life, and the Spirit reveals the truth of God. By faith we become obedient to Jesus's commands, and one of the most important commands are "go and make disciples" for the hearts prepared to receive His gospel.

You will find Jesus's Great Commission in Matthew 28:18–20. Can you see why God the Holy Spirit is so important in the life of the disciple? Without Him, you would neither desire to be obedient to Jesus nor to do the will of the Father. Consequently, the absence of God's Spirit means a person is still dead in their trespasses and sin, living a self-serving life, and the works are really of no value to one's personal aspiration to eternal life.

Walking by the Spirit is an action of the disciple living to please God. It is a place where distractions decrease, and obedience to God and His Word increases. Walking develops trust in God the Holy Spirit, step by step along the path of this life on earth. He gives you the ability to conquer the flesh, as "the flesh sets its desire against the Spirit, and the Spirit against the flesh" (Galatians 5:17).

As a disciple, you must continue to resist your flesh. We will keep this fleshly natural body until God raises us with a spiritual one, 1 Corinthians 15:44 confirms God's promise. The more we grow in the knowledge of God through His Word, the more the Spirit of God gains control over our thoughts, words, and deeds. There will always be a battle between your flesh and Spirit. The desires of the flesh were once in control of your thoughts, words, and deeds and wants it back! If you would peel sin away, you would see either your flesh or Satan behind the sin attempting to destroy your relationship with the only true God, Jesus Christ, and all the others in your life! Believe it or deny it ... your choice!

There may be some readers whose flesh is in control right now. Remember, God identifies those deeds of the flesh in Galatians 5:19–21. If you recognize the practice of any of these deeds, know the flesh is winning the battle for your soul, for right now. You must turn, alter your battle plan, look to the Spirit of God, and He will give you the ability to begin to fight more intentionally so you can WIN the fight!

Here's a promise from God. Claim it when you need strength or power to fight the sin in your life. It is Isaiah 40:29: "He gives strength to the weary, and to him who lacks might He increases power." The more you desire to fight sin, and live a life pleasing to God, the more He will increase your strength. You can expect it on every occasion. By God's providential will, He will uphold the weak in spirit, even those who are fearful or afraid. He equips us by His power. Our might comes by way of the Holy Spirit. This my friend is the closest I can describe this indescribable power from God to you!

This combat against the Spirit is to recover what the flesh has lost, and you must fight with the power provided by the Holy Spirit. This warfare will continue until ultimate sanctification becomes a reality.

When walking by the Spirit becomes a constant in your life, you are finally able to restrain yourself from being continuously overcome by the desires of your flesh.

The Spirit creates a freedom and an ability to recognize those deeds immediately, as you become more and more aware that they are opposed to God. Galatians 5:17 says, "For the flesh sets its desire against the Spirit, and the Spirit against the flesh; for these are in opposition to one another, so that you may not do the things that you please." So, in other words, your "self" sets its desires against God, and they are in opposition to each other. So, fighting against God, you will lose. Because the things you please in self are not the things that please God.

Thank God for His Spirit because, as you have read, sin can consume your life and everything good in it, and it is not until Jesus saves you and makes you His disciple that you begin to experience victory more than defeat. Believe it, it's true. These victories are moment by moment, hour by hour, day by day, month by month, and year by year, all *the way* to your last physical breath on this planet! Praise God! First Corinthians 15:57 confirms our victory in Jesus Christ.

If you have been running from God, STOP! It is time to walk! God desires for us to have a repentant heart for the sin we commit, a heart willing to turn around, and begin walking toward Him. Psalm 51:17 says, "The sacrifices of God are a broken spirit; a broken and a contrite heart, O God, You will not despise." It is time to reflect on what God the Holy Spirit has done, is doing, and will be doing in your life, now and forever! Ask Him to walk with you, and you will be amazed at what, and how, He will illuminate your mind as He teaches you His truth and wonders, and how He will carry out His plan of redemption through you, His disciple.

Suffer You Will

Jesus endured a tremendous amount of suffering, both physical and spiritual, for *all* His disciples. The physical was the flogging, scourging, being nailed to the cross, and because of the extremity of it, death. The spiritual was the rejection, abandonment, and the forsaking of Him by God the Father. This must have been one of the most horrific things that could ever happen to Jesus. He, the Father, and the Spirit are one. Now this loving relationship was broken apart, just like the one in the garden of Eden. Jesus stepped in my place, your place, as we have broken the relationship with God because of sin, and He has restored it by suffering through it. *PRAISE* GOD, *THANK YOU*, JESUS!

Jesus gave it *all* for His disciples! Following Jesus requires *all* of you! Believe me, it is either all in or all out. There's no gray area here, either. The way involves suffering, and we must look to Jesus as the example to follow in His steps. First Peter 2:21 says, "For you have been called for this purpose, since Christ also suffered for you, leaving you an example for you to follow in His steps." When you face suffering, as all disciples will, God's Word provides many passages to read and meditate on, knowing it will only be for a little while compared to suffering for all eternity. Even Paul, when saved, was told he would suffer for Jesus. You will find Paul's salvation story in Acts 9. Remember what James said about our lives in James 4:14? "You are *just* a vapor that appears for a little while and then vanishes away." So, what part of this vapor is the suffering? For some, it could be their entire life, while for others, a season, but suffer you will.

As Jesus's disciples, we are commanded to carry our own cross. That's biblical. In Luke 9:23, Jesus commands, "If anyone wishes to come after Me, he must deny himself, and take up his cross daily and follow Me." Jesus makes it very clear: I must live a life where my selfish wants and desires are denied. In other words, the craving for ... lusting for ... outbursts of anger for ... desires for ... must all be nailed to my cross. I must pick it up, and I must do this daily. All should expect, that since Jesus's cross involved pain, ours will too, there's no escaping it.

Why would any of Jesus's disciples think they would be absolved from suffering? Therefore, walking by the Spirit is so especially important. It is not in our nature to desire suffering, but here are wonderful promises to grasp, treasure, and write on the tablet of your heart, because you will suffer.

Yet in suffering, you will find strength. Hebrews 5:8 states, "Although He was a Son, He learned obedience from the things which He suffered." Have confidence you will learn obedience. James 5:13 reads, "Is anyone among you suffering? *Then* he must pray..." You learn to pray. First Peter 2:20 states, "But if when you do what is right and suffer *for it* you patiently endure it, this *finds* favor with God." You find endurance and favor.

It is hard to imagine one could grow during times of suffering, but you do grow spiritually. First Peter 3:14 states, "But even if you should suffer for the sake of righteousness, you are blessed." You find blessing. And then 1 Peter 5:9 reads, "... knowing that the same experiences of suffering are being accomplished by your brethren who are in the world." You find you are not alone. The most amazing promise is found in 1 Peter 5:10: "After you have suffered for a little while, the God of all grace, who called you to His eternal glory in Christ, will Himself perfect, confirm, strengthen *and* establish you." You can expect God Himself is able to mend or repair, by strengthening us to stand firmly on the rock of Jesus (Psalm 18:2)! The only way to live faithfully through suffering is by the power of God the Holy Spirit! Thank You, God the Holy Spirit!

Fruit Produces Yield

The Holy Spirit produces the fruits (characteristics) of the disciple. Galatians 5:22—23 confirms the fruits of the Spirit: "But the fruit of the Spirit is love, joy, peace, patience, kindness, goodness, faithfulness, gentleness, self-control." These fruits will be present, active, working, and lived out in your walk as a disciple of Jesus. Jesus is aware of the impact of the Spirit's fruit in the lives of His disciples and others. He also makes it very evident all will be able to distinguish between those who have the fruits of the Spirit, and those who do not. Jesus said in Matthew 7:16a "You will know them by their fruits." And this means more than apples, grapes, and pears!

It becomes more apparent in the observer of the disciple. The disciples themselves, as a matter of fact, when they see love for God and others, joy, and peace in circumstances and events which would previously have produced unhappiness, misery, and /or strife. Now, we have the power to overcome. We have patience with others when impatience and shortness would have prevailed. Kindness in the place of cruelty.

Goodness where evil thoughts and actions were prevalent. Faithfulness instead of wavering or deception. Gentleness replacing insensitivity. Self-control compared to actions and outbursts of anger from being frustrated or agitated resulting in losing your temper, and commencing with hateful thoughts, words, or actions. The Holy Spirit develops characteristics in the disciple we could not have been generated on our own.

Yes, sure, a person could offer a kind word or a nice action from time to time. But time to time does not reflect the image of Jesus. He was not a time to time kinda of man; He was an ALL the time man! If your life reflects a time to time demeanor, it says something else about you, as you profess to be a believer and a disciple of Jesus Christ. I no longer must try to live a life by the standards, trying to prove myself worthy or acceptable. I am acceptable in the sight of the Almighty God because I AM in Christ and His Spirit dwells in me!

I have asked other disciples, from time to time, "If Jesus was sitting across from you in the car, at the dinner table, at the restaurant, or at any other entertainment, would you act any differently?" Most people said, "yes!" "I asked, why?"

They responded, "Jesus is right there!"

"If you are proclaiming to be His disciple," I said, "His Spirit is living in you. Why should you be any different?" It makes me wonder if they believe, and if they believe in what Jesus said about where His Spirit would dwell. His Word says that they will dwell in us! Jesus's Spirit is not detached from Him; He is one; one body and spirit, and His Spirit is living in His disciples as well. So, Jesus lives in us. Therefore, we must live as His Spirit is living in us, and our living must be with faithful confidence as we carry our cross, we will be following in His steps.

How does the Holy Spirit accomplish this work in a disciple? First, the disciple must be born of the Spirit. In John 3:5 Jesus says, "Truly, truly, I say to you, unless one is born of water and the Spirit he cannot enter into the kingdom of God." Then, the disciple is baptized with the Holy Spirit (Acts 1:5). The Spirit leads, (Romans 8:14), and, as promised, begins to teach and put into motion new desires, reading, studying, and meditating on the Word of God. You begin to pray for self and others, activating understanding of the things freely given to us by God (1 Corinthians 2:13). What an overwhelming new-found joy!

Even Paul, with the challenges of imprisonment, beating, stoning, and shipwrecks, would testify it would not have been possible to endure, *but for* the power of God the Holy Spirit! It was by the Spirit's power working in all disciples throughout the history of the world, the gospel spread to lives and throughout history. We learn to endure and persevere by God the Holy Spirit's work in a disciple of Jesus Christ. The Holy Spirit not only helps in our weakness, but also prays as we do not know even how to pray.

Have you ever been confronted with a situation or a friend or person, and you did not know what to pray for or even how? Have confidence, the Holy Spirit knows and intercedes for us in our prayers to God (Romans 8:26). Do you remember the fruits of the Spirit? He also gives us abilities. Abilities to understand and apply the Word of God to our lives. You will come to know God's will and plan for your life. The ability to communicate the gospel, demonstrating compassion for others, forgiving and asking for forgiveness. These abilities are *activated* in you, believe that! It should raise questions when these abilities are underutilized or not present at all. You will pray, learn, grow, hear, see, serve, move, act, and respond in obedience to the promptings generated by the Spirit of God!

The Helper

In conclusion, Jesus warns us in Luke 9:62: "No one, after putting his hand to the plow and looking back, is fit for the kingdom of God." Well, it is God the Holy Spirit keeping your hand on the plow, and your head looking forward. With our sinful nature, it is a certainty we would take our hand off the plow and look back. You know you would if you are willing to truthfully admit it.

But for God the Holy Spirit, and His faithfulness to the Father, Son, and the disciple, we keep in step with moving ahead and pressing on, with the plan of God to make the only true God known, and to preach the *Good News* of Jesus Christ. The Holy Spirit plays a vital part in the life of the disciple. You see, without the Helper, you are lost, lacking direction, with no purpose, drifting aimlessly, destitute, blind, and most importantly, spiritually dead.

In each waking day, by each step, you should be thankful and grateful for God the Father's love, grace, mercy, and generosity, and for Jesus asking the Father to bestow the gift of the Helper in your life as His disciple. Jesus's commands for His disciples are tremendous and extremely important, for souls are at stake. Only those who possess the Spirit of God can faithfully carry out their assigned work.

As you grow in understanding of the importance of your calling as a disciple, it should create in you a desire to live in such a way that your life is pleasing to God. You are preaching the gospel in season and out of season, and faithfully doing the will of the Father.

I would be remiss as a disciple of Jesus not to address something you should be aware of. One can speak against or blaspheme Jesus and be forgiven. If one speaks against or blasphemes God the Holy Spirit, they will not be forgiven. Believe it, it is true. Many may claim something different, and the topic could be associated with "forgiveness" of all sin. Well, there is one where forgiveness by God is refused; thus, a potential conflict arises. But whenever there is a conflict pertaining to the Word of God and one's interpretation of it, the Word of God is what breaks the conflict. And whatever God says, transcends man's opinion!

Here is the passage to confirm what God says about those who speak against or blaspheme God the Holy Spirit. Matthew 12:31–32 says, "Therefore I say to you, any sin and blasphemy shall be forgiven people, but blasphemy against the Spirit shall not be forgiven. Whoever speaks a word against the Son of Man, it shall be forgiven him; but whoever speaks against the Holy Spirit, it shall not be forgiven him, either in this age or in the *age* to come."

We must understand what the word blaspheme means. It means to curse or swear against. One may wonder why God would hold this sin against humanity forever. It is not good to sin against a human messenger of God, yet it is unforgivable to sin against God's divine messenger, the Holy Spirit. This confirms a corrupted and unrepentant heart hardened by the deceitfulness of sin. It has no desire for forgiveness, and results in God's wrath. This leads to eternal condemnation and separation from God forever.

The power of God the Holy Spirit opens the heart of the unbeliever to respond to the gospel. The Holy Spirit teaches and provides us instruction on righteousness and holiness, as we respond in love through obedience. It is God the Father at work, through the power of the Holy Spirit, creating the ability in the disciple to love like Him. Without the power of the Holy Spirit, you are not capable of loving others like God loves you or them.

I pray for you now, God the Holy Spirit will come to you, as He did me!

A Prayer for You:

God the Holy Spirit, I, with so many others are so thankful for Your presence and work in our lives. We know, without Your continued teaching, direction, promptings, wisdom and understanding, we could never complete the work ordained for us. I know in my heart, with my sinful flesh, I would look back after putting my hand to the plow. It is only by Your power working in me that I can continue to press on. It is by Your desire and faithfulness to the Father we are obedient to complete this work today. I know, the ecumenical community does not fully address the importance of Your work in our salvation. Without You, there is no life change, because You are the One who has the power to make the dead come to life! We should be quite aware that we cannot do anything about yesterday, and we should not worry about tomorrow, as it has enough troubles of its own. Teach us to live each day in a faithful way and let all we do be pleasing to the Father as You make us useful vessels for the kingdom of God.

I pray this prayer for all disciples, and those you inspire to read the words in this book. I pray my words encourage them to look to You for strength, ability, knowledge of God's Word, and applying it as they live it out. Create a desire in them so they become the hands, feet, and mouths that proclaim the gospel of Jesus.

We pray You will take this prayer as You intercede for me and them, making our prayers a sweet aroma to the Father, and He will answer our prayers through You. I ask You, God the Holy Spirit, to baptize

_____. Please do a mighty work in them. I Know by the truth of the Father's word, that all disciples must be born again, and new birth only comes by Your power! May their hearts be filled with the unspeakable joy when You create a new life in them! I ask and pray this things Jesus's name. May the Spirit of God be with you always because God has promised He will be with you forever! Amen.

Reflections

REGENERATION...

"Truly, truly, I say to you, unless one is born again
he cannot see the kingdom of God." (John 3:3)

ARE YOU BORN AGAIN?

One may not think this work of God is a necessity, and that all one must do are some religious works to justify eternal life. Oh, I was blind to this truth of God as well! I thought all I needed to *do* was the rituals I learned in Catholicism. It did not matter how I was living if I did the sacraments, the work for me was done. I had no idea what born again meant, and I was in desperate need of it! But one would expect that if you are spiritually dead, then being made spiritually alive would be totally mysterious to a dead man.

I remember sometime in my late teens or early twenties; I was asked by several people on numerous occasions if I was "born again." My answer each time was, "Are you a Catholic?" They responded, "no," and I confidently said, in all ignorance, "You're the one going to hell, because unless you are a Catholic, you are not one of God's people. Did you know that Peter was the first pope?" Imagine that … blind and did not know it.

So, what is this "born again" about? The short answer is that we are born on this earth, and this is our humanity. Then we must be born from above, our spirituality. This is when God imparts life into the person, who was born spiritually dead, and makes them spiritually alive. I suspect many were like me—just live as good as you can, hope your good deeds outweigh your bad ones, and God in His mercy lets you into His kingdom. Well, this may be a perspective to have, but based on God's Word, it will not be a perspective to save; it's a perspective of judgment. My sinfulness was so depraved, I thought and believed I could be good enough in my own righteousness and God would accept my filthy rags and allow me into His holy presence. NOT! There must be a change of the spirit, nature, values, doctrine, and beliefs. It is a new work of God through spiritual faith in you, which would be comparable to a new birth.

John 3:1–21 is titled "The New Birth." It is an immensely powerful passage on life change coming to you when you become a child of the living God, and one of Jesus's disciples. Jesus makes it truly clear life change only occurs when one is born of the Spirit. In writing *Walking, The Way*, God made it obvious to me, and I pray God the Holy Spirit makes it obvious to you. Know that it *was* God, *is* God, and *will always* be God doing the work in His people, PRAISE GOD for His work!

How can anything dead regenerate itself? It can't. It has no life to regenerate from. It must be made new. Ephesians 2:5 and Colossians 2:13 both say the same thing: we are spiritually dead, and *He (God)* makes us alive in Jesus Christ! God made it a fact. It was the power of God the Holy Spirit regenerating Jesus to life after His death and burial. He was dead, and the Spirit's work brought Him to life, and He rose. Therefore, it will be by the power of the Holy Spirit Jesus's disciples are born of the Spirit; "born again," and made alive, just like Jesus. He was dead and made alive. When we see Jesus on the last day, we will see His head, hands, and feet. Do you have enough confidence in your faith to ask Jesus to show you His back? The truth of who He is and what He's done will become a frightful reality for many, and for the few, an awe-inspiring moment. We have faith in Jesus; we too are "buried with Him in baptism" and will be "raised up with Him through faith in the working of God" after our physical death (Colossians 2:12). Thank You, Jesus!

Nic at Night

Nicodemus was a Pharisee who followed the law and was a ruler of the Jews. As a ruler, he knew the law and followed it "religiously." Have you ever heard someone describe a person as "very religious or a devout

Christian?" This could surely have been said about Nicodemus. He had seen and heard of the works of Jesus and went to see Jesus at night to learn more about Him. He went at night, for fear his "religious companions" would not approve if he was seen with Jesus in broad daylight. One should always be discerning regarding their "companions" who have influence in their life. You will know if they are living life biblically or religiously by their opinions, guidance, biblical advice, if any, and counsel. Nic was living out the old worldly saying: "birds of a feather flock together!"

Jesus answered, "Truly, truly, I say to you, unless one is born of water and the Spirit he cannot enter into the kingdom of God." John 3:5

When Jesus speaks with Nicodemus in John 3, He makes it clear the *only* way to enter the Kingdom of God and live eternally is by the power and work of God, Himself. Man's efforts, no matter what they are, not even if it is the sincerest, will match up to the work of God the Holy Spirit. *The Way* to enter the kingdom of God is to be *born again*. You *must be* born of the Spirit, a sign of new birth.

Then, like today, people were taught they must do the traditions and rituals by works, following them carefully to prove their worthiness to God. There is much to be said and discussed about the differences of both religious sects. One sect was in control of the synagogues, the Pharisees. The other was the Sadducees, who were friends with Rome and were holding fast to the Roman laws. This discussion is about something different. If you desire to know more about the Pharisees and Sadducees, which made up the Sanhedrin, please research them, because you will find different theological perspectives on what each sect believed and practiced.

Going to the heart of the matter, what Jesus said was needed for man to enter His kingdom was spiritual birth which must come from God. Thus, you have a physical birth, born on this earth, and you must have a second birth, born from heaven to enter it. Traditions, rituals, and any work performed by man's own effort cannot create the new life Jesus calls for, to be in the presence of God, because these traditions, rituals, and efforts do not provide the full understanding of one's need for spiritual birth.

Today, you may hear the term "legalism," meaning, rules and regulations attempting to achieve salvation. It places focus on one's own efforts, versus the need for the work of God through grace and faith to be completed in their life. The simplest way to look at it is:

Man can produce man, for a natural life. But only God can produce Spirit for an eternal life. Jesus mentions both means of regeneration for this eternal life, and they are of water and the Spirit.

To be born again, you must experience washing and renewal by the Spirit of God. This really confirmed for me why I could not *give* my life to Christ. I was dead in my trespasses and sin, flawed, polluted, and corrupted. Why would a holy and righteous God want someone to give their flawed, polluted, and corrupt life to Him? Therefore, God the Father required sacrifices without blemish for the forgiveness of sin. Jesus, the perfect sacrifice, had no flaws or corruption. Hallelujah to the Lamb of God!

God gives man a new heart and a new spirit. Those two working together creates this new man. Now, this new man possesses the ability to renew their mind from the bondage of sin and begin to understand the love God has for them. Jesus freely laid down His life for us. Therefore Galatians 2:20 must be a memory verse for all of Jesus's disciples! Because Jesus loved you so much, He gave His life for you! AMAZING LOVE!

Anyone can possess significant teachings and knowledge, even accomplish phenomenal works from man's perspective, but lack the work of the Spirit, and fall short of entering the kingdom of God. Just like Nicodemus, I was clueless. So I will ask:, Have you been born again, or, are you leaning on the work you have done to *achieve* salvation?

A Disciple Who's a Surgeon

Consider this analogy. There was a cardiothoracic surgeon renowned for his ability to perform minor and major surgery on the heart. He possessed the skills and abilities to solve or mend the most complicated heart problems any cardiothoracic surgeon faced. With years of study and performing thousands of surgeries, he was blessed to handle some of the most sophisticated procedures.

He had his normal staff, and those he met along his travels. He was one of the most sought- after surgeons in the world. You know, the heart is a vital organ for life, both physically and spiritually. When someone needed this work, they requested him. Hearts sometimes can be repaired, and others require replacement. And if replacement is required, the recipient hopes for a proper match, and a skilled surgeon to do this extraordinary work.

As a cardiothoracic surgeon, he completed all kinds of procedures, but his specialty was the complicated transplant. Although he was highly successful, financially secure, and cared for his patients with true empathy and compassion, he was a humble man. He never condemned people for what they might have done to cause their heart complications. He always was available to encourage and teach his patients, and staff. He traveled the world to perform procedures on the young to the aged, and he possessed a burning desire for his Lord and Savior Jesus Christ, and the people God put into his path. He understood it was God who blessed him with his talents and gifts, and he desired to honor God with his life.

He knew his life was a mission; yes, it was his work, but also, as a disciple he knew he was to be obedient to Jesus's command to "Go and make disciples" along the journey. He lived his life as Jesus intended for His disciples. He was a disciple who was a surgeon, versus a surgeon who was a disciple. So his focus was spreading the gospel wherever he traveled, no matter if it was locally or the other side of the world. That's biblical, as Acts 1:8 says, "and even to the remotest part of the earth." This was why he believed his life was a mission, because he got to go places and see people most do not know even exist.

but you will receive power when the Holy Spirit has come upon you; and you shall be My witnesses...

Acts 1:8

Although very capable and having performed thousands of surgeries, he lost patients along his journey. Whenever it happened, it grieved him very deeply, but he understood God has a plan for all men, and his work was not the end result of God's plan. Even with the most valiant effort to attempt to repair the most damaged heart, he understood he did the work, but it was God who performed the healing.

Without his God-given skills and abilities, he would never travel to places where God used him. It is the same in our life, when circumstances, events, or sickness happen, and God leads us to places we normally would not go. As a result, when we respond in faithfulness, God uses us as His vessel, and we respond by living out the gospel, the *Good News* of Jesus Christ. Our life is the instrument God uses to spread His gospel.

The cardiothoracic surgeon had numerous favorite Bible verses, but he saw Psalm 139:16, as the verse most applicable in his life and work. It says, "Your eyes have seen my unformed substance; and in Your book were all written the days that were ordained *for me*, when as of yet there was not one of them." He had Psalm 139:16 in his home, on his bag and doctor's coat, his office wall, and car.

He knew and expected God would lead him to be anywhere to meet anyone at any time. He never knew who the next person would be, but he lived each day in anticipation. He would not know they existed before meeting them, but he trusted in God's promises. He knew, based on his understanding of Psalm 139:16, that there was a prearranged date and time for all things under heaven. That's biblical! Ecclesiastes 3:1 confirms this truth; it says, "There is an appointed time for everything. And there is a time for every event under heaven." He had complete faith, trust, belief, and hope in Jesus Christ and God is true to His Word.

On this day, he was visiting a long-time friend who was in the hospital several hundred miles from his home. He desired to love on his friend in his time of need. The friend's ailment and hospital stay were not associated with any heart complications. The cardiothoracic surgeon lived out God's Word in his life daily. His love for God and others was evident in his daily walk.

He did not go to give advice or to ensure the friend's doctor was completing his responsibilities correctly, or to see if he was receiving the proper care from the staff. No, he was just visiting his friend, a fellow disciple in his time of need. The whole purpose of his trip was to go and love on his friend and pray with, and for him, while he visited. He was not asked to go; he just went.

He has seen the work of God in his life, and in the Spirit of Psalm 139:16, anything God was performing in his life and the lives of others, could be expected. Can you live your life in full anticipation of God's work in your life? Or, do you believe life happens by coincidence, chance, and luck? The doctor knew this day was unplanned as he saw it. However, he knew there is a book, and in the book were written all the days ordained for him. He learned to expect anything, anywhere, or anybody known or unknown, to happen. This passage created conversation in his home, office, airplanes, trains, buses, and even in the operating room.

On this ordained day, there was a man who was getting ready for work. He felt a bit under the weather. He was uncertain as to what was wrong with him. However, he still *had* to get to work. You know how demanding work can be; regardless of the circumstances, you must be there. His wife prepared breakfast; however, he told her he did not have a big appetite. He gobbled down a little bit of food and said, "I gotta get to the office. I got loads to do, and I do not want to be there twelve more hours again today, and I know you do not want me to either." He expressed his thankfulness for his spouse's patience with his most-of-the-time demanding schedule. He had missed or been late to numerous important engagements, yet she would just smile and express her love for him. Again, his wife asked him, "Do you feel okay?"

He said, "No, but maybe something I ate last night has me feeling this way." Again, he stated, "I have a lot of work to do, and I need to get to the office." He kissed her goodbye, backed his car out of the driveway, and proceeded down the same road he has driven for sixteen years. Alongside the road there was a hospital, facing the highway near an exit. Numerous times in passing, he noticed ambulances pulling into the emergency room section, and at times wondered what was wrong that required an ambulance.

He was about a mile away from the hospital, when suddenly, he got a pain in the left side of his chest. He still drove, and the closer he got to the hospital, the farther the pain radiated down his left arm. He felt a need to at least pull over and go into the hospital to get checked out. As he drove off the exit and into the entrance of the hospital, the pain intensified. As he pulled up to the door and stopped, he rolled down his window and yelled to the passersby, "Please get help. I am having a heart attack!" The stranger ran inside and yelled out, "A man in the car is having a heart attack!" The emergency room staff immediately rushed out, got him, brought him in, and ran an EKG test to confirm what he feared.

The treating nurse said to another, "Hey, I saw that famous cardio-thoracic surgeon visiting a friend today? I saw him in the hallway early this morning. I know he met with the Chief of Staff and with the other surgeons yesterday. None of them are here, but he's here. We need to page him! This man appears to be having a massive heart attack!" The charge nurse prepared the man to be taken in for surgery, and the cardiothoracic surgeon was paged.

At the same moment, the cardiothoracic surgeon was in prayer with his friend. In his prayer, he asked God to be used this day, that God would be glorified in his life as He has so many times in the past. A page comes over the loudspeaker for him. He looks at his friend and says, "Strange, I do not have anything planned today in this hospital. Why are they paging me?"

His friend replied, "Hey, you know you just quoted Psalm 139:16, and you said there are days ordained. Sounds like this could be one of them. Even when you walked into my room to visit me, was a day ordained. I did not plan on you being here. You did not say you were coming in advance, yet you walked into my room and what a sight for sore eyes it was to see you. It brought joy and gladness to my heart. I think you should respond just like you responded to me."

The surgeon immediately got up and went down to the ER. The ER staff doctor showed him the EKG report. He looked at the man who had already passed out due to the pain, and said, "Based on what I see, there is an immediate need for surgery. No time to waste. Prep him now! Take me to the OR suite!"

They wheeled the man into the OR, and just as the surgeon was getting ready to make the incision, the heart monitor indicated a flat line. The dreaded solid tone pierced the ears of all in attendance, and the staff immediately went into code blue protocol! The cardiothoracic surgeon was just standing there, looking around the room, as everyone was hurrying into position. He said, "Stop right where you are!" Everyone froze, thinking some other emergency had happened.

He said, "Let's look at the man, we have three minutes before it is absolutely necessary to get oxygen to the brain! Let's go thirty seconds and see what's going to happen to this man." The nursing staff looked at each other in total amazement, thinking, *how can the cardiothoracic surgeon think this man, whose heart had stopped beating, initiating a code blue is going to do ANYTHING?*

One nurse said, "With all due respect, doctor, he has flat-lined, and his heart has stopped!"

He replied, "Yes, it is true based on one principle, but let's give him another twenty seconds, and see what he is going to do. I promise, we will not go beyond seventy-five seconds before proceeding with surgery. However, let's confirm his heart has stopped, agree?"

"Yes, doctor," they said in unison. "We would all agree!"

The cardiothoracic surgeon responded, "Based on science, yes, he's dead, as his heart has stopped beating, and he is no longer alive. Do you think it is possible this dead man could make himself alive?"

Again, in unison shaking their heads, "No Doctor!"

The cardiothoracic surgeon said, "He surely would have done it, or something already if he was going to do it, agreed?"

They said, "We have seen this before. Unless we shock him now, he will never come back!"

"I see," the cardiothoracic surgeon said. "Now we are at one minute; we have fifteen more seconds, get the paddles ready and epinephrine, and then we will proceed." Everyone's eyes were fixed on the clock, awaiting the fifteen seconds. Immediately, it became evident to everyone in the room that this man could not save himself. The surgeon requested the paddles, the system charged, and he provided the electronic shock to the heart. Immediately after the shock, the heart started beating, erratically, yet beating. He turned to the staff and said, "One of my favorite Bible passages is Psalm 139:16," and he quoted it with passion: "Your eyes have seen my unformed substance; and in Your book were all written the days that were ordained for me, when as yet there was not one of them.'"

"I had no plans today to perform surgery. I came to the hospital to visit my friend. Yet in God's book there's a day ordained for me to be here—not only to perform surgery, relieving this man of his physical ailment, but also to talk to you. I never met you before today; let's proceed."

He went on to say, "It takes an external power to make the dead come to life! Do you see this dead man? Did you know that we are all spiritually dead when we are born into this world? All have a need for an external power, like the paddles to give you spiritual life!" He went on to preach the gospel.

He preached on Ephesians 2:1. "'And you were dead in your trespasses and sins.' And 2 Corinthians 5:17 states, 'Therefore if anyone is in Christ, *he is* a new creation; the old things passed away; behold, new things have come.'" The staff were amazed, as they watched his hands work meticulously as he performed the surgery. It was as though there were two people in their midst: a disciple of Jesus Christ and an exceptional surgeon!

He continued with both the gospel and surgery. "Can you all see how Ezekiel 36:26–27 applies here? God's Word says, 'Moreover, I will give you a new heart and put a new spirit within you; and I will remove the heart of stone from your flesh and give you a heart of flesh. I will put My Spirit within you and cause you to walk in My statutes, and you will be careful to observe My ordinances.'"

He continued with Ephesians 2:8–9, quoting, "'For by grace you have been saved through faith; and that not of yourselves, it is the gift of God, not as a result of works so that no one may boast.' This man if he was able, would have made himself alive and could have boasted. But now, being dead, he will have nothing to boast about, as it was God who saved his life.

I do not know each of you personally," he said to the staff, "where you are in your faith or even if you believe in our Lord and Savior Jesus Christ. Do you believe Jesus Christ is Lord and believe He's Savior for all? If you believe, then you see the work of God, and this day is ordained for us. I am here today to tell you, not only as a cardiothoracic surgeon, but as a disciple of Jesus Christ, each day is ordained for us to go out and share the Good News of Jesus Christ. I am extremely interested in talking with anyone about the passages I quoted today, and new life in Jesus Christ. Know that, I am a good listener as well, if you are willing to talk. I would love to hear how God has used you in your work here in the hospital, or anywhere you go." He said, "That's biblical, according to Hebrews 10:24.

"...and let us consider how to stimulate one another to love and good deeds..."

Hebrews 10:24

Most importantly, I am not going to leave town until the patient recovers and is conscious, as I would like to have a conversation with him. As I conclude this surgery, which isn't as complicated as some I have done in my life, I am glad he responded the way he did. It is God in His mercy." He quoted Ephesians 2:4: "'But God, being rich in mercy, because of His great love with which He loved us,' has given the ability to provide an opportunity for this man to now experience life. So I am going to conclude, go back and finish my visit with my friend and tell him the wonderful things God has done in my life, again today!

I will leave you my card and look forward to any time you would like to have a conversation. You can contact me whenever you can, knowing, as it says in Colossians 3:16–17, 'Let the word of Christ richly dwell within you, with all wisdom teaching and admonishing one another with psalms *and* hymns *and* spiritual songs, singing with thankfulness in your hearts to God. Whatever you do in word or deed, *do* all in the name of the Lord Jesus, giving thanks through Him to God the Father.' Thank you for being responsive and forgive me if I made you alarmed in the early aspects of this serious situation. But I know it's God who is at work in us 'both to will and to work for *His* good pleasure.' Oh, that's Philippians 2:13."

If you were to really look at this story with a fresh set of eyes, could you see love expressed? How about obedience in responding to one's calling? Could you see faith in God's promises, or the belief everything is biblical? The use and power of scripture memory? The anticipation of

God's work to be lived out in one's life. The association to the external power from the paddles, and being born again by the power of the Holy Spirit? Could you see the gospel being lived out and spoken? Could you stand before God and say you are living your life as Jesus's disciple, which is like the cardiothoracic surgeon, and Jesus's other disciples mentioned in His Word? What would Jesus say to you in response to your asking Him if you are living your life like His disciple should be living? Are you born again, and if not, do you desire to be?

The "Reflection" section at the end of this segment will give you a place to jot down the work needed when you ask the Holy Spirit to reveal to you what you need to do to become obedient to His promptings and live the life Jesus intended for His disciple, you.

Out of Darkness into Light

It is Jesus Christ who truly inspires us in life's circumstances, events, and trials. These circumstances, events, and trials, like what was communicated in the analogy, are what confirms "for it is God who is at work in you, both to will and to work for *His* good pleasure" (Philippians 2:13). "*For I am* confident of this very thing, that He who began a good work in you will perfect it until the day of Christ Jesus." Oh, this one is Philippians 1:6. Both passages verify one sure point: it is God doing the work! It makes total sense to me. *If we are watching Jesus as He watched the Father when He was on earth, then we will do as He did, and we will end up where He is!*

The story of the cardiothoracic surgeon is designed to remind the disciple of the new life they have in Christ! It is also for anyone who is not a disciple of Jesus yet, who desires new life in Him. Like the cardiothoracic surgeon, wherever the disciple travels, they are to be about the work of Jesus, living out and preaching the gospel! Yes, we are to perform our work tasks, but we are to also perform our duties as a disciple to preach the gospel wherever we go! Second Timothy 4:2 says, "preach the word; be ready in season *and* out of season; reprove, rebuke, exhort, with great patience and instruction." I share the joy and happiness with all those whose life has profoundly changed by being born again by the Holy Spirit. You will find that you will have more spiritual conversations than mundane ones.

When one is walking in spiritual darkness, whatever one does is pleasing to oneself, because there is no desire to please God or others; it is all about self and satisfying the desires of the flesh. As hard as I tried to control the deeds and desires of my flesh, I couldn't, and I failed miserably. Sure, there may have been times of restraint or abstinence; however, sin was still prevalent in my life, and practiced. God knew I needed a life change or I would destroy myself and potentially others. I needed to be regenerated, born again, and given new life in Christ.

For some disciples, God may have used a catastrophic type of event to bring about salvation, or you may be someone with whom God used other means; after all, He is God and knows what we need—Him! Either way, regeneration by the Spirit is needed. This new creation is a life where the heart, mind, and spirit are no longer in the same condition as they were when spiritually dead; we become a new creature!

This new life in Christ brings freedom, the ability to ask and grant forgiveness where grudges were held. No longer does sin reign in my life. This new life in Christ and the promise of the Holy Spirit dwells within me. Does my sinful human nature change? No, but by the power of the Holy Spirit, the disciple gains new abilities, and one of the greatest abilities given by God is the ability to say no! No, I want to remain faithful to God! I tell you; I have quoted Proverbs 18:10— "The name of the Lord is a strong tower; the righteous runs into it and is safe"— numerous times. Thank You, Jesus!

This new life does not eradicate the flesh. *By the power of the Holy Spirit, you control your flesh, versus your flesh controlling you.* God makes no promises to remove the environment where sin exists. There are few occasions where sin would occur by my thoughts, words, or deeds. However, as it says in 2 Corinthians 5:17, "the old things passed away!" The old things here are pertaining to my perspective of how I viewed sin, others, and myself. How there was no life in the sin I was freely choosing to live out. My likes and dislikes changed, and I experienced the removal of total captivity and bondage by sin.

Our entire perspective and understanding completely change. Paul references the Christian's walk in Ephesians 4:17–32, specifically where he describes the "old self" (Ephesians 4:22). He talks of the futility of mind, darkened in understanding, excluded from the life of God, ignorance, and a hardness of heart.

I know it is difficult for people to see themselves this way.

The truth is you are not alone. Everyone is the same—that is all but one, Jesus Christ! It truly requires the power of God the Holy Spirit to regenerate a person for the new self to be created. Only in the new self can one understand one's deeds are because of a sinful nature. Sin entices and carries us away through "the lust of the flesh and the lust of the eyes and the boastful pride of life" (1 John 2:16).

We must be rescued from spiritual darkness and transferred into the kingdom of God the Father's beloved Son, Jesus Christ, which leads to spiritual life. I pray you will be born again by God the Holy Spirit as you read and ask, "Is it me, Lord, needing to be born again?" I ask this in the name of our Lord and Savior Jesus Christ, giving thanks through Him to God the Father.

This should cause you to desire to do the work of an evangelist and anticipate the work of God the Holy Spirit in your life, as it would be for the cardiothoracic surgeon witnessing someone who is dead regenerated to new life ... amen?

A Prayer for You:

ABBA, I love You and thank You for today. This is the day the Lord has made. Let us rejoice and be glad in it. I thank You for life, true life in Jesus. I know without Your work in me, I am still a complete mess, full of darkness and sin, living far from You.

New life in You is so wonderful. There are so many things I want to ask. My mind is flooding with all the different people who will be reading this line as I am writing it. Create a desire in them to want to know for absolute certainty, as I did, if they are someone who needs to be born again, and that You are alive! Make Your presence known to them and remove all their doubt. Give them the ability to ask, "Is it I, Lord, is it I who needs to be born again?" Answer them, Lord, when they ask. You make it clear, without rebirth by Your Spirit, there is no life. I pray You move, God, move and show them your truth by the power of your Spirit. Regenerate them as their eyes are reading these lines, and may their heart leap for joy over the new life which can be found only in You, as there is no life apart from You!

I know that in my own sin and depravity, I would have never chosen You. It took Your work to make me just like You made Adam by Your breath of life. Breathe the breath of life into them. By Your love, breathe the breath of life into them right now. I trust and believe in every word and promise You've said, and I claim, "Ask anything in My name and I will do it," right now, this moment for me, and right then for them.

ABBA, I know in my heart You are looking upon me as I sit and pray and write out this prayer for them, and You will see them as their eyes skim across these words. Please make them NEW! I thank You for the new life. I AM alive because of Your saving grace. I AM so thankful for your grace, love, and mercy! Make them a new creature and let them live out from this day forward; they are alive because You have entered their life, and they will never be the same again!

Make them your disciples. Create a desire and passion in them to read, study, and meditate on Your words, truth, commands, statutes, and ordinances. And forever be mindful of Your warnings. Give them the ability to believe, give them a new heart and spirit, and put Your Spirit in them so that they will now become a faithful disciple of Jesus, and love others as You love. Provide, sustain, forgive, and encourage me to follow You and do the will of the Father.

I love how You love; I thank You for listening and responding, and I AM asking in Jesus's name, amen.

Reflections

PRAYER...

"Sit here while I go over there and pray. [...] remain here."
(Matthew 26:36–38)

WHY DO YOU PRAY?

Humanity will fall into one of the following categories of praying to God: only pray when you want or need something, or pray when you need Him to move when you think He should; pray sometimes; pray when something bad happens; ask someone else to pray to God; never pray at all; or pray as an instinctive part of your life as a disciple? Which category would define your prayer life?

I used to be one who did not pray at all, because I was so ashamed, I did not even consider asking God what I needed to do, from His perspective. My way of thinking was work it out the best way I knew how. And as you have read, *I was the worse counselor I could have as a patient.*

You know the most interesting thing? Living this way, by not trusting God and praying at all, I always ended up in the same place; discouraged and where I first started. I couldn't see in my spiritual blindness; I was headed around the mountain again, living in constant discontent, for over thirty years. There were times I did not even consider praying, as sin was so rampant, and by the nature of it, it kept me from being in relationship with God. Refusing to pray, which is possessing a rebellious heart, thinking I did not need God, I did not reach out to Him, so I continued to walk aimlessly in despair within my spiritual darkness and sin.

The devil lost his relationship with God. Do not be deceived—he aims for you to lose yours if you have one. And if you don't, he will try to prevent you from having one with God at all. This deception is truly happening—ask around or better yet, test yourself. Do you see excuses or reasons for not praying to God as evidence of the deception of Satan at work in your life? Believe it, it is true. Be encouraged, though, God already knows. But let me give you hope. He desires to have an intimate relationship with you, where you have open and constant communication with God, directly. Prayer is *the Way* to accomplish it.

HINDERED?

If you are like most, you will not want or accept a hinderance in any way, shape, or form. To hinder means to delay, deter, obstruct, stall, or impede. *If you face hindrance in your job, you will not accept it and push back with all your might. No one wants to be treated this way, especially if it is on the job where you put forth the most effort! And if hindrance happens to a loved one, especially a child, then you'll be pushing and yelling even more against any hindrance affecting them.*

Everyone deserves to be treated fairly, assisted when needed, and free to advance. Any hindrance, and wrath and fury come blazing forth.

Sin was so dominant in my life; I did not think God would want me in His presence anyway. And the truth be known, I did not want to be there, as sin had me in its clutches. I was enjoying it, and it was a continuous practice.

Here's what I learned with the fresh set of eyes given to me by God. God commands me to live with Bonnie in an understanding way. There are no acceptable excuses. Either I do, or I don't, no gray area! If I don't, my prayers are hindered. You know the interesting thing? He doesn't say "disciples" He says "husbands!" God is talking to disciples who are husbands. It could be easily read as only the unbeliever's prayers, but why would an unbeliever pray to God, they wouldn't.

If you are a disciple who's a husband, a good memory verse to put in your life memory bank is 1 Peter 3:7, which says, "You husbands in the same way, live with *your wives* in an understanding way, as with someone weaker, since she is a woman; and show her honor as a fellow heir of the grace of life, so that your prayers will not be hindered." So let me caution you: disciples be attentive to what God is saying. If you are proclaiming to be one of Jesus's disciples and you are not living with your wife in an understanding way, your prayers *are* hindered.

Before being born again, I was not living with Bonnie in an understanding way, nor was I showing her honor. I couldn't. I did not have God's love and grace in my life. My lips were moving, but there was no sound coming out of my mouth. Why would God listen to a heart full of sin and respond in faithfulness when I was not even faithful to Bonnie, nor Him, because I was not one of His disciples? I understand now why He didn't.

When disciples who are husbands are not living biblically, could it be God looking and saying, "His mouth is moving, but I cannot hear a word he is saying?" Or does He instruct the angels to sing louder because their voices sound so much sweeter to Him than the voice of a husband who is verbally, psychologically, or physically abusive; who withholds his affection; who attempts to continually control his wife's every movement; who is deceitful; who is an adulterer? Remember, when God says, "living with her," this encompasses every fragment of one's marriage.

This type of behavior is opposed to what God says love is in 1 Corinthians 13:4-8a, so God's love is not flowing through your life to hers; therefore, your prayers *are* hindered. Can you see now why God was not moving when you *seemed* to ask in all sincerity? Hmmm, I pray this really gets someone to think, to evaluate what you are seeing and how you are living.

The disciple is always attentive to their wife's body language and words. How is your wife truly responding? Is she free to express herself to you? Can she speak openly without your ridicule or wrath? If you have the courage to ask her, then ask her! If asking isn't necessary, and you are not living with her in an understanding way, know, all this time your prayers have been hindered. You will not be able to ignore it anymore. You must face it. Repent so that the channel of communication moves past your ceiling, and the singing goes back to its normal tone. God will hear and respond to your plea for Him to listen, and He will move, as He is faithful to His promises—if what you are asking in prayer is for

His sovereign will to be carried out in your life. This is the only way to restore the Christlike conduct Jesus commands in your marriage.

Upward and Sideways

Have you ever considered Adam from this perspective? Adam and Eve were the first married couple, representing the oneness in the Trinity. Becoming one flesh is so much deeper than the fusing of the actual flesh of our human existence. Two people cannot become one in the physical but, in the beings, the spiritual, as the two are fused together as one. What you find in every marriage established in Christ is one man and one woman fused together, and there is also a fusing of the Trinity within the marriage. It creates the most wonderful bond ever known to humanity. It is truly a mystery as to how God accomplishes it, and when He does, His love flows freely, vertically and horizontally.

Are you familiar with the story of Adam and Eve? If not, you can find their story in Genesis 2 and 3. Here is a perspective worth considering. If you are familiar with their story, would you say, based on Adam and Eve's actions, that Adam is living with Eve in an understanding way? Adam stood by and did nothing. If he did nothing, then no, he was not living with her in an understanding way. God entrusted Adam to be Eve's spiritual leader. He was to love her, as Christ loves him, which would be the church, us, now. He was to live with her in an understanding way. Adam should have known of his responsibility. He needed to communicate to Eve all the wonderful aspects and his relationship with God. The Bible doesn't tell us how long Adam walked with God before Eve was made from Adam's rib. But there were a lot of animals to be named.

If he did, at the first sign of temptation, which results from lust, he should have *moved*. God's relationship with Adam was so rich it should have caused Adam to act. Adam walked and talked with God daily. I understand the significance of God's and Adam's intimate relationship. If God desired it with Adam, He has not changed—He desires it with us as well. Do you desire to have an intimate relationship with God and experience it daily? Adam was accountable to God, and so are you and me. We are to teach our spouse everything we know about God. We have the same standard and accountability with our wives as Adam did. We are to be her spiritual leader, her disciple, and God is expecting us to be like Him; as He leads us, we lead them. We, like Adam, express the love we have for God and His for us. We make it known we are living based on God's provision, as Adam should have reminded Eve. Are you being the disciple God calls you to be with your spouse?

There is nothing greater than the love, grace, provision, blessing, and wisdom of God. Do you think Adam was watching her because he *was* "with her"? He should have stepped in, in an understanding way. He should have loved her back to the faithfulness God was showing them. And in love, Eve would have responded in love and submission to God, and Adam. How are you as a spiritual leader (disciple) with your spouse? Do you let her fend for herself? When necessary, are you stepping in, in love, and loving her back, so she responds in love and submission to God and you?

There is no gray area in marriage. You will either live by living out the Word of God in your life, or live as the world does, and not. Many people when they have "tied the knot," have filled the void of loneliness. Now no longer alone, they communicate their standards, expectations, and demands. They make sure their wife understands her role in the marriage. How she must submit and respect him. They claim that her failure to give him what he desires and deserves is not biblical. Some use the Bible as the means to justify behaviors, his and hers. A husband might claim his wife's actions are unbiblical, regardless of how he is treating and talking to her.

This creates a conflict. It begins to develop within the hearts of both, and it becomes clearer as the conflict grows. Sin begins to move in. It attempts to destroy the marriage. Anger, pride, and selfishness begin to invade their hearts. So he treats her as he pleases and screams, "that's biblical!" And she's not living by God's Word. Please understand, this is not loving like God loves, nor living with her in an understanding way.

Adam was banished. Our prayers are hindered. I am so grateful and thankful for the mercy and grace of God. He could have cast me into hell. He and I both know there were millions of times when He could! Because of His love, grace, mercy, and patience, it makes me say,

"THANK YOU, JESUS!" I say it every time the thoughts of my old self come passing through the corners of my mind. Did you ever consider that your prayers are hindered? If so, you should know what to do. Immediately, repent and ask for forgiveness from God and your spouse. Jesus is faithful and righteous to forgive and cleanse us. Your spouse begins to grow in the knowledge of God's Word. You do this through your work as a disciple of Jesus, by the power of the Holy Spirit. She will imitate you as you imitate Jesus! Your relationship grows deeper both vertically and horizontally!

A Dwelling Place For Prayer

Prayer was created to be an intimate part of our relationship with God. It is the way of speaking with God, and Him to us, as we listen intently when He speaks. Prayer gives us the means to directly communicate with God, and because of the work of Jesus, we no longer need humanity to be the go-between for absolving sin to receive forgiveness from God. As I have stated before, one will not be aware of another's struggles or the sin they may be dealing with themselves. God tells us we have Jesus, "who is at the right hand of the Father, who also intercedes for us" (Romans 8:34). The Trinity is intimate in all aspects of their existence. Our lives must be just as intimate as theirs, if they live in us, and we in them.

Prayer provides us the opportunity to pour out our heart and soul to God. God is the only one who fully knows and understands us individually. We should live knowing God will listen, because He truly loves us and wants the best for us. In prayer, we draw near to God, and He draws near to us. Prayer should encompass so much more than petition and pleas; there must also be prayers of praise and thanksgiving, which should be just as expressive as when our prayers are for some other immediate need.

We are called as disciples to pray for others. We must live with faith and confidence, knowing that God inclines His ear to hear us and will respond in whatever means He deems fitting for the circumstance, event, or trial. We must trust that He knows what everyone needs, and we respond in faith, even when His answer is not what we have asked for Him to do. Prayer is the instrument which maintains and nourishes our relationship with God—sometimes, prayer is just plain ol' talking and expressing your heart to our loving Father—but always focused and directed toward the sovereign will of God being carried out in our lives and the lives of others.

Prayer has been a natural characteristic, attribute, and action between Jesus, the Father, the Spirit, and His disciples. If prayer was not an important trait in Jesus's life, then I would expect Jesus would have never gone off to pray alone. He would have just stayed in constant contact with His disciples. While it is important to do the work of a disciple in spreading the gospel, I am testifying, it is just as important to keep in constant contact and communication with God, who *is* the source of your power. And if it is a trait of Jesus, then He expects, in our imitation of Him, it must be the same in us as we journey through this life. Know this: a light bulb only burns when it is hooked up to the power, and the power running through it is the source making it beam!

God's house is the house of prayer, and our bodies, which are the temple of His Spirit, are to be the same—a temple of prayer. It is a phenomenal blessing to know the Spirit of God dwells within our human existence. What does your prayer life look like? Did you complete any reflections on what category best described your prayer life in the opening paragraph? Do you understand the significance of constant communication with God in all aspects of your life? If prayer is other than instinctive, then pray and ask God what you need to change so that your prayer life becomes what Jesus intended for it to be.

Remember, a bulb without the power running through it from the source is ineffective for radiating light in the darkness surrounding it. You are the light He describes in Matthew 5:14: "You are the light of the world." Knowing what you know, and what you knew about the extent of darkness in yourself, you should have a great desire to beam in every place the Spirit leads you. In other words, illuminate everywhere to everybody.

Being Alone with God Is Nourishment

Have you been spiritually starving for nourishment? Are you famished and feel that you are lethargically wasting away to lifelessness? Do you keep attempting numerous things to satisfy your spiritual deficiency, and nothing moves your spiritual gauge off empty?

There is hope, and this hope is in the only One who can provide the spiritual nutrition, giving you the fuel to endure and persevere.

Jesus knows the power of prayer. It worked for Him, so it would only make good sense to look at what He did so that we can imitate Him and have the same result as He did. And if He did it constantly, He would expect His disciples to follow Him and do as He did! If prayer was so important in Jesus's life on earth, do you think He still prays? I would expect He does, and more than we know. But we will find out on "that day." He did, and it was for you!

Before we look at the following passages, I know if we were to ask His disciples, they would say, "Jesus prayed with us all the time." Once He taught them how to pray, they prayed all the time. These passages emphasize Jesus's need to pray to the Father, and it required time alone to accomplish it. Scripture says, He went to a secluded place by boat, mentioned in Matthew 14:13. Mark 1:35 says He rose early in the morning and went to a desolate place. Jesus went up on the mountain to pray, as it says in Mark 6:45-46. And He went further on to pray, also in Mark, 14:34-35.

Jesus was continually going to a desolate, secluded area or the mountain to pray. He understood the need and the importance of being alone with the Father. Jesus makes it blatantly obvious where and how we should pray, since most may not have access to a boat, secluded place, or mountain. Matthew 6:6-7 says, "But you, when you pray, go into your inner room, close your door and pray to your Father who is in secret, and your Father who sees *what is done* in secret will reward you." I would expect that every disciple has access to an inner room to pray. Jesus goes on to say, "And when you are praying, do not use meaningless repetition as the Gentiles do, for they suppose that they will be heard for their many words. So, do not be like them; for your Father knows what you need before you ask Him." This was an eye-opener for me. Jesus was saying that repetitive prayer is not what He desires to hear from hearts, be it silent or out loud. If prayer is following some "tradition or ritual" that repeats the same words hundreds of times, not one of them would be what He desires to hear. Jesus desires to hear the words from our heart, and meaningless repetition is a far cry from lifting up the soul and pouring out our heart to God. Solomon has good advice on praying in Ecclesiastes 5:2: "Do not be hasty in word or impulsive in thought to bring up a matter in the presence of God. For God is in heaven and you are on the earth; therefore, let your words be few."

I remember several months after the day of my salvation; I was on fire spiritually. This day, I had a conversation with a man who proclaimed he was a disciple of Jesus. He told me that he'd seen people like me, on fire, but over a short time my flame will fizzle out, just like most who act like me. He said it was all in my mind and questioned the true heart change. I can tell you; it was a punch right into my solar plexus, and spiritually I felt like I hit the floor face first and rolled up in a ball. It forced the spiritual air right out of me. It was like Satan was attempting to steal my joy of salvation from me, but the "seed" had fallen in good soil, and the root of the "seed" that was planted went deeper than I thought. Praise God!

I do not know what my face looked like when I got home, but Bonnie immediately recognized there was something wrong. She asked me what had happened, and I told her the story. When evening approached, I really did not have an appetite so just picked at my supper. When I went to bed, I had a tremendous amount of unrest, and I guess I experienced my first bout with doubt. Doubt can shake your spirituality to the core of your foundation. I did not sleep well, and about 3:00 a.m., I got out of bed, and Matthew 6 was on my mind. I will again testify that there is nothing better to occupy your mind with than the Word of God.

Up until this point, I would pray when I first woke up in bed, at the kitchen table, in the shower, on my way to work in the car, and in my office. I had never in my spiritual life gone into my inner room and closed the door. I guess one could say I was at the crossroads of my faith. You must believe this, as this is the truth. I would hope you believe, and if it is not true, that God would reveal that to you. Please know, I am not the only one proclaiming this truth about God.

I guess looking back now, what happened over the next five hours fully ignited my faith. When I walked into the inner room, I closed the door behind me. I did not just get down on my knees; I was laid out face down on the floor. It was the first time in my life I was completely humbled and submissive to God. I truly desired to know the truth! I needed to confirm that all of what I believed truly happened, and it was not just my imagination. It was the first time in my life I truly poured my heart and soul out to God. I needed to know if He was alive, and if He was, to please reveal Himself to me that day. I would have to say, as I look in the rear view mirror of my life, that this was a Psalm 139:16 moment. Jesus was ready for me, but I did not know what to expect from Him.

I did not see my next comment to God as an ultimatum. This is what happens when someone is at the crossroads of spiritual life and death. In the only way I knew how to communicate how I felt, I said, "Jesus, if you are real and alive, show me today, because if not, when I walk out of this room, I will never come back." This is the *all in or all out* frame of mind, and God knew this as well. He knows everything about us, and He knew that *if* all He needed to do was to reveal Himself, *then* I would love Him with all my heart. God is faithful to His will and Word and responds as He promises He will.

Jesus says in John 15:7, "If you abide in Me, and My words abide in you, ask whatever you wish, and it will be done for you." He and His words are abiding in me. And He says, in John 14:21, "He who has My commandments and keeps them is the one who loves Me; and he who loves Me will be loved by My Father, and I will love him and will disclose Myself to him." Jesus was doing exactly what He promised He would do. Amen? You must believe!

In response to my plea, Jesus said, "On the road to Damascus." His response was a bit confusing, as I expected him to say "Yes, I am alive." But "on the road to Damascus?' I did not even know what it meant. But I did hear something, and it was the voice of God. He did remove all the uncertainty and anxiousness and I went back to bed and fell off to sleep.

A few hours later, Bonnie and I were doing our daily devotional. I was about to proceed with our normal passages when I said to her, "Oh, I must read on the road to Damascus." You know how I knew it was not me? I did not even know how to spell Damascus. When I found it, it was in Acts chapter 9 and titled "The Conversion of Saul." After I read it to Bonnie, I explained the previous evening and then wondered how the road to Damascus was applicable in my life. Just like the foreword in this book for you, God used Bonnie to confirm His truth and works in me. Those same works Jesus did to convert and save Saul were similar works used to convert and save me. God removed the scales from Paul's eyes, as He did from mine. She fanned my spiritual flame when she said, "The Lord has saved your life, and this is a beautiful thing. You said, 'the Lord is speaking to you,' and I believe you!" PRAISE GOD!

The flame of the living God was on, and so was I. That was over sixteen years ago. Thank You, Jesus! So I will testify that there is something to be said about being alone with God. It confirms by the actions you demonstrate by faith that He is alive and is listening, and He will respond. But believe me, it takes faith to believe. If you have never followed the command of Jesus to go into your inner room, then I suggest you do so by taking the first step of faith and go in. *The next steps of faith become easier to take once you take the first one!*

As disciples of Jesus, we must imitate Him in desiring to be alone with the Father. You will see throughout God's Word the importance, worth, and need for prayer, and being alone with God. I have been alone with God for over two years now while writing of *Walking, The Way*. It has been the most exhilarating time in my spiritual journey thus far. As I am testifying to you through the words of this book, know I testify of God's work in me as a person also!

Prayer confirms our desire to be in unity with God, one on one. How many times as a parent does it bring you joy when your child asks to speak with you alone? In this time alone, they reveal their intimate thoughts, desires, and heart. Do you feel the same way, when a person or another disciple asks you the same question? Just imagine how the

Father feels when we have the same request of Him. God desires the same intimacy with us, and Jesus knew He needed the same time alone with the Father. We all do as well.

Being alone with God develops our intimacy with Him. We learn, grow, gain understanding, and feel God's unfailing love. He draws closer to us, and we to Him, as our relationship deepens and becomes more intimate. Our prayer life must contain prayers for the saints, the unbelieving, and ourselves. Prayer with and for others is a blessing, but it never takes the place of prayer in secret to God, which gives us the opportunity to open our hearts to God alone as He hears, and listens to His children. Psalm 116:1–2 is a promise you must claim as a disciple of Jesus; it says, "I love the Lord, because He hears My voice and my supplications. Because He has inclined His ear to me, therefore I shall call *upon Him* as long as I live." Praying alone to God confirms our relationship and our desire to live life deeply with Him. Disciples who are dads truly desire to live life deeply with their children, amen?

Prayer Is a Continuous Work

By now it should be blatantly obvious to you that Jesus PRAYED! Jesus is the perfect example on how often we should pray. First Thessalonians 5:17 says we are to "pray without ceasing." Jesus knows the importance and power of prayer and knew His need for it every day. And we should be the same because God knows we need it. Jesus knows prayer is required for the mighty work of the Father to be carried out in our lives. Whether it was in and through His life while on earth, or in and through our lives today, prayer is needed, all the time!

Jesus needed time alone with the Father to prepare for His trials. In the Garden of Gethsemane, He was preparing physically, emotionally, and spiritually to lay down His life for His disciples—them, you, me and every one of those following us. In our life as a disciple of Jesus, we will experience trials physically, emotionally, financially, and spiritually. Can you guess what you will need? I would think prayer would be the first thing coming to your mind.

Jesus prayed continuously, and we are called to imitate Him—all of Him. Ephesians 5:1 says, "Therefore be imitators of God, as beloved children;" God's plan for humanity is we "become conformed to the image of His Son," as it says in Romans 8:29.

Prayer is our lifeline and is a form of direct communication with God. Prayer is the same as any communication—it is between two or more people and it is bi-directional. Prayer requires both speaking and *listening*. When we are praying to God, we tend to do all the speaking. When our prayer is in petition form, we pour out our hearts, hoping God is listening, do we not? When we pray in faith by the work of the Spirit, we trust God is not only listening but that He will respond to our petition according to His will.

Jesus talked to His disciples directly, and He does today, because He is risen and alive. Do you believe this? Know He is the same; He has not changed, and that's biblical! Hebrews 13:8 says, "Jesus Christ is the same yesterday and today and forever." See it this way; *He did walk with the initial disciples; is walking with the present ones; and will be walking with all of them forever*! Jesus was faithful to His word, is faithful to His word, and will always be faithful to His word. Therefore, those in His time on earth were saved, there are those being saved today, and all will be saved when all of Jesus's disciples enter His kingdom. Can you see it now! He's the same, and I love that He is! And believe, He will always be who He said, is, and will be, amen?

Jesus's disciples know and believe John 10:27 is true. To hear Jesus's voice, you must believe in Him. You must have faith He will speak, and you will be waiting patiently for Him as you attentively listen for His voice. Are you actively listening, and patiently waiting for God to speak? When praying to God, be prepared to listen more than you do to anyone or anything else. God's words, written and oral, are the most important words you will ever read or hear! God's truth made known in His Word is our strength, the protector of our hearts and souls forever.

Have you ever been too busy to pray? Or do you pray, and your prayers are those of habit, following the same old pattern? Prayer to God is to be an expression of adoration, confession, repentance, gratitude, thanksgiving, and praise from a sincere heart. I have heard on numerous occasions people saying, "We'll just say a 'quick' prayer, for the sake of time..." This would be the same as calling someone just to say, "I called."

At times, just throwing up a quick prayer can lack substance and sincerity. I wonder what God thinks of our "I am too busy but let me toss this up to You so You can do something with it, and I can get on with what I need to do." I would imagine it saddens His heart.

We must always be mindful of the importance of prayer and our need for it. It is the most effective way to speak to God. If you have a desire to be in constant communication with your loved ones, where do you think you receive that desire? How many times have we just taken each day for granted and been too busy to pray? There is an old saying, which has been said in various ways: "Prayer is the tiny nerve moving the Mighty Right Hand of God." If you lived by this—would your prayer life be different when you actually saw God's Mighty Right Hand *move* in response to your prayer? Prayer is intimate communication with God, requiring faith, reverence, and full devotion.

Pray at All Times and Every Season

Prayer keeps us buoyant rather than sinking under the weight of the yoke or of the toil produced by trials. Praying, takes our mind off the circumstance and puts our focus on God. God becomes our focus because He is greater than any trial we could ever face. Our prayer life must be continuous, and we must be receptive to whatever answer God provides. Our prayer life honors God for who He is, what He's doing, and what He will do in our lives. God is always the focus of our prayers. Our prayers are a love language to God, and prayers are His to us.

Jesus gives a powerful promise on prayer in John 14:13, which says, "Whatever you ask in My name, that will I do, so that the Father may be glorified in the Son." Jesus confirms that the Holy Spirit will carry our request to Him and His answer to us—especially prayers for our work as a disciple by the power of the Holy Spirit. Pray for wisdom when facing tough decisions. Pray when in need of extending forgiveness or requesting it. Pray for strength in times of weakness. Pray when facing temptation, and when you need to encourage or rebuke. And most importantly, pray and ask the Spirit of God to move in the heart of an unbeliever when sharing the gospel. I pray for His inspiration in the writing of this book. I pray God will be glorified and will use it to encourage His disciples or bring salvation to someone ... you.

Praying is not a new method by which God's work is carried out. Prayer was prevalent in the Old Testament and the New, and has been an active part of Jesus's disciples' lives even today. Everyone doing kingdom work, facing difficulties or challenges, and in the face of certain death, PRAYED!

Abraham prayed to God, and God healed Abimelech, his wife and his maidens, so they bore children (Genesis 20:17). Isaac prayed on behalf of his wife because she was barren, and the Lord answered him, and Rebekah conceived a child (Genesis 25:21). Moses prayed, because God was angry with Aaron and was going to destroy him (Deuteronomy 9:20). As a result of Moses's prayer, God relented. Hannah prayed because the Lord closed her womb. Scripture says Hannah continued to pray; she was faithful to pray, year after year, and waited patiently for God (1 Samuel 1:12).

Samuel prayed to the Lord (1 Samuel 8:6). Elisha prayed in secret behind closed doors (2 Kings 4:33). Hezekiah prayed before the Lord (2 Kings 19:15). God answered Hezekiah's prayer through Isaiah (2 Kings 19:20). Nehemiah prayed to the God of heaven (Nehemiah 2:4). Job prayed for his friends (Job 42:10). Jeremiah prayed to the Lord (Jeremiah 32:16). Daniel prayed to the Lord (Daniel 9:4). Jonah prayed to the Lord (Jonah 2:1).

Can you see it? All of those who did mighty works of God prayed. So if prayer worked for those mentioned, why is it so hard for some to see prayer does work. Yet it is not a constant in some people's lives today. Could this be a reason God does not move in response to your prayers?

All of Jesus's disciples pray continuously. At some point, every disciple of Jesus will need wisdom, patience, forgiveness, guidance, understanding, discernment, self-control, faith, confession, repentance, and scores of other things to faithfully do the will of the Father. Prayer must be our first consideration before taking any action. Throughout Scripture, prayer was needed to overcome whatever the disciple faced.

Prayer requires faith as we wait on God to respond and move. God's answer may require us to wait, or to change our perspective or actions, for God to move on our behalf. Prayer involves patience, waiting on God in faithfulness, and knowing what Jesus knows that He who promised is faithful. Hebrews 10:23 says, "Let us hold fast the confession of our hope without wavering, for He who promised is faithful." For the most powerful work performed by God in and through man, *prayer paved the way.*

Reflect on These Remedies

In this life on earth, we will face all kinds of circumstances causing us to reach out because they are beyond our control. You may have already faced some, and there are others yet to be faced. It would be extremely difficult to list them all, and who other than God would know the where and when for each of us? Have confidence ... God is there for all of them.

You may be experiencing one, two, or several now in your life, or know of someone who is experiencing them. God's Word has all we need. The more you read, study, and meditate on it, the more you will find thousands of God's promises you can claim. I would say we all need to pray, and it should be without ceasing. Below are some passages to encourage you in your time for seeking God in prayer:

Guidance:	**Truth:**	**Fear:**
Psalm 32:8;	John 14:6; 17:17;	Luke 12:5
Proverbs 3:5-6	Ephesians 4:14-15	

Discouraged:	**Reading God's Word:**	**Crisis:**
Psalm 23; 42:6-11	John 5:39; Psalm	Psalm 121;
	1:2; 119:105	Matthew 6:25-34

Worried:	**Courage:**	**Forgiveness:**
Matthew 6:25-34	Psalm 27:14	Mark 11:25-26;
		Ephesians 4:31-32

Adversity:	**Anxiety:**	**Trust:**
Matthew 10:16-39	Matthew 6:19-34	Psalm 37:3-5; Proverbs 3:5-6
Death:	**Hope:**	**Purity:**
1 Cor. 15:54-56	1 Peter 1:13	Matthew 5:27-32; 2 Timothy 2:22
God's Protection:	**Confession of Sin:**	**Temptation:**
Psalm 91	James 5:16	1 Cor. 10:13
Fruits of the Spirit:	**Wisdom:**	**Love:**
Galatians 5:22-23	James 1:5-8	Luke 10:27; 1 Cor. 13:4-8a
Suffering:	**Doubt:**	**Patience:**
1 Peter 5:9-10	Matthew 8:26; 14:28-31; Hebrews 11	Hebrews 10:36
Disappointment:		
1 Peter 2:4-6		

There are numerous passages in which disciples prayed, and God did the work. One of my favorites is Elijah. Scripture says, in James 5:17, "Elijah was a man with the nature like ours and he prayed earnestly [sincerely and intensely] that it would not rain, and it did not rain on the earth for three years and six months." I gain hope and confidence in the Holy Spirit's work in me, because Elijah was a man just like you and me. God can and has answered my prayers, and He can and will answer yours, just like He has for all His disciples who continue in His Word.

When I asked Jesus, what prayer meant to Him, His response was "sustenance." From eternity past until forever, prayer is sustenance to Jesus. We should see prayer as food to sustain and nourish us, as it does Jesus. Make prayer a constant in your life. How would your physical body be without nourishment? I would expect you to say it would be malnourished. Well, you need to consider the impact on your spiritual life when it is malnourished due to the lack of prayer.

Our High Priest Prays

I hope you see the fullness of what Jesus has done, is doing, and will be doing for those who live out the Great and Foremost Commandment. Jesus laid down His life as a ransom for many, but before He did, He prayed for all His disciples, asking the Father to give them eternal life. He asked they come to know the only true God, and Himself. He requested for all His disciples to be filled with His joy (John 15:11). To live out His command to "Go and make disciples," the Father will put His Word in you, and you will have the ability to keep it, by the power of the Holy Spirit, as you *live out* your calling.

Take some time to read, study, and meditate on Jesus's prayer in John 17, "The High Priestly Prayer." It takes up whole chapter and is full and rich! If you want to hear the heart of your Lord, God, Savior, and Rabbi, praying for you, you will find it there. Read it numerous times.

I am learning John 17 as a memory chapter. This is Jesus's prayer to the Father as the mediator and intercessor for all His disciples. I love memorizing God's Word; it brings life and substance to my heart and soul. It is a great model to follow. It should bring tears to your eyes when you read it, and joy to your heart when you cite it!

Did you know, everything is YES in Jesus?

His High Priestly Prayer is one of adoration, thanksgiving, gratitude, acknowledgement, remembrance, and supplication. Jesus's prayer communicated and demonstrated His love for the Father and for His disciples—the initial ones, and us. He knows of the Father's love for the world and Himself, and He expects His disciples to love just like they do!

He expressed thankfulness for the Father's gift to Him, His disciples, all of them, from the beginning of the gospel message until a new heaven and earth appear. Jesus pours His heart out to the Father for us, and His prayer contains numerous elements. The ones standing out for me were when He prayed for Himself, prayed for His disciples, petitioned God, and asked the Father to keep, sanctify, unite, and be glorified in Him, you, and me. This is a prayer for strength and guidance. He is teaching us how and what to pray.

When we pray, our prayers must be in faith, with an open and honest heart. I've heard it said, "God desires a holy heart, versus holy actions." Our prayers must be Christ-centered, focused on the will of the Father, and led by the Holy Spirit. You must fully believe you can approach God with confidence, and this truth is confirmed in Hebrews 4:16, which says, "Therefore let us draw near with confidence to the throne of grace, so that we might receive mercy and find grace to help in time of need." As a disciple, we will always need to draw near to the throne of grace, for ourselves, and for those we are discipling.

I would think most desire to have "help in time of need." And in order to be a vessel for God to anyone, especially when you are discipling, you need wisdom, discernment, and understanding, as you are discussing life with a person who is an unbeliever and your response to their inquiry must be seasoned with salt. Yes, there may be times when you are struggling because of a trial, and you need mercy and grace to endure, make it through, and continue to grow spiritually. Be sure to spend time in prayer before, during, and after.

Jesus also requested protection from the Father to guard His disciples and, most importantly, to keep them and us in the world. We are to be the words, action, and truth, by teaching future disciples. If it had stopped with the initial ones, there would be no one to teach you and me. We must be faithful to Jesus to carry on His words to the hearts prepared to receive them. The life of the disciple is to be the focus of our prayer life when we are entrusted with the duty to make disciples. If you were to stop and meditate on all the Father, Son, and Spirit has done in your life, you should want to express the same adoration, thanksgiving, acknowledgement, remembrance, petition and supplication clearly and enthusiastically as Jesus did.

Jesus's prayer demonstrates the perfect bond of unity within the Trinity, and in us. This unity of love is perfected in us through the Father, Son, and Spirit. Our love for God must be with all our heart, soul, mind, and strength, as it says in Deuteronomy 6:5, and Matthew 22:37. Our lives are lived in imitation of Jesus's love. As the love of

God flows through us to others, we become pleasing in the eyes of the Father. Our love for our neighbor surpasses the love we have for self. No longer should any of Jesus's disciples have the perspective of a "quick prayer for the sake of time." Nor can we be too busy by letting distractions interfere with our prayer life and our time alone with God. I pray you spend time in intimate communication through prayer to God. Remember, Jesus prayed and poured His heart out to the Father for you. It should be out of love you pour your heart out to the Father *through* Him.

A Prayer for You:

ABBA, I love You and I thank You for this day and the time You granted for writing this segment. It is surely Romans 2 for me as well. Your Word is a great reminder and made it clear to me when I teach another, I am teaching myself. I have learned to pay close attention to the words proceeding out of my mouth, and You know this. You have placed me on the journey of learning, and I hope it goes on forever! Please forgive me for the times when I was unfaithful and chose to push off time for intimate communication with You alone in prayer. I know the workings of this book have come by the power of Your Spirit working in me. I am humbled by Your love, grace, mercy, and forgiveness.

Today, I pray You create a desire in all disciples to see prayer to You as You see prayer to the Father—sustenance for our spiritual existence. I know without the work of Your Spirit, none of this is possible. I ask You to lead and inspire those disciples to see and hear the message You have placed on my heart through the words of this book, and Your calling on their life.

I pray Your Spirit will move in their lives, giving them the ability and spiritual eyesight to recognize the importance of what You are calling us to do on this earth. How we respond communicates to You what we perceive as the importance and the accountability of Your calling on our lives as disciples, and our responsibility to live our calling out daily.

I know as we see the work of Your Spirit moving in our lives, we marvel at Your sovereign will being lived out in us just as You planned. Let our lives glorify You, Lord, and by the power of Your Spirit, we move in the lives of the people You have ordained to receive the gospel as we preach the Word, and do the will of the Father.

I pray we are useful vessels You use to glorify the Father. I am so thankful and grateful for all those whose eyes are opened and will be opened, as they read the truth of who You are and what You command us to do. I ask and pray their hearts are kindled anew with desire to love, serve, honor, and worship You in all they think, say, and do.

I pray for all of those you lead to reach for this book who are not Your disciples. I pray and ask, by Your command that their eyes and ears are opened to receive what You are saying that Your Spirit comes upon them, and that You save them like You have been doing from the beginning of the world.

I thank You for this time and opportunity to bring forth a work worthy to You and pleasing in Your sight. Please use it to glorify the Father. I ask all of this in Jesus's name, AMEN!

Reflections

TESTIMONY...

And the testimony is this, that God has given us eternal life,
and this life is in His Son. (1 John 5:11)

FREE AT LAST

It would be easy for me just to tell you the wonderful work of God in my life and call it a day and that sometimes, it is totally fine just to say, BUT GOD! Because at the end of the road, when I am standing at the judgment seat of Christ, this will be my testimony. It was You, and I owe it *all* to You. Many times when talking about life change, all I have to say to someone who has been delivered from the bondage and captivity of sin is, BUT GOD, and they fully understand the context and significance of what I am saying.

Captivity by sin can be ravaging and is destroying lives every moment of every day. Not only those of the person who's in bondage, but also those related to them. These painful parts of our life are there to share. I expect it is God's way of allowing us to testify to another about the effects and destruction sin can have in one's life. Although we hate the damage and destruction it caused us and those we love, sometimes it is necessary to open the channel of this painful part of our lives to help another avoid it or be freed from it, and to offer hope by the work of God they also can be free from this captivity.

You read the preface, and I hope your response would be, "David, you were not alone, I was there, too! PRAISE GOD for deliverance and the light of Jesus Christ!"

I believe it when God's Word says, "the god of this world has blinded the minds of the unbelieving" (2 Corinthians 4:4), because the deceiver used illusions and me to do it. When you are existing in spiritual darkness, the only thing you can see is yourself. How else could I be blinded when I could actually physically see?

There is no doubt life change occurs in Jesus's disciples. Yes, it brings joy and gratitude when they are no longer held captive in the bondage and slavery of sin. We are FREE! We are free to love, free to give, free to serve, and free to experience peace, joy, happiness, kindness, faithfulness, gentleness, and self-control in all relationships. These relationships extend from the home, work, and wherever we go. A tremendous amount of love, joy, and happiness fill the heart of the disciple when the Holy Spirit regenerates and transforms their life into a new creature. Jesus Christ becomes our life as we die to self.

Not until Jesus freed me, did I understand the magnitude of sin's bondage and captivity in my life. As a result of God's work, this biblical truth is real in my life. John 8:36 is this truth: "So if the Son makes you free, you will be free indeed." This gives me a totally new understanding of Dr. Martin Luther King's proclamation: "Free at last, free at last, THANK GOD ALMIGHTY, I AM FREE AT LAST!" Rest assured, I will proclaim this truth as well ... and add, THANK YOU, JESUS!

The Testimony that Really Matters

There are thousands with stories of slavery to sin. And for those observing, it is hard to believe anyone could live in such enslavement, or how can escaped captives be enticed to return voluntarily? They cannot see the freedom they could live in if they could only break the chains of captivity. I know. I've failed at it miserably.

Even though I was a slave to sin, when something destructive happened, I wondered how I could have let myself get so far gone. This is the deceptiveness of sin. I seemed to always look at others, never myself, as it was always their fault that I acted the way I did. I was blind to my chains of enslavement, deceived into believing I was free to choose whatever I wanted, and whatever I chose would be good for me.

It doesn't matter what the "so far gone" conditions are. They could be immorality, impurity, jealousy, envy, anger, alcohol and drug addiction, stealing, lying, and the many others keeping one bound to this earth. It is normally in the secrecy of your mind you ask yourself, "How could I live like this?" What I failed to notice were my spiritual chains and bondage.

With all the different opinions, religions, and beliefs out there, if there ever is a testimony one should believe as the truth, it must be the testimony of God Himself. Yes, the God of the universe, the Creator has a testimony, and you will find it in His Word, the Bible. Remember, we all have a fallen nature, so if we are dependent on opinions, religions, and beliefs created on man's wisdom, then the potential for deception exists. Man is capable of being deceptive and will deceive numerous people. Satan, even more clever and crafty than man could ever be, will deceive many. He was crafty enough to deceive man in the Garden of Eden, and he is no different today. Therefore it is vital to have one truth we can trust, and this truth is the testimony of God.

A testimony is an authentication of a fact. The fact stated in 1 John 5:11 is, "And the testimony is this, that God has given us eternal life, and this life is in His Son." In other words, there is no eternal life outside of Jesus, because there is only eternal life in Him. Therefore, you must be in Jesus, and He must be in you, for you to live eternally with them. God has an eternal purpose for man, and His purpose is to be in relationship with humanity forever. In His sovereign will, He will ensure the journey of this life will prepare us for eternity and lead us to Him.

We only have two options: believe this testimony as truth, or believe it to be a lie—there's no gray area. You must be on one side of the truth or the other. For one to disprove a lie, one must have the truth. What other means does one have to disprove this truth and render it a lie? There are only two means for verification. One is God's Word, and the passage to support God's testimony is John 5:32, which says, "There is another who testifies of Me, and I know that the testimony which He gives about Me is true." But if you are one who does not believe the Word of God, then you must be taking the position what God says is a lie. Remember, it is one or the other, truth or lie.

The other means to confirm if this truth of eternal life is true will be on the last day of your life on this earth. It may be the most horrific way to find out that God's testimony about Jesus was true, and you refused to believe. What do you suppose the consequence would be if it is true? Do you think you can live forever with Jesus's decision about your unbelief in Him?

Hebrews 3:19 says, "So we see that they were not able to enter because of unbelief." Unbelief is a sure-fire condemning sin, especially since God has made Himself evident to all humanity. As a result of unbelief, the heart is closed, and the spirit and soul are prevented from entering the kingdom of God. Hence, no eternal life. Again, do you believe this truth?

The truth: Do you believe God's truth about Jesus and your need for Him as your Savior? Or do you believe eternal life will be based on what you have done, with the hope your life was good enough for you to live eternally? Stop and consider what you believe, and if what you believe is not consistent with God's Word, then recognize you are heading to the above-mentioned most horrific moment. Believe me or believe God; it's true!

It is a Way of Life, Not Mere Words

In our society, most people associate a person's testimony with a court proceeding. In legal proceedings, one's testimony is given under oath and they verbally profess to tell the truth, the whole truth, by placing their right hand on the Bible. Isn't it interesting, most do not believe the Bible is true, yet it's an instrument the courts of law use as the means to ensure the truth is communicated? I wonder what the judge would do, if someone said, "I do not believe in the Bible," and refused to place their hand on it to testify. Would the judge allow them to proceed? I wonder what would happen when they refuse to take the oath? I am certain many lawyers know the answer to this question. With the placing of their right hand on the Bible, they are swearing to the court they can expect the truth from their lips. If it is only the outside of the Bible confirms that what is said is the truth, why do so many not believe what's on the inside, yet place their hand on it?

An interesting observation: the oath is stated to the witness, and it ends with "so help me God." The witness is required to affirm that they will comply with the truth of their testimony. The swearing of an oath is supposed to validate the testimony they give will be with greater care and is the truth. If they are to struggle, God should intervene and assist with the production of it. But the truth is, it is what fills the heart of the person testifying determining if they will speak the truth or tell a lie when questioned. If the love of God and the truth of His Word is not filling the heart of the one testifying, it increases the potential for deception, and the witness is muttering mere words.

The disciple's testimony must be greater than just mere words. Our life, not just our words, must reflect God's testimony about His Son as we live out Jesus's promise of eternal life. We live by faith in God's promises, and it is in believing that His truth comes to us and proceeds through us to others. We who believe grasp onto the Son of God and His Spirit. We live our lives in full expectation of receiving the promised inheritance of eternal life. It is brought forth in the gospel, and we live out and preach the truth, the testimony of God, to all we encounter. In other words, our walk is the gospel alive in us, and how we live it out authenticates its truth, as we disciple everywhere the Spirit of God leads us.

The disciple's testimony is about so much more than the bondage and captivity of sin. Everyone, before being saved by Jesus, is bound in the slavery of sin and all need to be saved. Romans 3:23 says, "all have sinned and fall short of the glory of God." Therefore, every new disciple is someone delivered from the bondage of sin. Their testimony is about the salvation and deliverance resulting from God's work, not their own.

When the Israelites were being pursued by the Egyptians, God parted the Red Sea because they were trapped and needed freedom. We are like them, trapped in sin and facing certain death. Without the work of God in their lives and ours, we have no freedom. Without the work of God in man's life, there is no eternal life, only judgment and eternal separation from God.

Our testimony proclaims all the wonderful and amazing works Jesus has done in His ministry on earth, in ourselves, and all those who are to follow us. These works will be accomplished through the power of the Holy Spirit. Salvation is a wonderful blessing and gift from God. To know and believe God in His infinite love, grace, and mercy, saves; thus, making all who are saved proclaim that it is truly AMAZING GRACE! This is my testimony, I was blind, but now I see.

Jesus's disciples' testimony is really about what happened after their foot touched the sand on the other side of the Red Sea. It could be easy for me to say I was free when my foot hit the sand, and end of story, but, there's more to it than that. It is always about the saving power of Jesus, and the freedom found in Him comes when you reach the other side, where your first steps of freedom begin.

Jesus asked me, "What happened when your foot touched the other side of the Red Sea?" Here is the answer I wrote to His question. I learned sin was prevalent in my life. I was being held captive and captivated by it simultaneously. It was extremely appealing to me, and I enjoyed the pleasures of it.

I rarely considered the consequences and the destruction it could, would, and did bring into my life. My sin affected and infected the lives of those around me. The snares of sin commence as minor and appear to be controllable. I proceeded with a false sense of confidence, not realizing I was blind to the depth of it.

As sin continued to compound itself, it grew in enormity, intensity, and severity. I began to recognize it was influencing my thoughts, words, and deeds. At this point, I had no self-control; I began to sink deeper into its clutches as it sank deeper into my heart. I could not escape and needed to be rescued by You.

Jesus, I know You already knew. When You gave me a fresh set of eyes to see and brought me into Your light, I realized I was free! While standing there, I realized it was me! I was the culprit all along; please forgive me.

I saw the wonderful work of God when He removed my heart of stone and gave me a heart of flesh. God, through grace, gave me a new spirit, and put His Spirit in me. I received spiritual faith in Him alone to believe. He made me into a new creature, and the old man and his ways passed away as I passed between the walls of water to my salvation. I have been reconciled to God, and my transgressions, though many, are forgiven and remembered no more. I began to learn to freely love God with all my heart, soul, mind, and strength, and others with the love of

God present now in my heart. I began to believe every word proceeding from the mouth of God, as my faith was now completely in Him for His deliverance.

The disciple's testimony should address sin's captivity, as any unbeliever will be able to relate to it. It is also designed to tell of the wonderful works of God, and their new life in Jesus Christ. The gifts of grace, faith, eternal life, promises, and the truth of His Word permeate through every part of the disciple's existence. The first disciples' testimony demonstrated what life in Jesus Christ would be and how it looks. You see, it was a way to communicate what they saw Jesus doing in the lives of people. There were physical healings, yes, but it was the spiritual healing of all the others who did not have a physical ailment, but were like me, spiritually poor and dead that made a strong impression. As stated, all of God's work and power is through God the Holy Spirit. Life change truly occurs when the Spirit of God comes upon you and you are born of the Spirit!

Over the past sixteen years, I have seen God's will carried out many times in my life. As I continue to learn His will was being carried out even when I was far from Him. I trust in the promises of God because His Word is true, and it continues to renew my mind, strengthening my faith, hope, and trust in Him alone. It is about the new life and self, created in Jesus. It's about deliverance, love, and forgiveness—what Jesus has done, is doing, and will do from the day of your salvation, until He calls you home or He returns in glory. I claim and believe this promise of God, stated in Philippians 1:6, "*For I am* confident of this very thing, that He who began a good work in you will perfect it until the day of Christ Jesus." Therefore, I am a disciple under construction, continually growing, living out my calling, awaiting with confidence for the day I will see Jesus as He is! Thank You, Jesus!

God Can Restore What the Locusts Have Eaten

I should have been a statistic like so many others whose marriage and family relationships were destroyed because of the practice of sin. The life I was living, and the plethora of sin controlling me, scorched the life right out of my marriage. I had no one else to blame but myself. The way I was speaking and treating my family was far from Christlikeness. BUT GOD, through His love, forgiveness, grace, and mercy, restored my marriage and my relationship with my daughters.

The first sign of my life change was a need to repent and ask for forgiveness from God. I needed to seek forgiveness from Bonnie and my children. God created a burning desire to read His Word and saturate my mind with it. He knew what occupied it, and it would take being renewed to cover up the brand of the images of pornography. I found the more I read His word, the more it started to influence my thoughts, conversations, and discussions. I began to see the need for use of it in the discipling of myself, Bonnie, and my children. I started to love in a way that was not familiar, as there were no conditions and expectations set; and therefore, disappointment from the unrealistic expectations started to fade away.

I learned I could freely forgive any sin committed against me in the past, and this forgiveness would include the present, and future. I acknowledged my sin against God, and when I do sin, I continually seek His forgiveness. Psalm 32:5 says exactly how I felt. It says, "I acknowledged my sin to You, and my iniquity I did not hide; I said, 'I will confess my transgressions to the Lord'; And You forgave the guilt of my sin."

God the Holy Spirit has given me the ability to memorize His Word, and I have written it down on the tablet of my heart. I can see the Holy Spirit is working and His fruits present and active in my life. I am learning why His fruits start with love as I work toward self-control. I love to serve God and His people, and it brings tremendous joy when I can love and encourage another. I have learned how to pray and the importance of it, and how to work as Jesus's disciple. I am living in obedience to Jesus's commands, and I desire to do the will of the Father. I am thankful Jesus saves, and I am thankful God has entrusted me with His gospel, because I know it is the power of God for salvation to everyone who believes. Remember Romans 1:16–17?

Here's what I mean when I say God can restore what the locusts have eaten. I do not know if you have ever seen what a crop looks like after it is been ravaged by locusts; it's devastated. Our marriage had the signs of a field of corn demolished by hail. It was severely damaged, and although it had hints of life, there would not be much to take to market, and our yield would be a loss for sure. If you have never seen a picture of what the corn resembles, then check it out. For the farmer, the hopes of harvest are gone. For the marriage, the hope for restoration is gone, and like the corn, the only alternative is to plow it under. With marriage, the finality of divorce is almost inevitable because of a hardened heart, full of the sins of selfishness, pride, and bitterness, which get in the way of any reconciliation. Without forgiveness, the hurt and pain continues to fester and eat away all the goodness the relationship did contain. So, plow it under!

When the hail hits, it is normally in the summer, and harvest is in the late fall. Even if you tried to replant, the growth cycle would never be completed in time. If sin is not eradicated from the center of a marriage, and the two refuse to have Jesus as their focus of existence, then there is no real hope for growth and life of these two spiritual beings who were once one flesh. However, when Jesus becomes the center and focus of your life, you begin to see new growth! If you were to see this field of corn, there would not be new stalks growing out of the damaged plant. There would be a new plant growing right next to the damaged one. In other words, in the marriage, although they are the same people on the outside, there is new life, a spiritual one, and growth in this *new self* on the inside. True love from God begins to exist between the two because they no longer must manufacture love. It is now God's love flowing through me to her, and through her to me.

There is now patience, kindness, and consideration. She is now more important than me. The necessity to needle her in response to disappointment ceases. There's encouragement, and the desire to keep score or track of the wrongs suffered stops. Now these new hearts freely forgive, and when forgiveness is needed, both freely do, without any hesitation. It becomes a marriage God intended, and joy and happiness fill the air of the home that used to be flooded with yelling and profanity. There is peace, prayers, and praise to God for His saving power and life change echoes throughout the home where the Spirit of God now dwells.

It is All About Him

There are a lot of people who from birth, and then through adolescence to adulthood—which, happens by the grace of God—seem to maintain the mindset of "it is about me." In all truthfulness, which becomes evident by one's behavior with this sinful nature, they keep self at the center and forefront of their mind and lives. Selfishness has caused more problems and broken more relationships than anything else. Because even at the root of sin is self.

Here is a perspective to consider, which also will serve as confirmation of the sinful nature and the problem of self-centeredness. In Genesis 3, titled "The Fall of Man," specifically verses 1–6, "you" is used six times and "your" is used once, for a total of seven. So one would have to say, it is all about "you." This (you) is what Satan uses to blind "your" mind and deceive "you." Verse 6 has some very profound words which feeds one's selfishness. They are "good," "delight," "desirable," and "took." Can you see how sin can progress? It starts with perspective, and then creates the action, and we act in response.

If sin was unattractive or bad, caused discontentment, and was undesirable, would you partake in it? I would hope your answer would be no. But with the deception of sin being good, delightful, and desirable, a mindset is created that plagues us all. If it did this to Adam and Eve, it sure will us. I know I can only speak for myself. I would hope you would testify; I am not alone. But I must testify that it was never about you, and will never be about you. It is all about Jesus … always was, and always will be!

One of my favorite books of the Bible, the book of Colossians, sets out for us how and why it's all about Jesus. I would like to identify and emphasize with the bolding of this truth. Colossians 1:15–20 says:

> **He is** the image of the invisible God, the firstborn of
> all creation. For **by Him** all things were created, *both* in
> the heavens and on earth, visible and invisible, whether

thrones or dominions or rulers or authorities—all things have been created **through Him** and **for Him. He is** before all things, and **in Him** all things hold together. **He is** also head of the body, the church; and **He is** the beginning, the firstborn from the dead, so that **He Himself** will come to have first place in everything. For it was the *Father's* good pleasure for all the fullness to dwell **in Him,** and **through Him** to reconcile **all things to Himself,** having made peace through the blood of **His cross; through Him,** *I say,* whether things on earth or things in heaven. (bold emphasis added)

Fourteen times this passage references Jesus. How many times does it reference "you?" Zero! So, may I say, and you should be in agreement, it is *not* about you. *It is all about Him!* Amen?

When the apostles testified to the unbelievers of their time, it was all about Jesus. We should imitate them, as they imitated Jesus. His message was all about the Father. It is Jesus who has done the mighty work of God in the lives of all His disciples. If you are proclaiming to be a disciple of Jesus and no one knows you are, then you should ask yourself, why you are not doing your work as His disciple. Remember, He *will* hold you accountable, and He promises He will. Here is a promise for all of us to be mindful of, found in Revelation 22:12, which states, "Behold, I am coming quickly, and My reward *is* with Me, to render to every man according to what he has done." In other words, Jesus will be looking at your work, and what you have done with what He has entrusted to you. Is it for Him, or are you only focused on yourself?

As with all disciples, each knew they once lived and were held captive in sin. Sin either controlled or dominated their life. You will hear out of the mouths of those delivered from the clutches of sin those two words, **BUT GOD!** Two words at the heart of every disciple's testimony, and the gospel. They know it was not them and their decision; it was God … always was, and always will be. When you read the Bible, you will see these two words appear, "**but God,**" which reveals and confirms His work! The following are some examples for you to meditate on:

- Genesis 8:1, "**But God** remembered Noah;"

- 2 Chronicles 20:15, "for the battle is not yours, **but God's**;"

- Psalm 49:15, "**But God** will redeem my soul;"

- Psalm 73:26, "**But God** is the strength of my heart and my portion forever;"

- Mark 2:7, "who can forgive sins **but God** alone;"

- Luke 16:15, "**But God** knows your hearts;"

- Acts 13:30, "**But God** raised Him from the dead;"

- Romans 5:8, "**But God** demonstrates His own love toward us;"

- 1 Corinthians 1:27, "**But God** has chosen the foolish things of the world to shame the wise;"

- 1 Corinthians 3:6-7, "**But God** was causing the growth;"

- 1 Corinthians 15:38, "**But God** gives it a body just as He wished;"

- 2 Corinthians 7:6, "**But God**, who comforts the depressed;"

- Ephesians 2:4, "**But God**, being rich in mercy;"

- 1 Thessalonians 2:4, "**But God** who examines our hearts;"

Can you now see "**but God**" and what this means when spoken by the disciple of Jesus Christ? The disciple's testimony must give all the glory to God, for His love, mercy, grace, forgiveness, and work, **BUT GOD!** God is doing the work. Ephesians 2:10 says, "For we are His workmanship, *created* in Christ Jesus." Philippians 1:6 declares, "*... that He who began* a good work in you will perfect it until the day of Christ Jesus." (emphasis added)

The Message: Jesus Saves

The testimony of the disciple expresses the gratitude of God's *saving* power. It's Christ who *saves* His disciples not in our sin, but from our sins. He *saves* me from the guilt of my sin by His death on the cross.

He *saves* me from the control of sin by His Spirit and His grace. In *saving* me from sin, He *saves* me from His wrath and the curse placed on humanity at the fall of man. He *saves* me from all the despair created by sin, now and forever. He *saves* me from my flesh and its evil desires. *Jesus saves ...*

With the work of the Spirit, the unbeliever will respond the same as the unbelievers responded in Acts 2, "What shall we do?" (Acts 2:37). As it says in John 6:44, "No one can come to Me unless the Father who sent Me draws him." The disciple must continually sow the gospel. We do not know when or whom God will save, or when He will use our testimony and life as a vessel in His divine plan of redemption.

God saved us and allowed us to grow in the knowledge and understanding of the depths of His love and scope of His grace. The disciple becomes a child of the only true God. In doing so, Jesus commands, "GO" and spread the *Good News*! In other words, go tell the world of the amazing love God has for them. How does the disciple know the true testimony of Jesus Christ? God gives it to them. And when you are sharing your testimony, someone may ask, "What is eternal life?" How would you answer? I am certain there are many different answers, but let's be good Bereans. You can find the reference to the Bereans in Acts 17:10-15. They were "noble-minded, receiving the word with eagerness, and examining Scriptures *daily* to see whether these things were so." So go and look it up if you question what I have quoted Jesus saying. Jesus answered the question of eternal life in John 17:3, saying, "This is eternal life, that they may know You, the only true God, and Jesus Christ whom You have sent." It goes well beyond just securing a place in heaven for yourself!

Therefore, the testimony of Jesus's disciples contains a confession of their sinful life before salvation, the need and desire to repent of their sin, and the wonderful saving power of God! This is confirmed in 2 Peter 3:9, which says, "The Lord is not slow about His promise, as some count slowness, but is patient toward you, not wishing for any to perish but for all to come to repentance." The Lord calls us all to repent for sin committed against Him. God in His mercy is allowing time for you to acknowledge, confess, and repent of your sin.

BRAND-NEW LIFE

People have asked me, what this "new life," and becoming a "disciple" of Jesus Christ is all about. Why does it seem those who know have this "way" about them? Because we know we are saved by grace through faith, and it's not of ourselves; it's a gift of God, not because of works, as I paraphrase Ephesians 2:8–9.

This new life possesses an eternal security in Jesus Christ, no matter what! We know and live with a salvation secure in Jesus. Romans 8:35 says, "Who will separate us from the love of Christ? Will tribulation or distress, persecution, or famine, or nakedness, peril, or sword?" And verses 38–39 of chapter 8 say, "For I am convinced that neither death, nor life, nor angels, nor principalities, nor things present, nor things to come, nor powers, nor height, nor depth, nor any other created thing, will be able to separate us from the love of God, which is in Christ Jesus our Lord." PRAISE GOD! The disciple of Jesus is SECURE! This generates a tremendous amount of confidence and security in our walk and work as Jesus's disciples.

This new life generates a heart of service as we imitate Jesus. Mark 10:42–45, clearly communicates what Jesus felt about serving others through love. This is also a passage to commit to memory. With this new life in Jesus, there is a genuine willingness to serve in *whatever* capacity the church needs, trusting fully in the Holy Spirit to prepare, teach, and equip the disciple to perform the tasks or duties as needed.

It's about giving and serving God in gratitude for the newness of life, and the gift of His Spirit, the new heart, and the love of God now flows through the disciple. What a wonderful thought to possess, knowing you will spend eternal life in God's presence! If one seriously examines oneself and see sin as God see sin, it should create a heart filled with thankfulness and joy for the forgiveness of sin committed against a holy and loving God.

It becomes obvious for all the world to see the life change occurring in Jesus's disciples because, as with most people since the first converts, everyone who had witnessed how they lived before are now witnessing someone who appears the same on the outside yet they were walking, talking, and living differently. This life change occurs from the inside out, and now this new life is a means to proclaim one's testimony as to what happened to them on the day of salvation.

Those who have been saved by Jesus Christ are set apart from those in the world, and God describes who His people are and what they have become to Him. First Peter 2:9 says, "But you are a CHOSEN RACE, A royal PRIESTHOOD, A HOLY NATION, A PEOPLE FOR God's OWN POSSESSION, so that you may proclaim the excellencies of Him who has called you out of darkness into His marvelous light; ..."

With the light of Christ beaming within you, you now are charged with a command to love—not only those who love you, but also your enemies. But most importantly, our utmost love should be to God in Christ. Jesus tells us of what our expression of love should look like, and it is by keeping His commandments. Jesus said, in Matthew 28:19-20, "Go therefore and make disciples of all the nations, baptizing them in the name of the Father and the Son and the Holy Spirit, teaching them to observe all that I commanded you; and lo, I am with you always, even to the end of the age."

You should be living and exhibiting confidence, knowing the only true God has forgiven you and chosen you to be His disciple. We are to be a voice in a wilderness, a light in the darkness, an ambassador for the living God, bringing forth the *GOOD NEWS* to all the world. *IT'S ALL ABOUT THE SAVING POWER OF GOD!*

He who has the Son has the life; he who does not have the Son of God does not have the life (1 John 5:12).

Now GO, proclaim the *GOOD NEWS* of Jesus Christ, and His SAVING POWER for you and them. Amen?

A Prayer for You:

ABBA, I love You and thank You for today. I know, there is no testimony than the testimony of eternal life that is only found in and through Jesus. Your Word is the testimony of You. How You have created all things, and all things exist by Your power and work. Every disciple's testimony is the life of Your Son, Jesus. And there is no testimony greater that can save. I am so thankful for Your work in my life. I was not deserving of your grace and mercy, yet You love me and saved me.

I pray for all who are asking questions regarding what true life is in You. I ask You to make Yourself known to them so that they can have eternal life and be freed from the bondage and captivity of sin.

Lord, give them eyes to see and ears to hear the truth of who You are and what You have done for them. Open their hearts to receive what has been communicated. Give them a new heart and place Your Spirit in them so they can live a life as Your disciple, proclaiming the good news of Jesus.

Life change in You is a beautiful story of Your amazing grace, and You are still saving lives today. I pray and ask You to use this section to provide understanding of Your work, which creates life in the dead. Give them the ability to understand this truth, and their testimony will be less about themselves and more about You and Your saving power.

Thank You for listening, guiding, and responding to my prayers. I ask You to grant my request to touch the life of one more today. I ask and pray in Jesus's name, amen.

Reflections

TRIALS

"You are those who stood by Me in My trials ..." (Luke 22:28)
"Consider it all joy, my brethren, when you encounter various trials ..."
(James 1:2)

TRIALS EXPOSE THE MASQUERADE

No one wants or looks forward to the trials of life—spiritual, physical, emotional, or financial. It doesn't matter the trials' frequency, variation, or magnitude; it is always a blessing to have someone standing by you as you live through it so that you need not face it alone. Trials have their way of penetrating the surface and piercing the disguise projected, revealing the truth of who one really is, and what one believes. When they do come, these trials touch every aspect of our lives and the lives of those around us.

Many believe their trial is unique to themselves, although trials may have similar circumstances, or even events, because the common factor for two different disciples may involve a commonality of faith, trust, or courage for example. Though the trial is unique, the result is spiritual growth, and it always involves you, others, and God. God truly desires for us to grow spiritually and have an intimate relationship with Him and others when we do. We must keep an eternal perspective in mind for our growth and development to have its full effect. This will enable us to see faith in others and ourselves as we watch God in action.

No matter what the trial will contain, rest assured you will grow into Christlikeness. Know the result desired is for your trust and intimate relationship with God to grow, as well. So, *expect and anticipate God to deliver on His promise to conform you into the image of His Son.*

Some trials can create a state of powerlessness, so when we are placed in a trial which challenges our own power, we feel we have lost control or have no control of the trial or even our lives. In reality, though it's God revealing to us we have no power in our own strength. So, when we are powerless to control, the question arises as to why God would place us in trials revealing our powerlessness. The truth is, He wants us to look to Him and His power to endure.

Questioning God versus trusting Him, and directing our focus solely on the trial and not His comfort, direction, wisdom, and teaching, could be one reason God allows the trial—so we become aware of our need to totally look to and depend on Him. Also, placing our focus solely on the trial could negatively influence the stability of our faith, spiritual strength, belief, confidence, and trust in God alone and could affect our usefulness as His disciple.

Think of the void in the lives of the disciples after Jesus's death. Keep in mind, they walked with Jesus every day for three years. They were mesmerized by the words of God coming out of His mouth, just as we are with His written Word. I am certain God touched every emotion, thought, and belief in their existence. They'd seen and experienced the amazing works of God through Jesus, others, and themselves. And now, after a short time, He's dead.

Only after Jesus's trial, crucifixion, and resurrection did the disciples fully understand what Jesus had said all along. Would they stand with him? No. Would they do everything He asked, at that time? No. The proof and result are realized after the trial. What about their lives? Did the trials they faced after Jesus's ascension confirm all what Jesus said to them, and what they discovered and learned about themselves? Yes.

It confirmed their true faith and trust in Him, as they lived out 1 Peter 2:23, which says, "and while being reviled, He did not revile in return; while suffering, He uttered no threats, but kept entrusting *Himself* to Him who judges righteously." I would suspect, since all where martyred except John, that they knew how Jesus walked through His trial, and they imitated Him by not reviling but by suffering without threatening, and by entrusting themselves to Jesus because they knew He would judge righteously.

Why would the disciple's trials be any different than those of anyone else? Could it be possible the disciple may face more trials than those who are not Jesus's disciples? Based on Scripture, yes, and 1 Peter 4:12 confirms we will face the "fiery ordeal." Jesus's disciples must face trials with the proper perspective and mindset. We live as we know and believe in our heart, mind, and spirit, God is at work for our good and His glory. The result is that you become like Jesus, in whom the Father is well pleased. Do you desire to be pleasing to the Father, reflecting the image of Jesus to Him and others? I would hope your answer is yes, but again, be mindful of what Jesus is calling you to be and do.

Read "Preferment Asked" (Matthew 20:20–23) about two of Jesus's disciples, who wanted to sit at His right and left hand on the throne of God. When you peel away the question, you see selfishness. And Jesus, with a phenomenal approach, requests of them their commitment first; then He agrees to give them His cup. However, sitting on His right and left is not His to give, because the Father prepares it.

I can only imagine their faces as they looked at each other and wondered what they had gotten themselves into. In other words, when we say we will do something, we must stand up and act when the time comes. If you have whispered in the quietness to the ears of Jesus, "In my heart, I desire to be like You," you should expect He will do what is needed to make you like Himself. And He will expect you to give all of yourself to accomplish it. It took all of Jesus to accomplish the will of the Father.

Trials have their way of forcing us to our knees, as God exposes our weakness and makes them known to us. One would suspect that when one is brought to their knees, prayer should immediately follow, as one surrenders to the will of God. At times, we yearn for God to intervene and rescue us from a trial. However, have you ever considered it could be God initiating the trial? If you have a tough time believing He would, read Job 1:8. And you know the amazing thing? God did not have to say much, just "Have you considered my servant Job?" And because of His work or His allowance, He is right in the middle of it with us already. If we lose sight of God's sovereign will and focus on anything else, the trial could cause us to spiral downward into deep despair versus reaching up to Him in faith, hope, and trust.

When anyone is consumed with despair, anguish, suffering, or sorrow, there is a tendency to want to isolate themselves, which is one of the worst actions anyone could chose to take. Instead, in times like these, we must draw near to God and press into Him, His Word, and His people, as He will give us strength in our time of weakness and uncertainty. There is a promise I found which is a good memory verse to remember for when living through a trial. It's James 4:8a, which says, "Draw near to God and He will draw near to you." God will give us hope, endurance, and perseverance when all we can see, seems to be anxiety or worry, that leads to hopelessness. *MOVE towards Him*!

Trials Produce Results

Why are trials brought forth? This is a question which plagues myriads of people, and Jesus's disciples are no different. Why would I need a trial? Many would exclaim the following perspective: "My life is fine where I am at, and I really do not need or desire any additional tests, whether spiritually, relationally, physically, emotionally, or financially. I am good at maintaining this pace of life, and it is fine, thank you very much." Just remember, God desires for His children to grow and develop spiritually by living out the fruits given by the Holy Spirit.

Why does God allow trials? This was a question I asked Jesus when writing this segment. I am certain many of His disciples are asking this same important question. I was right there with the rest of them. When He responded, His answer was concise and profound. He said, *"God has a plan for your life, and trials prove and produce the result."*

In the numerous discussions over the years, many confuse temptation with trials and tests. Temptation results from lusting. Know, lusting is not only associated to sexual immorality. To lust is to yearn, desire, and long for … it could be for power, money, and self, which all lead to idolatry, and idolatry is the sin. Therefore, when one is enticed by their own lust, the downward progression begins. Temptation comes because of lusting, read James 1:14-15 and you will see the spiral and the consequential result.

Trials and tests are the "verifier" of the truth. Trials confirm how you will move. If you will move closer to God, or away from Him. So, *trials prove where you stand and what you will do.* Tests reveal self, and you will either fail or pass, no gray area. God even says in Malachi 3:10 to "… test Me now in this …" and God moves revealing His faithfulness to His own Word. So, He moves, and you find out for certain God is faithful, because the test is about His faithfulness to His Word. And when He does, He will pass the test you gave Him! When God tests you, what do you think the results will say about you? Remember there are two vast differences from temptation, trials, and tests.

Temptation is in the darkness of one's mind; causing one to act in secrecy, isolation, and withdraw from others. Thus, one avoids or is lured away from God's presence, and the solidarity found with and in others. Trials & tests on the other hand, are in the open for all to see. This results in inclusion of disciples coming together, united in love and Spirit in response to the trials and tests of another disciple, and they in love bear the burden of another. And God's Word, works, and will is lived out in the lives of His people.

So, tests reveal self to self and others! If you are to test yourself, what will the "evidence" (results) of the test say about you? *Trials and testing are designed for spiritual awareness and growth.* As God uses *both* to transform the *old* to the *new*, believe it, it's true!

The Spirit then led me to read Romans 8:29. It says, "For those whom He foreknew, He also predestined *to become* conformed to the image of His Son, so that He would be the firstborn among many brethren." In other words, these trials of life are designed for you to be conformed to the image of Jesus. We are only a fraction of what we will become when we enter eternity. Trials could be our boot camp. However, it is not a short duration for a set period like military boot camp. Trials could be for one's entire life or may come in seasons. Trials are always going to be implemented when there is a need for spiritual growth. And like any plant, tree, or bush, growth is a constant, if it is nurtured and pruned. So, expect trials to be a constant since spiritual growth is a requirement.

Why would trials require suffering? Suffering shapes and fashions us, like the potter shapes his clay. I suspect clay would harden just sitting on the table, but once forged by fire, it is solid, through and through. Look at what God's Word says in Romans 5:3–5 about suffering and what it produces: "Not only that, but we rejoice in our sufferings, knowing that suffering produces endurance, and endurance produces character, and character produces hope, and hope does not put us to shame, because God's love has been poured into our hearts through the Holy Spirit who has been given to us" (ESV).

I will ask you: How do you make a lump of clay into a pot? You must shape it. Because it is in the form of a lump; although it is clay, it is useless for the purpose the potter desires. For the potter to change it from a lump to what he desires, he shapes it. It is not always clay the designer shapes, but to shape any object or person, he forms, molds, whittles, chips, sands, scrapes, presses, and buffs it to a shine. How do you purify silver or gold? You refine it. You use heat to remove any impurities. God refines to remove the impurity of sin in our life. God causes or allows trials to develop the Christlikeness He desires in all His children. How else would you know you believe, have real faith, and trust in Him, unless you go through a trial, and come out refined on the other side?

And You Think You Can Do It Yourself

Here's an analogy for you to consider, when one thinks they can shape themselves and do not need God to complete His work in them.

The potter is a master craftsman and is renowned for his creations of fine and unique pottery. He has the wisdom, knowledge, and expertise to shape any lump of clay into beautifully designed vessels. Day after day, he has proven his skills to fashion without the use of instructions or formulas. His vessels are being used everywhere in the kingdom, from the lowly in the village, to the king in his palace.

The potter walks into the room and as he does, the clay, laying in a pile on the table, immediately says to the potter, "I am going to be a cup!"

The potter responds in a loving tone, saying, "I think you would do well to be a bowl."

"NO!" Snaps the clay, "a cup!"

"So you say, so you say," says the potter.

The clay becomes very indignant and attempts to convince the potter it is quite capable of the shaping process and will show him.

The potter glances around the workshop full of his numerous creations, and while doing so says to the clay, "I have some advice for you since you are so adamant and confident you will be able to shape yourself into a useful vessel." He redirects his attention back to the clay and in an unyielding voice says, "First of all, you are deceiving yourself, as your usefulness will only happen when you are a bowl versus what you perceive you should be. Here's my advice if you are willing to listen."

"I am listening," the clay responds arrogantly, "but I have my mind made up and will proceed with my plan right after you finish, and you will be amazed at my handy work."

Saddened by the clay's pridefulness, the potter could do three things. Ignore the clay and toss it into the furnace, let the clay attempt to make a mess of itself, or proceed with his work and make the clay into the useful vessel he intended from the beginning. The potter truly desires for the clay to be all it can be, so the potter imparts his wisdom to the clay. "When you make yourself, you need to make sure you have the proper amount of water to mix and get the correct consistency to begin to shape. Too much or too little water, and you lose the ability to form yourself. And you will become a useless lump and no good to anyone at all.

You must figure out how you are going to get the wheel started, because without it, shaping is exceedingly difficult. If you are successful in starting the wheel, you must use the proper speed. Too fast and you will find yourself flying all over this room and will not be useful to me or yourself. Two slow and your shaping will be extremely difficult, and you will be of no use to anyone.

When you set the oven's temperature, it must be accurate to ensure the hardening process is completed correctly. If the oven's too hot, you will dry too quickly and become brittle and shatter at the first impact. If the heat is too low, you could lose your shape. But most importantly, when you put yourself in the oven, you better be able to get yourself out! Too long, and you will burn up, turn into particles, and your only usefulness will be to coat the bottom of the bucket absorbing the slop thrown into it. With my work and making you a bowl, you will hold all kinds of food, and at times even water. You will be useful daily to the king and could serve at festive occasions. So you see, from everyday use to celebrations, you will be useful to me, yourself, and others. Now, I will ask you, do you wish to be a bowl or what you think you should be?"

Consider this as you look at your life. We are born with a sinful nature, whether you admit it or not, and are influenced by our flesh, the world and Satan. It begins in the early years of our lives. And as we are shaped, we begin to look to ourselves as the means to accomplish what we want, need, or desire. We are told and taught it is good to develop our self; after all no one will have a greater interest in our lives than ourselves. Yes, parents, siblings, and other family members do have our lives in the bandwidth of theirs, and some do faithfully fulfill their duties entrusted to them by God. Others, if they have the same deep-rooted selfishness, are only concerned with their own needs, wants, and desires. They only impart what is needed for you to exist, and what is provided will assist you just past survival.

Why would we think, with a true sense of real uncertainty, we would be successful in shaping our own spiritual lives better than God who knows all things? If you were able to see the hearts, and the deep thoughts of all who live separately from God, I wonder if you would be astonished to learn their lives were not as *all together* as they portray them to be. Their life is just a disguise because they believe they have been the ones who have brought forth life by the decisions they've made. They are just putting on the masquerade for the masses, so they can blend in on either side. In their pridefulness, they are the clay telling the potter they can shape themselves without any work from His masterful hands, only to find themselves caught in the furnace, unable to free themselves. God knows what we need more than anyone else. He knows we need Him. He lovingly and faithfully has our best interest in mind. And you know the amazing thing? He knows us even better than we know ourselves.

By the skillful work of the Master Potter, God, will make and shape His disciples into useful vessels, not only for ourselves, but also for

Himself and others. Living life in an intimate relationship with God creates a spiritual bond in which God imparts life through His Spirit resulting in constant change and growth forever. You are unique and there are not two bowls alike! By how you are shaped, you become resilient and useful in your walk through this life. When you respond and are obedient to the teachings and promptings of the Holy Spirit, your nature and disposition are continuously being developed into a more Christlike person. You develop spiritual confidence, courage, faith, and hopefulness. You learn even more about the love of God, which is displayed in your testimony, and His work is carried out in and through your life. Your life is now on display for the world to see. When people attempt to shape themselves they are a cups. When God is shaping you, you're His bowl. So I will ask you: Are you a cup or a bowl?

Add Another Plate

I remember a young disciple, I'll call him J, approached me one day to ask for prayer, as he was going through a trial. He had a ton of questions, and I welcomed them all, because he was on fire with his newfound faith. By the inspiration of the Holy Spirit, I fanned his flame. Each question started with "why?" He was trying to discern why he would need a trial. He had only been a disciple for a brief time. But when is the best time for a trial? I would think it would be right after this new life begins. It gives you immediate knowledge of how God has changed you. You know how you would have responded in the past, yet, now, as a new creature in Christ, you respond in Christlikeness versus selfishness. After he was done expressing himself, I prayed for wisdom, asking God for a way to communicate to J so he could understand that trials are necessary and good, and it was really God who was at work in him.

Here's what the Holy Spirit gave me to communicate to J, as he was seriously into working out and lifting weights several times a week. There was no question about this, as his physique had muscles bulging everywhere, and he looked strong. As a result of his passion and commitment to personal training, it made sense the Holy Spirit would use this example as J could surely relate to and understand the connection between weight training, trials, and discipleship. The answer to my prayer was this analogy.

A man sets out to train today, and he has been working on his bench press. He had initially started out lifting only the bar (forty-five pounds when empty) and grew in strength to one plate on each side. For those who do not know, each plate weighs forty-five pounds. His continuous commitment proved beneficial and he was progressing, as he initially started with just pressing only the bar. The Lord was his spotter and had assisted him with the proper form and technique to develop strength and endurance. As he progressed, he began to press the bar numerous times with the proper form and technique without any difficulty.

This day, when he was going to do the work out, he faced a new trial. There was a twenty-five pound weight added to each side. Over time, he eventually was able to press this weight as consistently and effortlessly as he did the empty bar. It seems in our walk as a disciple, most want to stay pressing the bar because it is a weight we can handle, and we can accomplish the exercise mindlessly, and without any real effort. This perspective would be the same as being saved and just walking through life, looking for the narrow gate, and passing by all those in need of hearing the gospel. As time went on, he continually showed improvement until he was doing well with the bar and one plate.

God is fully aware of our ability. He knows us and what we're capable of handling, and that's biblical. Psalm 139:13 says, "For You formed my inward parts; You wove me in my mother's womb." One day, when J went into the training room, he noticed another plate has been added to the bar! Immediately, he felt a sprinkling of doubt, as he had never attempted to press two plates. The Lord recognized this uncertainty and reassured him that He would be there to spot him, as it was time to grow!

J recognized that this trial was intended to produce growth, strength, and endurance! I wish you could have seen his face. His whole perspective changed about his trial. It surely had a lasting effect, as each time we saw each other, he would say with enthusiasm, "Add another plate!" He told me one day that he has used this analogy when discipling another young man, as they were experiencing a trial. PRAISE GOD for

His faithfulness to respond, for Him using me as His vessel, and for J's response to his calling to disciple another!

God desires for us to look at trials as a means for us to grow spiritually, and not as a form of punishment. Did you realize you can also grow from discipline? Sometimes a trial can be a form of discipline as well. So can you be like J and look at the trials of life as a means God uses to justify the end, so that you will be like Jesus? Expect God to bring about a trial, regardless of the weight, possessing the attitude to "add another plate" so that you can get stronger in Him! Remember, the Spirit is there to spot you, and He expects you to put forth the effort and trust Him when you reach your sticking points. So, press on my fellow disciple, press on!

Expect Them to Be Diverse

Trials in our life will come in numerous ways, times, and intensities. Believe it, it's biblical. James 1:2–3 says, "Consider it all joy, my brethren, when you encounter various trials, knowing that the testing of your faith produces endurance." Know this: if you are one of Jesus's disciples, and He had various trials in His life while walking on this earth, you should expect them yourself if God's plan is to conform you into the image of His Son, and you desire to be like Him. Remember, they are designed to equip us and—regardless of the ease, difficulty or seriousness—God is fashioning us into His image. I looked back and wondered why I went through the trials of my life. Did I think it was fair? No! But you know, I can sit down with anyone who has lived a similar trial and talk freely about God's deliverance from the bondage of bitterness and hatred. As you can see today, it has not stopped, nor will it, until Jesus returns. So *if* I am called for this purpose, *then* I am to live it out, and press on myself, leaving those ill feelings and experiences behind.

Remember Psalm 37:4? You can count on God to be faithful to give you what you desire, because He desires the same for you, which is to be like Jesus in all aspects of your life as His disciple.

Have confidence when facing life, and be like Jesus. He looked to the Father for His strength,

Delight yourself in the Lord; And He will give you the desires of your heart.

Psalm 37:4

work, prayer, endurance, and trust. When we respond the same, our results will be the same. Jesus looked to the Father for everything. Are you? My "in other words" would be, to walk like Him, talk like Him, pray like Him, love like Him, extend grace like Him, forgive like Him, be obedient like Him, and be faithful like Him. It did not matter what the trial was or its variation, or intensity. Jesus knew the Father was with Him in the midst of it, and in faith Jesus believed and trusted the Father would bring Him out the other side. He knows that the work of the Father and the Spirit is always good. And He knows He would be better than when it approached Him. The lesson to be learned is; *Jesus is the standard*. It will take more than one trial in our life on this earth, possessing a sinful nature which will be with us the entire journey, for us to be like Jesus.

James 1:2 mentions the word "various," and the word speaks volumes all by itself. Various means numerous, different, diverse, or assorted. It makes me wonder why it would be necessary for God to allow or cause a *variety* of trials. His work is so perfect, He surely could just bring forth or allow one trial, and it would accomplish what He intended, right? Yet, on the other hand, it makes total sense because of the multiplicity and complexity of our minds, heart, spirit, and faith; it requires a variation of trials to work and develop all of them!

In athletics, the classroom, or our vocation, we accept tests and trials as normal, to identify areas of opportunity and develop multiple aspects of strength, endurance, and perseverance. Discipleship is no different while we live and work in a world full of evil and darkness. We are called daily to fight spiritual battles. Surviving and pressing on in spiritual warfare requires testing (trials) to prepare and equip you to persevere and be a useful vessel to God.

Notice the words *trials* and not *a trial*. One should expect there will be more than one trial in your journey as a disciple of Jesus. It could go on for longer than one presumes; so, you should anticipate that as well. It's foolish to think you will live life without trials as a disciple of Jesus. Without trials, you would never know what Christlike attributes are lacking in your spiritual arsenal. It takes various trials to develop and grow your spirituality, because this is *the Way* God intends for His disciples to live, work, and grow.

The lack of trials in life could affect one's faith and walk as a disciple, and how one endures and perseveres. Real substance could be lacking, and the truth be known, it will be all an assumption from there. These nuggets of truth confirm how I should live in the face of them. God's Word provides *the Way to* approach and handle trials. This leads to a surety and a confidence as we anticipate *true spiritual growth*.

Trials Produce Faithfulness

Consider this: Shadrach, Meshach, Abednego, Jesus, and the Holy Spirit's work. These young men's real names are Hananiah for Shadrach, Mishael for Meshach, and Azariah for Abednego. You can find their life stories and this reference in the book of Daniel. What I want to specifically address is their trial. They are commanded to bow down and worship an idol. If they fail to worship the idol, they will be cast into a blazing furnace. They have a choice: love God with all their heart, soul, mind, and strength, worshiping and serving Him only, or worship and serve the idol. Their *trial* involved *faith and obedience*. Hence, *various …* The question they faced, as we will, was whether they would be faithful and obedient to God or not. Afterall, their life was at stake! Jesus already knew the answer for them and us, as He was waiting in the furnace for them! Jesus will be waiting in the trial for us, as He promised. He will not leave us as orphans; He will come to us, as I paraphrase what Jesus says in John 14:18.

However, it is not only in the earthly realm Jesus references orphans; it's also in the spiritual. Being left as an orphan means you have no one who really loves you, who will impart their life to you. Blessed are they who have extended family who can step in and bring love and nurturing into their lives. Therefore, we look to Jesus's promises to come to us. He did when He walked with the initial disciples, He has come to us in His spirit, and He will come for all of us at the end of the age. Believe me, no one will love you like God loves you! This is a great promise to hold onto when you come face to face with your trial. Know, God is with you in it, because you are not an orphan, and you are not going through it alone.

If Hananiah, Mishael, and Azariah had a trial regarding faith, you are not exempt from one either, so expect it. If you were to look at it from just the physical realm, they were face to face with certain death, because defiance of the "powers that be," depending upon their citizenship, could lead to death. Execution may have been a widespread practice in the early days of history, where no one could do anything about it. It may not have been masses of people put to death for their belief in the only true God of the Bible, and it may not be a frequent practice today, but it's still being practiced.

Think of death and faith in a simpler way because most will not be thrown into a furnace to prove their faith to themselves, although a test of faith could involve a person's career. It may not be a physical death, but it could mean a tremendous change to your way of life or standard of living if one goes against the powers that be. What if you believe your employer is practicing business strategies and objectives to increase their profitability that are unbiblical? What would you do? Do you just go along with it, as you know you need your job? Do you remain faithful to God and resign, knowing what His Word says about how you are to live as His disciple? Would your decision confirm that what you cherish means more to you than God? Do you think what you have is because of you, or God? Does this job give you life, or does God?

Here's another point to consider. We are presently living through the removal of God and His Words from our society. And as time goes on, it gets even worse. Not only is there no longer prayer in school, but a day is coming when prayer will no longer be tolerated anywhere else— not at your job, in public places, or even in your home. The freedom you have come to live by will surely change, especially if Jesus's disciples just stand by silently and watch evil have its way. Today, we may not even consider the magnitude, but for the sake of discussion, it is possible. Technology is capable of anything, and constant monitoring is not a farfetched idea anymore.

In addition to the removal of prayer, there are to be no more Bibles, and all the ones in book form are to be surrendered. And because of the control of technology, electronic versions are disallowed. What would you do? I expect that if you are to attend church, it will only be the church of the powers that be. I will ask again, what would you do? It may not come in this present culture, yet it is not a farfetched idea. But what about our children's children? They may not be far away from this reality. How would you, and most importantly they, respond to a trial of this magnitude? How would you prepare them to be able to prepare their children? Can you see why discipling our children is so important?

Hananiah, Mishael, and Azariah knew in their hearts they would serve the only true God, regardless of the outcome. They had lived, tasted, and seen that the Lord is good, and took refuge in Him. They lived out Psalm 34:8, which says, "O taste and see that the Lord is good; How blessed is the one who takes refuge in Him!" Do you know the amazing thing? They were captives, so you would think the decision would be easier, right? It would seem that if they were free, the decision would be simpler, but then again, maybe not.

Living in true spiritual freedom by the grace of God empowers Jesus's disciples to go far beyond what they think they are able, compared to someone who is held captive in the bondage of sin. Hananiah, Mishael, and Azariah's decision was a life or death decision. For most, the decision is obedience or disobedience to God and His Word. They were willing to live or die for God, as it was totally up to God and all right with them. Now consider this: *All* the rest of the people, nations, and men who were in bondage fell and worshiped the idol to save themselves. That's biblical. Matthew 16:25 says, "For whoever wishes to save his life will lose it; but whoever loses his life for My sake will find it." Sometimes trials require us to give our lives for the sake of the gospel. Are you willing to give your life for the sake of the gospel?

Because of their faithfulness to God, and their defiance of King Nebuchadnezzar, the king wanted to display to all who were watching what he would do to anyone who defied him. In response, he commanded the furnace to be heated seven times hotter, ensuring their bodies, when thrown into the furnace, would be instantly destroyed. This is a great testimony of these young men's faith and trust in God. You can find their response to the king in Daniel 3:16–18. It would only seem natural for them to want to hold on to the most precious thing they possessed—their own lives. It was obvious, so the king commanded them to be thrown in. The amazing thing observed—from their faith, love, and obedience to God alone—was regardless of what God chose as the outcome, they would remain faithful to Him.

Can you live with the same faith in God, regardless of what God chooses as the outcome for your life, or the lives of those you love? It will tell you the truth about your faith, trust, and obedience to God and if you fully trust in Him alone.

I would be remis not to mention the work and power of God the Holy Spirit in the midst of their trial. As disciples of Jesus, the Holy Spirit's work and power is in us as well. We have access to it just like they did. Do you believe this truth? There was no gray area here either; they would either perish or live.

Without the Holy Spirit's power, they couldn't withstand the searing heat of the furnace. This fire was so hot it consumed the men who were carrying them to the entrance of the furnace. Imagine the faces of Hananiah, Mishael, and Azariah when they saw the men perish right before their eyes … and they survived.

Think of the joy they must have felt when they landed in the flames and saw Jesus standing there waiting for them. Consider the joy you will experience when you are looking to God amid your flames and heat from your trial, knowing it's Him who's keeping the flames from consuming you!

God is amazing. Do you agree, or, do you think this is just another *story*?

Know that God is greater than any element because He created them all. It was by the Spirit's power and plan of God they were able to stand amidst the flames and not be consumed. When we are in the presence of God, and His Spirit is at work in us, we should have hope and confidence our trial will not consume us, but even if it does, we must remain faithful to God, knowing God is waiting for us in our trials as well.

God Is Glorified in and by Trials

Have you ever wondered how God could be glorified in death, even the death of a child? I can only imagine as a parent the experience and the extent of the pain and anguish resulting from the loss of a child at any age of life. It must be excruciating and a burden of loss to bear for years. You may be someone who has lost a child, and if you are, consider this perspective on the loss of life. God may choose to use a child's life to save another's. It could be as close as a family member or as distant as anyone who may be associated in one way or another. It is through God's love for humanity He desires to save. Therefore, Jesus died—to save the lives of many. Therefore, if God desired to save, and you are called to be an active part of His plan to save, would you question God's motive for His saving grace?

Many do not really consider how horrific hell and the total separation from God must truly be. Therefore, most just seem to want to ignore the truth of what God says does exist. And what do we do as His disciples? Aren't we called to spread the gospel and give our life if necessary, for *it* as well? So who is in control of one's life in giving it for the gospel, man or God? If we are in agreement with God's Word, then it is God who decides what He does for the salvation of the lost. God desires to bring the wonder of eternal life to the unbelieving. And Jesus is "The Way" … God the Father accomplishes His divine plan of redemption for humanity. Therefore, life is given for Jesus's sake, just as Jesus's life was given for our sake, yours, and mine. Wouldn't the life given to save a life be just like Jesus, who gave His life to save you? What a blessing it is if God chooses you and your child to save the life of another, one who did not know of the saving power of God until they witnessed His work in you and your child. Your testimony to others of the grace of God in your life is confirmed in you and them through love and forgiveness, where needed. Was Job any different than anyone today? He lost his whole family.

What about death of an infant, toddler, or adolescent? How does one endure through this type of trial? What a trial this is in someone's life. I expect no one prepares for a trial of this magnitude. Parents who can make it through a trial of this degree must possess a fervent love, having complete faith and trust in God and His will for everyone's lives, including their child and their own. Only by the love of God and the power of the Holy Spirit are the parents able to stand as they hold fast and comfort each other in such a demanding trial. In their strength, they may even disciple others by the display of their love, faith, trust, and hope in God. We must always keep our focus on eternity versus this life, as this life is a *vapor* compared to eternity.

Of course, there are several variables involved. I would suspect it has a lot to do with the relationship of the child with the parent or parents. If the child has grown into adulthood, and there is no relationship, the possibility exists their parents may never know and may not be affected at all. But the loss of the child could be what God uses to draw them to Jesus because of their brokenness.

If they did find out, there could be tremendous sadness, depending on the heart of the parent, and if it is not a new heart given by God, this news could lead to depression and regret over their failures in their role as a parent. They may harbor guilt for not pursuing their child to apologize, as it may have been the parent's action toward the child when they were younger causing the break in relationship. And now, with the loss of life, they will never have the opportunity to reconcile. This creates a burden to bear. God, in His infinite love and wisdom, could use this burden of guilt to draw them to Jesus.

If the relationship has been growing both relationally and spiritually between the child and their parent or parents all the years of their life, then the absence of their presence, calls, hugs, voice, notes, and most importantly the time spent together, is also lost for this phase of life; it leads to grief, sadness, and despair. There seems to be a progression when faced with grief. Initially there is disbelief and refusal to accept it's actually happening. This extends to anger, leading to a form of depression and a hollowness in one's existence. One then wants to separate oneself, which can lead to hopelessness, as one struggles to find God's purpose in what has happened in the life of one's loved one and themselves. Strength, purpose, perseverance, and endurance can only be found in Jesus to accept the will and work of God in the lives of all involved.

They know with Jesus there is always hope, they will see their child again when they themselves arrive at the narrow gate which leads to eternal life with God. So, they do not continuously focus on the temporal, but they look to Jesus, and His promises of raising them up on the last day to eternal life with Him. God is glorified for His saving grace in the life of their child and themselves.

If the love of God is not present in their hearts, there is a tendency to blame. They may blame each other, someone else, or even God, stating, "Look what you've done to cause me this grief" when they feel the loss of life may be related to the actions of another human being. Or, in anger, they question God, and ask, "Why would You do this to me?"

Would your perspective change from questioning God to praising Him when you arrived at the judgment seat of Christ and saw your child wrapped in the warmth of God's loving arms? I would hope your answer would be, "Yes, I would." It is only natural to expect one to live what we think is a full life. But again, it will be our definition of what a full life is, based on our life and those around us.

We must trust that God knows what is best for all, what He deems as good, and what He deems full compared to humanity's perspective of it. We have been conditioned to believe we work and then retire to a grand old age, only to slip quietly off into eternity. Is this how it should be? What about all the people in the world who suffer their entire lives, and close their eyes to this world never to experience retirement? Why, other than through deception, does someone believe they are a privileged people and should live in this life and world trouble-and-trial-free? If you have this perspective, then you should really stop and think: *Why is* God *not growing me into Christlikeness through the trials of life?*

Our faith and love for God must be strong enough to know and trust that all life from the womb to old age is God's, and He will do with life as He chooses, and we must accept His ways and truth. God makes His point clear in Isaiah 55:9: "For as the heavens are higher than the earth, so are My ways higher than your ways and My thoughts than your thoughts." Our minds and thoughts are only what we have learned on this earth, and we must set our minds and thoughts on God. And without the work of God's Spirit, you will never be able to accomplish it through your own work, nor can the world give it to you! Colossians 3:1–2, gives us the instruction as to where our seeking must be: "above, where Christ is seated at the right hand of God."

It is not my choice, nor in my power to think I could stop or thwart God's sovereign, decretive, efficacious, and permissive will. All we can do is walk alongside each other in Christ as the Holy Spirit works in and through us as we love one another as God loves us. And when you have an opportunity to disciple someone who has lost a child, then glorify God for giving you and them the opportunity to love and encourage each other. Could you see and are you willing to look for the blessing in this kind of trial?

Have hope! Although the infant or small child did not have the life to come to know God's love, mercy, and saving grace as Jesus's disciples know it, I believe Jesus's atonement for sin is sufficient, and God the Father in His love and mercy would see Jesus's blood as full payment for those never capable of believing. God's Word is clear regarding when life begins, and we are born of the seed of Adam. Life and sin begin at conception. We are born in sin. It is in our bodies, soul, and mind, and the roots are in our hearts. David confirms this biblical truth in Psalm 51:5, which says, "Behold, I was brought forth in iniquity, and in sin my mother conceived me." This does not mean that David's mother was committing a sinful act when he was conceived. It means that the sin is passed from Eve to all wombs carrying the sin from the fall. Sin equals defiance. Have you as a parent experienced defiance in your child? I know I was a defiant child, and would confirm through the truth of God's Word, I was surely a child conceived and born in sin. I was born out of wedlock; and also carried the sin of Adam.

How would you respond to the question of choice? If given the choice of whether you could have your child a brief time on earth compared to spending time with them forever, what would you choose? I would hope you would choose forever, because one could only imagine the extent of pain and sorrow of having them a long time on earth and then losing them to condemnation forever! You will see an example of how the loss a child's life brought life to another through the wonderful work of a transplant. Now the heart of one is beating in the chest of another.

You Just Never Know

A disciple told me a story of a man who came to a city and was in a cab having a conversation with the driver. The passenger communicated that he was a heart transplant recipient. It must have got the passenger's heart racing when the cab driver's darted in and out of traffic on the way to his destination.

The driver asked, "When did you get the heart?" The passenger told him the date and place. The driver asked the passenger if he minded making a short detour. The passenger was leery at first but agreed, as he could see that the driver had a sincere look on his face and tears in his eyes when he looked at him through the mirror.

Shortly thereafter, they arrived at a residence, and the driver asked the passenger if he would accompany him to the front door. Since it was daylight, the passenger was nervous, but there was an air of anticipation as to why the driver brought him to this house. So he followed the driver to the porch, and stood at the front door. The driver rang the doorbell, and as the door opened to the residence, the driver introduced the passenger to the mother of the young man whose heart was beating in his chest.

With tears in her eyes, she asked if she could approach the passenger, and in amazement, he agreed. She gently placed her ear on his chest to hear the beating of her son's heart in his chest. God is amazing; *the life of one gave life to another.* I am certain, there are people who are so thankful to God for all of the organ donors across the world, where a loss of life for one, meant life to another. I am certain there are so many stories of life given from a life taken. Doesn't it sound just like Jesus?

Could the same be said for sickness requiring a lengthy hospital stay? Why is it at this time and at this place? Yes, you may from time to time visit someone at the hospital. But in visiting you come and go, and surely would not have been at the hospital for a long period of time. When we realize we are always on mission as a disciple of Jesus, we must always be about the will of the Father. We do not know when and where the gospel will be received; therefore, we must be faithful to sow on every opportunity where the Spirit of God leads us.

Life change could occur to someone on the hospital staff, a family member within the same family, or an unrelated person in the same ward as the person who is ill. You are the keeper of God's Word, and now you are in their presence. Without the illness of another, and even yourself, you would not have been in that place. It's truly Romans 8:28 working every day in the lives of God's people and others, who by the testimony of the disciple of Jesus, brings the light of Christ into the darkness of another's life.

Trials Produce Victors

I was talking with Curtis, a disciple of Jesus Christ. God yoked us together several years ago. I am thankful to God for placing Curtis in my life. Our relationship is founded in Christ, and I believe it is an eternal one. Curtis is a great encouragement to me. Curtis is blessed with a beautiful and loving family.

Zachary is one of Curtis's sons. Zach was born with spina bifida, which means there is an incomplete closing of the backbone and membranes around the spinal cord. Zach is living out his trial. He is confined to a wheelchair, has had brain surgery, has suffered through cancer, chemo, and seizures so strong they fractured three vertebrae in his back. Imagine this. Zach has a 3.2 GPA, and Zach's family is in constant prayer for him, and he for them.

Zach's a scholar athlete

You want to know how? Zach believes as his family believes, and lives out Philippians 4:13, that he can do all things in Christ who strengthens him. Zach hunts, fishes and travels internationally. He attends the University of Missouri. He is on a scholarship and plays for the university's wheelchair basketball team. One would expect that without the blessing from God on Zach's life, if he did attend U of M, he may have gone to a game or two and cheered, but he would not be in the locker room before, during, and after games. He may have built a relationship with a player if it was God's will for him to do so. But Zach is on the team, going places where God has ordained him to go. And he is responding to God's calling on his life and going!

Prayer is a constant for Zach, and for his family members, friends, and grandparents who are praying three generations deep. There is sacrifice involved for all, and they live faithfully and obediently to God, because they have seen God's faithfulness and work in their trial. Living their lives is not about how much money they can accumulate in the bank. It's not about their future financial planning. It's about glorifying God in their daily trials, and living out His biblical truths in their lives.

It is about salvation and the hope they have in Jesus Christ. It takes a family praying together, staying in one accord, one faith, one hope, to one Lord, living one day at a time to make this happen.

"Come to Me, all who are weary and heavy-laden, and I will give you rest."
Matthew 11:28

People may believe the Bible is full of just stories, and you may think this is just a story; however, go to the link below and you can see the wonders of God's work in Zach's life. Now if this is true, then you must believe God's Word is also true! My question to you is: Do you believe? Zach and so many others are living examples all around us of the power of our loving God, who will be right in the middle of the storm with you.

They live out this hope as a family in Jesus—when Zach is struggling with pain, suffering, and complications. They know there is a time coming for all of God's children to live in eternal life where Zach, like all, will have a life with no more hurt, pain, suffering, and no more death. There is a perfect body for Zachary and every other child of the only true God.

You may have ailments and complications and there is nothing the medical field can do; have hope—there is a perfect body waiting for you in glory when you are a disciple of Jesus Christ. Thank You, Jesus! Many disciples pray continually for God to be glorified in Zachary's life and their lives as parents and siblings. There is prayer for strength and endurance for the many trips to the hospital and the long nights and short days. Yes, at times it can be extremely overwhelming, yet they charge ahead with hope, looking to Jesus all the way, praise God!

I have heard Curtis say numerous times, "God is using Zach's life to develop godly character in me and my family, empowering us to praise, worship, rejoice, persevere, serve, stay faithful, and have hope!

My hope is in Jesus, and I will not be disappointed." Zach influences and encourages his friends, family and others by his determination and willingness to press on and live a life pleasing to God.

You want to know how they know? When they hear out of the mouths of others watching them the words, "Watching you and your family suffer with Zachary gives us hope, because we do not know where you get the strength to persevere," they immediately proclaim the goodness of God. It is a wonderful opportunity for the family to live out the truth of their belief in God, and they proclaim the gospel of Jesus Christ. Zachary is a blessing in their family, just like the rest of their children, given as a gift from God.[4]

I am compelled to mention the children with special needs around us today who are born with physical impairments, learning deficiencies, emotional instability, inability to communicate, and behavioral challenges, as well as those with a mental illness. These people may look fine on the outside but are turbulent and chaotic on the inside. You may be one of them, know someone, or have a relative with this type of trial. Do you shun them when you see them? Do you engage and love them as Jesus loves you? Do you feel pity for them, or can you see the blessings of God in their lives? Can you see how God is glorified in their lives, or do you see it as a curse? Do you have any idea how many lives are eternally touched by those who live their entire life in a trial? If you haven't, you should get to know someone; they are a beautiful blessing from God.

---

4   Mizzou Rec, *Mizzou Wheelchair Basketball: Zach Steger* (March 7, 2018): https://youtu.be/Kfd-1xyhYSI.

You Gotta Be Just Like Him

When a trial comes forth, do you find yourself asking this question of God: "Father, if You are willing, remove this cup (trial) from me." Have you ever felt this way when faced with a trial which *seemed* too much to bear? Do you remember what Jesus said, when you repeated His words? You can find His response in Luke 22:42. Jesus knows the need for our deliverance and salvation. Jesus knows the Father's will, and His suffering and dying was a part of it. Trials are to make us like Jesus, and God the Father expects us to respond the same as Jesus responded as we imitate Him and as Ephesians 5:1 is actively lived out in our lives.

Here is another perspective to consider. God may choose to test your love for Him. Read Deuteronomy 13:3. Yes, this one is about love. God's testing is a sure way of confirming to yourself if you will keep His commandments or not, or if you love Him or not. When you look back, you see faith, growth, trust, God's love, will and the Holy Spirit's intervention. You see His work developing obedience, strength, perseverance, character, and hope. You see weakness become strength. Through the work of God, you learn the truth about yourself. You begin to see and recognize in yourself and others, the same characteristics present in Jesus, who "is the image of the invisible God" (Colossians 1:15). You are being made to look and act like Him, as we learn no trial will weaken our faith in God, but only strengthen and confirm it. We are being trained in the likeness of God and learning of our own level of obedience.

Here's a promise in God's Word I would surely claim when the trial involves suffering. It's found in 1 Peter 5:10, which says, "After you have suffered for a little while, the God of all grace, who called you to His eternal glory in Christ, will Himself perfect, confirm, strengthen *and* establish you." It is a wonderful work and gift from God when God Himself makes Himself fully known to us and refines, enhances, builds up, and validates His disciples. God is true, and He desires for His disciples to be true as well.

God knows how difficult trials can and will be. The strength, endurance, and perseverance you will need and get from God directly will help you to press on. This is a phenomenal work from God Himself. Do you see why reading, studying, and knowing God's Word is so important? Do you believe and understand that God desires for us to know and learn of His attributes? If you have never read 1 Peter 5:10, you would never know of this wonderful promise from God. But again, it takes believing! Can you now see why the god of this world does not want you to know this about the only true God of the Bible?

Those who are walking by the Spirit live out Christlikeness through actions of love, compassion, comfort, counsel, help, and assistance in our time of need during the trial. Their expressions of love lighten the burden of anguish, despair, suffering, and sorrow caused by the trial. It is amazing how God works through His people to reassure you that you are not alone, nor are you the only one experiencing a trial of this kind, and intensity. If you remember anything I have written in this book, it's this! Jesus says in Matthew 11:28–30, "Come to Me, all who are weary and heavy-laden, and I will give you rest. Take My yoke upon you and learn from Me, for I am gentle and humble in heart, and you will find rest for your souls. For My yoke is easy and My burden is light." Why would we go to man when we can go directly to God? You have no idea where the person/humanity is in their own life, nor what fills their heart, but God does, and this would be why He commands us to come to Him.

Why go to the leaf when you can go to the root, which is the source of life to the leaf. Why go to the creature when you can go to the Creator? Do you see my point in these questions? Sometimes during trials, man wants to provide many different remedies, when all we may need is rest. The only place where one can find complete rest is by resting in Jesus, amen? Jesus tells us to "learn" from Him, and I fully believe that if Jesus wanted us to go to anyone other than Himself to learn, He would have told us. Do you believe that?

His Pain, Your Gain

Cogitate on this. Read and study the crucifixion of Jesus. Most would say it was the most horrific event to happen in a person's life. And yes, the amount of pain and suffering He endured, if you only focus on the human element, was horrific. Obviously, He was the only One for this job, as no one else is qualified. Revelation 5:1–9 confirms this fact. Yet if you are able the see the fingerprint of God in and through Jesus, immediately it becomes the *most wonderful*!

I asked Jesus, humanly, was it worth it? His answer was "YES! It was worth it for *your* sake! The pain is a faint memory to the love and joy coming from pleasing the Father and being faithful to Him. The Father's love has been poured out into My life, and now I AM pouring my love out into yours!" If you desire to see how our Savior dealt with this trial, you can find it in Luke 22:42–45a. You will see prayer, humility, love, and obedience to do the will of the Father. How do we learn to view life and trials in a biblical way, versus humanly? I'll give the answer: look to Jesus (Hebrews 12:2)! Jesus is the perfecter of our faith. Who else do you know who has accomplished this? No one; it's really *faith alone in Christ alone*!

Who Surrounds You?

It makes me smile and fills my heart with joy when I hear about a fellow disciple enduring a trial. Many disciples come together in prayer. Some disciples who are praying may not even know the disciple directly. This demonstrates the power of the Holy Spirit moving in the hearts of Jesus's disciples within the community in Christ, and you know that God is glorified amid the trial.

Look at all the lives being touched by another disciple's trial. This prepares all of us for trials. Some may be in a trial themselves, yet during their trial, they lay it aside, to pray for another. This is love for the brethren. They follow the commands of Jesus to "love one another" as Scripture says in John 13:34. This also leads to spiritual growth as the thoughts and prayers of another replace their own. Have you ever been in a trial and found out another disciple of Jesus were in a trial and needed encouragement and prayer? When you lifted them up in prayer, you laid your trial aside to focus solely on them. Through this work of discipleship, you receive peace and comfort in your own trial, and God's Word came to life. Philippians 4:7 says, "And the peace of God, which surpasses all comprehension, will guard your hearts and your minds in Christ Jesus." Remember, the heart is the seed of the mind, so if the heart is protected, so is the mind. But again, you gotta believe. Can you see why believing in God is so powerful?

Trials move others to respond in prayer, love, encouragement, and support, and God is glorified in the life of His people. This is the importance and value of other disciples in community with you. This enables everyone to reach out and communicate to one another, so everyone can continually live out God's truth in their lives. Galatians 6:2 tells us to "bear one another's burdens." How do you accomplish this unless you are in true biblical community? The answer is, you can't, unless you are. Biblical community, as present in Acts 2, is more than just a "social gathering." They were fully devoted to Jesus's teachings, loved Him, and one another. True biblical community is truly living life together in fellowship with each other, and not just "going through the motions," or "checking the box," because the church says, we must live in community as believers in Jesus to represent to the world we are living as Christ calls us to live.

We are all called to "bear one another's burdens" (Galatians 6:2), and in doing so, we are fulfilling the law of Christ, and His Word becomes a *reality*. It is pure and genuine love versus the disguise of lip service. Have you ever mentioned your trial to someone, and they immediately said, "I'll be praying for you"? It seems they never give you another thought, because there is never any follow up to check on you. Do they say it out of habit, or because it is the "right thing" to say? You should know that no matter where you are or when it is, there is never any better time than the *present* to pray! If someone needs prayer, **then pray**! If you are going to love, *love them now!*

First Corinthians 2:9 is one of my favorite memory verses. It says, "Things which eye has not seen, and ear has not heard, and *which* have not entered the heart of man, all that God has prepared for those who love Him." It is a magnificent promise of God revealing to us, by His Spirit, the life He has prepared for those who love Him through Jesus's life, death, and resurrection. As disciples, our hope rests and depends upon Jesus Christ, His righteousness, and His saving power! I will ask you: If you could see the finished product of yourself, would you respond differently to trials? Imagine, if you will, that the trial came, and even in your finite mind, you try to assess the full extent and impact of the trial, only to find out you barely scratched the surface of what God was doing in your life.

Then God, in His love and mercy, reveals His entire plan, when we see Him as He is, as it says in 1 John 3:2. What do you suppose your response would be then? Would it be, "I had no idea this is what you could make out of me Lord?" And think of the spiritual growth you could have if you were praying faithfully, and your heart and mouth were full of thanksgiving and praise to God. I am not saying one should not ask for wisdom or direction from God, but it would be much more pleasing to God to ask, "How can I serve You, Lord, in this trial? Lord, what are you teaching me, as your servant is willing to listen, and do as You say? Lord, please reveal to me what You desire for me to know and learn."

> "Beloved, now we are children of God, and it has not appeared as yet what we will be. We know that when He appears, we will be like Him, because we will see Him just as He is."
>
> 1 John 3:2

Trials develop faith, prayer, humility, patience, perseverance, endurance, maturity, joy, compassion, understanding, gratitude, and thankfulness. As a result of this work by the Holy Spirit, your life and testimony come alive to share with those God has placed in your walk along your path of life. You share His gospel with enthusiasm with everyone you encounter. You can and will relate intimately with those who are currently enduring a trial. We become a living witness, testifying of God's work in and through our lives to theirs. I hope and pray you see your own trials from a different or new perspective and will approach those imminent trials with a different mindset, and viewpoint. Keep your focus on how God is and will be glorified in their lives and yours, and how their life and yours is a blessing to so many others encountering trials. Your spiritual confidence will grow when you see the works of God in and through Jesus's disciple's life—you!

I close this segment with these three passages you should have as a reference when facing a trial. They are good ones to commit to memory and will serve as a constant reminder of the promises of God, His faithfulness, and the truth of His Word.

> **Hebrews 12:1**: "Therefore, since we have so great a cloud of witnesses surrounding us, let us also lay aside every encumbrance and the sin which so easily entangles us, and let us run with endurance the race that is set before us,"

> **Romans 5:3—5**: "And not only this, but we also exult in our tribulations, knowing that tribulation brings about perseverance; and perseverance, proven character; and proven character, hope; and hope does not disappoint, because the love of God has been poured out within our hearts through the Holy Spirit who was given to us."

> **James 1:12:** "Blessed is a man who perseveres under trial; for once he has been approved, he will receive the crown of life which *the Lord* has promised to those who love Him."

Remember, spiritual growth and your development into Christlikeness results from your faith and trust in God when facing the *various* trials in life! You must have faith, be loving, trusting, believing, hoping, enduring, persevering, praying, encouraging, listening, and asking with full confidence in God, knowing God is at work in you, completing His sovereign will in your life. As you grow as a disciple of Jesus, you can and will be a blessing in someone else's life, as they see the hope you have in Jesus. You are called to live out 1 Peter 3:15: "but sanctify Christ as Lord in your hearts, always *being* ready to make a defense to everyone who asks you to give an account for the hope that is in you, yet with gentleness and reverence." God the Father is glorified in and through your life as you do the will of the Father in the lives of humanity, amen?

A Prayer for You:

ABBA, I love You and thank You for today. This has been an amazing segment for me to read, study, and meditate on. You have brought to mind what You call us to do as Your disciples when in the face of a trial. Nothing happens outside Your sovereign, decretive, efficacious, and permissive will. Help us to know, understand, accept, and live by this truth.

I thank You for Your Spirit's work in me, giving me the ability to communicate Your truths, who You are, what You desire, how You love us, and what You expect of us as Your disciples. Trials can be so overwhelming, but I guess this is why You bring them forth or allow them to occur. They cause us to look at ourselves, as You make everything evident and without question. They cause us to press deeper into You, and I claim Your promise that if we draw near to You, You will draw near to us. Father, draw them to Yourself so they will look to You for comfort, peace, rest, wisdom, discernment, and understanding as they are either in or about to encounter a trial.

Your Word has revealed so much to us by Your wonderful works of faith in all the lives of those before us. They have loved You with all their hearts, souls, minds, and strength, and have trusted and demonstrated their total faith in You, and You have responded to them faithfully. Lord, I pray You will continue to do the mighty work in all Your disciples. I pray the words of this segment encourage, teach, reprove, train, confirm, enlighten, correct, and You convict the hearts needing conviction so that they will become a faithful disciple, and will be faithful and obedient to Your command to make disciples.

I pray for everyone who reads this segment. Give them a fresh set of eyes to see, and a new heart to believe, and to know and understand that the trials of life are for our good, and the various ones are needed to conform us as You planned. By the power of Your Spirit, give them the ability to see the work of Your hands, and the desire to be like Jesus more than any other desire they have in their lives. Give them the desire and ability to read, study, and meditate on Your Word, as Your Word is a lamp to our feet and a light to our path. Holy Spirit do a mighty work in them. I pray and ask in Jesus's name, amen.

Reflections

FORGIVENESS...

"... and without shedding of blood there is no forgiveness." (Hebrews 9:22)
"How blessed is he whose transgression is forgiven; whose sin is covered!"
(Psalm 32:1)

TO FORGIVE OR NOT FORGIVE, THAT'S THE QUESTION

FORGIVE! WHAT? NO WAY! They must pay for the sins they committed against me! This was deeply rooted in my heart, and it occupied my mind. I could have argued, had I known that it was a biblical stance, as Leviticus 24:17–21 is titled "An Eye for an Eye." So rightfully so, they need to pay, and I needed to get revenge!

Therefore, I am taking the law into my own hands, determining the punishment I need to impose, because they must pay the consequences. I set the standard, punishment, penalty, consequence, duration, and actions for their sin, because I do not like it, nor do I appreciate it. In fact, I hate it and them.

If given the chance, I WILL kill them!

They can say "I am sorry" a million times while crawling on their pitiful knees, but that won't cut it! They're right ... they are a sorry person, and I bet you they do not mean it anyway. I will choose when and where I accept their apology if I do. Then and only then, will I allow them into my presence.

I will never talk to them again; nobody sins against me and gets away with it.

Do any of these words sound familiar in your life, or in the life of someone you know? I pray not, as this is a far cry from what Jesus calls us to do in Matthew 5:38–39. But if you do, then prayer is needed, as is *the work of God to deliver you as He delivered me from this bondage.*

I would hope you would say instead, "This person must have really been hurt. And, they have so much pain, it is leading to bitterness and hatred." If this was you at one point in your life, and no more, PRAISE GOD for a new heart and the power of forgiveness through love! If this is you now, then read on. If you think you are trapped and believe or have been told you cannot break free, *read on.*

Those words were said repeatedly, by me. The sin committed against me hurt me physically, emotionally, and psychologically. I had a heart full of bitterness, hatred, and anger. No matter what, it was always there. There was no escaping it. But you must have hope. I was rescued and set free over sixteen years ago, and all I can say today is, BUT GOD!

You know the amazing thing? At that time I thought I was a Christian. I attended Catholic School, was an altar boy, and went to church quite often, may I say. I went more than my parents and siblings as a matter of fact. Can you imagine how many times I repeated, "If given the chance, I WILL kill them?" I will tell you—over and over again, I was reliving it repeatedly.

If you would have asked me then, should I receive eternal life, I would have told you yes. I had five out of seven sacraments—Baptism, First Communion, Penance, Confirmation, and Matrimony to my record. I had more *works (altar boy-serving in mass, funerals, and wed-dings)* than most ... far better than any with none, right? And believe me over the years in parochial school, I served a lot. So now, wouldn't those "good" works carry some weight in the eyes of God? Afterall, some knowledge and works regardless of the condition of my heart is better than none—right?

I knew of the teachings of the Catholic religion because I attended Catholic school. And not being a student of God's Word, I believed all of what was taught was true. *After salvation God made it clear to me, teachings are only beneficial to anyone when those teachings line up with the truth of His Word!* But it's easy to believe anything, especially when those teachings are taught by influential people, who have a perceived authority, and are very convincing. But the truth is when *any* teaching is not biblical you are misled. Did you ever consider that knowledge and works generated from false teachings are *fruitless* in the eyes of God? It is either the work of Jesus or nothing, believe that!

There is a surety of salvation in everyone the Spirit of God completes His work! You then believe and have faith alone in Jesus alone. There is no other mediator, redeemer, or Savior as Jesus's sacrifice is the finished work of God the Father. God's Word is the only infallible word—ever!

It makes me wonder how many others are deceived to think the works they do are good enough to satisfy God's wrath for sin.

God has a plan for every human being walking on the face of this planet (Proverbs 16:4). ALL will complete their "assigned" work. God's plan is from Jesus to Judas including you and me (Mark 13:34). Even the doorkeeper (assigned task) must be alert to open the door upon the master's return. Most importantly, *no one* born of the seed of Adam has equality with Jesus! And believe me, if you are living in anything other than *the truth*, you are being deceived and living in bondage. The difference is that some are bound tighter than others, but bound, nonetheless.

What do others see in you as the evidence of God's will, work, and plan being lived out in your life?

My friend, I am here to testify to you it is not about religion—It's about being saved and knowing the only true God *through* an intimate relationship with Jesus Christ. You become His disciple and begin your journey sowing the gospel wherever the Spirit leads.

My testimony to you is true, and I am speaking from the heart. I was a bitter man and held on tightly to resentment. This bitterness caused me to carry hostility toward others, and I continuously craved revenge. It was like being eaten up from the inside out. The more I kept it inside, the more it churned.

I must tell you, in those years, there were a few opportunities when I was presented with a chance to execute my revenge only to have it pass me by. These "missed" opportunities led to even more disappointment. Mostly I was disappointed in myself, because I did not act on the opportunity when it presented itself. This lack of action compounded my anger, bitterness, and hatred.

You know the sad part? I had thrown myself into the mix since I made a promise to myself, I would make them pay; and did not keep it! Not only did I hate them, but I even hated a part of myself. Believe me, living in this state of mind meant that it did not take much to ignite the flame of fire on the cannister of my anger.

If there was a sign posted, it would have read, "DANGER! CAPABLE OF IMMEDIATE EXPLOSION! PUSH AT YOUR OWN RISK!" Bitterness coupled with extreme hatred made me an incredibly angry man. There was going to be no forgiveness, only RETRIBUTION! How could I forgive them in my own strength? I could not, because I hated them, and my heart was deceitful, wicked, desperately sick, and my mind, polluted. So forgive them? *# % @ NO!

WHAT LIES BENEATH

You could look at your life and heart like the ocean. We see the surface, and it could tell us some signs, but that's just the surface. But what's happening below the surface is the real question? There's more happening than you could ever imagine, and it's either righteousness or unrighteousness. The surface may look calm, yet just below, there is a riptide. Riptides result from turbulent water, and although the surface is untroublesome, just below, it's deadly. Just like our lives; the surface, your face and demeanor, could be totally opposite than what lies beneath and is consuming your heart. And you know another thing? Someone could be particularly good at concealing how they really feel to those close to them who could help them the most. But it also could reveal the same, turbulent water above and below. Would you agree, based on yourself, and others you may know, that a person's life could reveal two entirely separate ways of living?

If you have ever gone deep sea fishing, you will know there are millions and even billions of fish we never see under the surface. People are just like the ocean. There are so many who give the impression they are "just fine" on the surface and they are passed by with a friendly nod or a pleasant smile. Most have no idea of what is going on below the surface, in their heart. Like the millions of fish below the surface of water, there are millions of people with problems being held captive by the bondage of sin. There are many who proclaim to be disciples of Jesus who pass by these people but who have no genuine interest into finding out what is going on below the surface in the unbeliever's heart. This is how the Holy Spirit works in the lives of Jesus's disciples. We may not know, but God knows, and He initiates attentiveness that leads us to engage. This is what confirms one is a disciple of Jesus. They are the ones who engage, and the person either breaks through their own surface, or the disciple dives in.

As a child, the abuse I lived through was physical, sexual, emotional, and psychological. During the years of abuse, this little boy made a life-surviving promise to himself. In doing so, I was unknowingly setting the roots of sin so deep in my heart, I learned self-extraction was an impossibility. Now with an unrepentant heart, due to being consumed by sin, forgiveness was NEVER going to be a choice because my heart was hard as stone.

The longer any person neglects the presence and practice of sin, the further the heart hardens. As the roots expand in size, they commence to slowly squeeze the life right out of the heart. These sinful actions committed against me were by no means my fault. Did they influence my life, there is no question they did? It was not the sin committed against me that caused my sinful acts; it was my own. It was my own sinful nature of pride, lust, immorality, anger, and drunkenness to name a few. This is sin's power through deception. Sin will get you to believe something different than the truth, so you will have an excuse, to never examine yourself for the real problem—you. So with the focus on one, and avoidance of the other, there was no escape for me from the hell I was living—that is, not until Jesus broke into my darkness with His marvelous light and saved me.

You see, living a life consumed by sin causes one to spiral downward viciously, day after day after day. When you are your focus, the only perspective you have is downward as you fall deeper into a "woe is me" mindset, and my chains got even tighter. I was extremely weak, and was only focusing on my bondage, captivity, and sin. And all the while Satan was attempting to destroy what God planned to make new. Through his deception, revenge instead of forgiveness will always be the best option. *As darkness envelopes and sin consumes*, the only option is revenge; in this state of mind, forgiveness is truly an unknown miracle, not available to the spiritually blind and dead.

And What if You Don't?

Jesus warns of the consequence of not forgiving in Matthew 6:14–15. It says, "For if you forgive others for their transgressions, your heavenly Father will also forgive you. But if you do not forgive others, then your Father will not forgive your transgressions." This is where Jesus warns of the failure to forgive and the eternal consequence. I must remind you: you will never be able to forgive in your own strength; you will need the help of God to do it. You must fix your eyes on Jesus, looking to Him for His strength for your forgiveness and the forgiveness of others. Believe that!

I will ask you, and your answer in your own heart should be based on what you believe, and how you live will determine if you are forgiven. First, do you believe what Jesus says? Second, do you forgive or not?

One must wonder how someone can forgive another when they sin against them, regardless of the type or extent. The answer is quite simple. The disciple gains understanding by the power of God the Holy Spirit, that the sins they commit against a Holy God are far greater than one or multiple people could ever commit against them.

"Test yourselves *to see* if you are in the faith; examine yourselves! Or do you not recognize this about yourselves, that Jesus Christ is in you—unless indeed you fail the test?"

2 Corinthians 13:5

This is God's unconditional love. He forgives. Thank You, Jesus! Consider this: Look at your whole life, every aspect. Could you even count the sins you committed against God and others, in your thoughts, words, and deeds? You must make certain if you are going to live outside of the grace of God and the forgiveness offered in Jesus, and refuse to forgive. God has every single one of them recorded.

The disciple of Jesus must be willing to freely forgive as many times as needed. Do you remember the word "unconditional"? Now this is where the proverbial rubber meets the road. It will surely confirm to yourself and others the condition of your heart, if you truly have a new heart, His Spirit, and a renewed mind. A mind transformed, and the Spirit of God is dwelling in you, gives you the ability to freely forgive anyone for any sin. Read 2 Corinthians 13:5, to *test* and *examine* yourself! You must be truthful and—just a reminder—God already knows your heart. You will not be fooling Him, only deceiving yourself.

BUT GOD, who gives His disciples the ability to forgive not only others, but also self! You know the amazing thing? Those observing see the attributes of God and His will being completed in and through your life. The Father and the Son are glorified in this, and you! PRAISE GOD!

Remember, if you do not forgive, God will imitate you, and not forgive you either. There will be no excuse you could ever use to convince God that your failure to forgive was justified. Remember, this would be disobedience, by not forgiving, and the consequence is eternal separation from God forever, in hell.

Cannot Keep Living like This ...

I was a living riptide. On the surface, I was giving the impression of being A-Okay, but below the surface, I carried a turbulent heart full of sin. I was being pulled down deeper and deeper, asking the question, "What about this sin committed against me? What am I going to do about it?"

I believed I should have taken matters into my own hands because my actions *were* justified. The actions against me were wrong, and because I never told anyone, I needed to fix it myself. It was against me, so I had to make it right. This was wrong and definitely not biblical. But common sense tells me that if I break the law, I go to jail. So if I kill them, although in my mind they deserved to be killed, I still go to jail. Therefore, whether I know God's truth or not, I break God's law without God's forgiveness, I go to hell.

In my mind these sins committed against me required more than just an apology. The attempt to apologize really could mean they feel bad, yet if the truth were known, they really couldn't care less. If they had really cared about me, they would have *not* done what they did in the first place! I understand now; my actions in the beginning never took into account the consequences.

It is the consequence of being caught, or exposed and held accountable, that causes one to apologize. Their apology may lessen the consequence, or potentially eliminate it altogether, but would surely depend on the severity of the sin committed.

Do you know there is a difference between an apology and asking for forgiveness?

Ponder this. It is natural for someone to say "I am sorry" when it's made known to them that what they've done was hurtful. This is especially true when they are face to face with a large, strong, angry madman with a hammer, or if this madman has his hands around their neck, squeezing like a boa constrictor, watching and waiting for the sign of life to flow out of them. I'm certain, and so should you be, the response of "I am sorry" would come fairly quickly, agreed?

Sometimes, an apology or asking for forgiveness will lessen the consequence of one's actions. The main difference is that where forgiveness is given there is no vengeance from the aggrieved party. Vengeance is left up to God if one is truly living out His biblical truths. Here is the remedy. God says in Romans 12:19, "Never take your own revenge, beloved, but leave room for the wrath *of God*, "for it is written, 'Vengeance is Mine, I will repay,' says the Lord." And with an apology, there is no guarantee vengeance will still not be carried out.

We must trust in the promises of God. If I had only known, I would have done two things: (1) forgive them, and (2) release the bitterness, and leave it up to God to handle the vengeance. However, in my spiritual blindness, I chose to do what I thought was right for me. Without any spiritual guidance and living a life of sin, I did whatever it was which seemed right to me! And you know, that is biblical, too, for Proverbs 14:12 says, "There is a way *which seems* right to a man, but its end is the way of death." Believe me, I paid a heavy price for my decisions.

Let me make myself perfectly clear. An apology has to do with the abuser's emotions and only releases the abuser's guilt. It does nothing for the continuing hurt, pain, and anguish for the abused. It is like an anchor hanging around the neck and is a constant reminder for the abused. And it really does not matter whether the apology is accepted—the abuser will feel better because they can now release their guilt. But there is a tremendous difference between being sorry and asking for forgiveness. As you can see, an apology has to do with one's own emotions, while forgiveness specifically considers the other person and the specific hurt (sin) caused to them.

Many want to link apology and forgiveness together, to say they are the "same" thing. Well, I am here to tell you they are not! When someone sins against another, the sinner should feel bad, but sometimes they don't. When they do feel bad, it could be because of the reaction they see or hear in the person (or people) against whom they have sinned. When the sinner does not feel bad, it is often because, in the sinner's mind, their actions or behaviors were needed or justified, and an apology wouldn't even be considered.

When I was stuck in this cycle, never did I consider God in all this. Yet it was God who had preserved my life! He preserved it for salvation, this moment, and all the following ones. Thank You, Jesus! I did not one time think or even consider how God had been hurt and offended by my sinfulness, regardless of this abusive life of mine.

Unless I was able to see my own thoughts, words, and deeds as sinful to God, I would never think I would be held accountable to Him for my evil. I was spiritually blind to believing, blinded by the deception of believing those five out of seven sacraments justified my salvation. Boy, was I so wrong! It was not until the grace of God illuminated my mind, and I became aware of the magnitude of my sinfulness to God and my need to *repent and seek forgiveness* from Him.

Myself Included

It was extremely easy for me to place all the sin I was committing on others, and just try to go on living, using any and every means to stuff it away. But I was not really living, just surviving. I was so consumed with my own sin, I blamed

"Jesus said to him, 'I am the way, and the truth, and the life; no one comes to the Father but through Me.'"

John 14:6

everyone else for my sinful predicament. I never even considered myself as the swindler. I did not realize the full extent of the sin of unbelief in my life and, in my spiritual blindness, I could only see their offenses, while mine were camouflaged in my darkness.

As I was moving aimlessly, walking and living in spiritual darkness through life, there was only one destination on that path. If God had left me in the domain of darkness, my path to hell was certain. But because Jesus came into my darkness and rescued me, the path is now eternal life. Although many want to claim multiple paths to eternal life, I will testify that there is no gray area here, either. There is only *the Way*, and it's Jesus Christ. Read John 14:6, where Jesus confirms this truth. No need to speculate. *It's only Him.*

There are only two final destinations for everyone born on this planet. One is eternal damnation and the other eternal life. So I will ask you: Where are you headed? It may be easy to respond, "Eternal life!" But look around. What markers do you see? It will bring a tremendous amount of joy to your life when you see the work of God the Holy Spirit and not your own as the means to your decisions. Celebrate with thankfulness in your heart to God, as you keep pressing on in your journey toward the narrow gate!

Yes, their acts against me were sinful, but so were mine. Yes, the sin of abuse was against me personally, but my sins were against me and God. The reality is, I was hurting myself more than what was done to me. This was clear in how I was living, and my sin was against God. I would not admit it, nor did I even consider it. I understood the need for God's and others' forgiveness, but how could I forgive myself or look to God for His forgiveness when I was pointing my finger at everything and everyone else? I was making excuses for my sin, just like Adam when He blamed Eve and God.

Through countless nights, I blamed myself for the mess I had made of myself. And you know, I was right—it was all my fault for my sin, for the damage and destruction I had caused. I could not use anything or anybody as my excuse. Remember what I said I learned when my foot touched the sand on the other side of the Red Sea? If you do not, I'll tell you: it was me all along.

If you truly look at your life, how many times could you, or did you say, "If I hadn't done this or that, I would not be where I am today"? Or, "This wouldn't have happened. It is all my fault." This happens *when you run out of people to blame, and you are the only one left.* This creates the tendency to beat yourself up, or beat yourself down, again and again. I want you to know that I was incredibly good at this internal condemnation by continually blaming myself.

No, this is where forgiveness of self applies, and only God knew I needed to do this!

How could I forgive others if I could not forgive myself? Many love themselves so much their actions toward others seem like hate. Some people are so selfish, they put themselves before everyone. Where others are expecting to experience love, they feel rejection, which gives the impression of or seems like hate. Remember, there is no gray area here. Either you will either love or hate. I did not love myself. Remember, because of my failure to execute my justice, I hated myself. You would not try to take your own life multiple times if you genuinely loved yourself, would you?

It takes a new heart, the love of God in this new heart, to begin to understand, in this same mind, the love God has for me.

When Jesus saves, you learn of your own depravity, and from depravity, sinful behaviors, and the result is always the same. Let me explain. Every part of me—my heart, mind, desires, feelings, and flesh—was contaminated by sin. As a result of sin, I lived out sin, and it infected all areas of my life. I always seemed to end up sad and disappointed. It was like repeatedly going around the mountain.

If you continue to immerse yourself in sin and its ways, you'll end up exactly where God says you will— "For the wages of sin is death" (Romans 6:23). Now you must decide if you will continue to live a life full of sin. If you do, then expect the same results as you have experienced so many times before.

If you are having trouble identifying the sin in your life, or in turning away from sin, or you desire to be free from the bondage

> "Therefore let us draw near with confidence to the throne of grace, so that we may receive mercy and find grace to help in time of need."
>
> Hebrews 4:16

and captivity of it, then reach out to God for help. You can approach His throne. Remember God's promise in Hebrews 4:16? If you do and believe it, God is waiting patiently to help you in your time of need! Get up and draw near to Him!

There was something important I had to learn about the depth and power of this wonderful gift of forgiveness from God. Remember, it is forgiveness through love which begins the healing. What I understood, after God's amazing grace came into my life, was I had a desperate need to begin to love myself, and then and only then could I forgive myself.

Sometimes it is easier to forgive others, and even ask for it, than it is to forgive oneself. One will never be able to forgive oneself or anyone else, without the love of God flowing in one's life. The sin committed against others should be less and less as we grow in the knowledge of God and the Holy Spirit's ongoing work in our lives.

When sin is committed, causing hurt and pain, seek God's mercy. Have confidence by the blessings and love of God that you can receive His forgiveness, when you approach Him with a repentant heart, and you will stand again. This is truly the worth and work of His Word! We can read it, and it serves as a constant reminder of His truths and promises. This allows us to rise again and continue to be a useful disciple for Him. Forgiveness is one of the real and true works being carried out in our lives—not only for others, but also for ourselves. This is what unbelievers see in our walk and testimony as Jesus's disciple.

One of the Greatest Expressions of Love

Believe it or not, forgiveness is one of the greatest expressions of love. It is love in action. It truly requires a person to look at themselves. It is natural to think we must look at others because of the sins committed against us. No, you must look at yourself. Before you take some time to fully examine your heart, first meditate on the following questions and the answers:

> How was Jesus able to ask for forgiveness for those who crucified Him? *Love.*

How could Stephen beg, "Lord, do not hold this sin against them," in reference to the very men who were stoning him? *Love.*

In Genesis 45, how could Joseph forgive his brothers for beating him and selling him into slavery? *Love.*

How does a parent forgive a person who committed an evil act against their child? *Love.*

How does a man preach the gospel to the same people who killed his entire family during a genocide? *Love.*

How does a wife forgive her husband for adulterous affairs? *Love.*

How does this little boy, now living inside of the man, forgive like those mentioned? *Love.*

How can a broken heart heal itself? I am here to testify, it can't; it can only be done when the heart is made new by the *love* of God, and when His *love* is flowing through the new heart. *Love.*

So do you hold onto resentment and bitterness? Are you angry and cannot find a way to release the anger? Do you have hurt and pain caused by the sin of another? Freedom can only happen through forgiveness, which requires the *love* of God!

When you read in God's Word about the lives of these people, and see and experience forgiveness in your life, it should cause you to either desire to forgive or to ask for forgiveness. Either way, there is always a need for forgiveness in this world, and the flesh we walk around in proves it. As God works in the hearts of His people, I can tell you that there have been countless acts of forgiveness throughout the world and history we may never hear about, but God knows! What makes these people respond with a forgiving heart and truly forgive another? Love. How is it others cannot, or refuse to forgive? The answer must be they have yet to have the love of God in their hearts.

In the story about Stephen in Acts, the writer mentions that Saul, who was later to become Paul, was standing at the place and witnessing Stephen's death by stoning. I often wondered if Paul was thinking the same thing as millions do today: *What is making these people act this way with a heart of forgiveness, even when they are being killed, or learn of the one who killed their loved one?*

He would find out later that it was the love of God. I have learned that the answer is quite simple: those who forgive have the love of God in their hearts. They know and understand the gospel and their need of God's forgiveness. I needed God's forgiveness more than I needed an apology or someone asking for my forgiveness.

Many mention the word "forgiveness" but do not understand the meaning of it and how God intended for it to work in our lives and the lives of others. Let us examine the word "forgive." It's made up of two words: "for" and "give." The word "for" means aimed at, intended for, designed for, meant for, and used for. The word "give" means offer, impart, transfer possession, and bestow. The giving of something to someone is not predicated on who may or may not deserve it. When done in love, they receive forgiveness without even asking for it. Believe it, it's true. In Luke 23:34, Jesus asks the Father to forgive those who crucified Him, because they did not know God's plan of redemption, and they were His instruments to assist Him in bringing it about. Those men did not ask Jesus for forgiveness.

I know that I did not deserve God's forgiveness, yet in love, He forgave me. And you know how I knew? The burden, bitterness, and hatred were no longer at the center of my mind, because God removed them when He gave me a new heart. Those who have sinned against me did not deserve it either, but as I understood the magnitude of God's forgiveness to me, I freely and lovingly forgave them. Although it was designed for them, it actually worked in me. It was the only way to begin to heal and grow spiritually. So forgiving was *used for* healing as I transferred possession of my hurt and pain to God. It may not have been in my heart any longer, but the thoughts of it were in my mind, so I gave even the thoughts of my hurt and pain to God, knowing He is quite able to handle it all; after all, all of it was nailed to His cross.

The Perfect Example of Forgiveness

I would like to address the two passages mentioned under the "Forgiveness" title. The first is Hebrews 9:22: "And according to the Law, *one may* almost *say*, all things are cleansed with blood, and without shedding of blood there is no forgiveness." The second is Psalm 32:1: "How blessed is he whose transgression is forgiven, whose sin is covered!" Both passages have two especially key details regarding my sin: blood and forgiveness. It takes one for the other to be activated.

Since life is in the blood, it will take blood, life, to seal the promises of God with His people. God explains it best in Leviticus 17:11: "For the life of the flesh is in the blood, and I have given it to you on the altar to make atonement for your souls; for it is the blood by reason of the life that makes atonement." Whether or not you believe in God and the work of Jesus Christ on the cross, you will need to face the reality of God's consequence for sin. His divine justice for sin is death. Sin results in spiritual death; there is no gray area here, either. On the day of judgment, you will either have a substitute or not when you stand before God.

Either I bring a million lambs to be sacrificed on the altar of God for my sinful thoughts, words, and deeds, or it is me. I must tell you, I do not own a million lambs, or goats, bulls, rams, turtledoves, or pigeons. And even if I were to have a few, in my spiritual darkness, I would have squandered it away on the pleasures the world has to offer, and then show up empty handed trying to plead my case with God. So if I cannot produce a sacrifice to God for my sin, then I am left to fall into the hands of the living God with no other sacrifice aside from ... myself. And know, you may be right there with me, unless you think you are exempt from the justice of God. You must know that you need Jesus, and so did I! If you do not believe in Jesus Christ, you are in a troublesome predicament already.

With the sacrifice of animals, blood is poured out to God. God required man, on man's own behalf, to sacrifice animals as atonement for the sins committed against Him. There is a day coming in which no one will escape the judgment of God.

The animal sacrifice was the substitution to cover sin. We are sinners and deserve death. There is no argument; you are born in sin, and we all sin in thought, word, and deed. You will be next in line for the cross if there is no sacrifice for you, because without the shedding of blood, there is no forgiveness. No forgiveness, no eternal life.

We will all stand before Jesus and be held accountable for it all—every thought, word, and deed. God is holy and righteous, sin has a penalty, and the penalty must be paid. As a disciple of Jesus, we can feel the effects of sin today in our mortal bodies, though it be temporary compared to those who die in their sin.

Have you ever felt guilt, void, puzzled, or detached from God? As a disciple of Jesus, when we sin, it does hurt God and grieve the Holy Spirit. But praise God, it will never separate us from Him! This spiritual death is eternal separation from God forever.

Living in this world today, it could be easy to say, "That will not happen to me," or "I am not concerned, because I do not believe it anyway." Either way, you will find out the truth, and these thoughts when opposed to the cross of Jesus, will be revealed as well on your fateful day of judgment.

Mercy, grace, and forgiveness come through the blood of the one perfect sacrifice of Jesus Christ. Animals do not compare to the blood of Jesus; it was human blood for humanity, shed for you and me, for the forgiveness of our sin. There is a great passage to read which addresses the "Results of Justification," and it is found in Romans 5, specifically Romans 5:12, which states, "Therefore, just as through one man sin entered into the world, and death through sin, and so death spread to all men, because all sinned" Romans 5:19 states, "For as through the one man's disobedience the many were made sinners, even so through the obedience of the One the many will be made righteous." And the "One" is Jesus.

The blood of Jesus covered our sin and depravity, and we receive forgiveness from God. Jesus, our great High Priest, understands our sinful nature and can sympathize with us. Therefore "the word of the cross is foolishness to those who are perishing, but to us who are being saved it is the Power of God" (1 Corinthians 1:18). Without Jesus being pierced for our transgressions, our sin is uncovered; there is no atonement for anyone, and all of us are dead in trespasses and sin. It will not matter what you say or do, no forgiveness from God, and you and I will spend eternity in hell, separated from God forever.

What will you say when God says your thoughts, words, and deeds condemn you? Here are some questions I had to ask myself. Have I ever had an evil thought? Have I ever said an evil thing? Have I ever committed an evil act?

Based on what I have told you, we both should agree that yes, I did. Then, without a doubt, I will be held accountable for my sinful thoughts, words, and deeds—all of them, every single one. And without Jesus, I should expect, God in His righteous judgment, will find me guilty of it all.

So I will ask: if you are going to live on your own works, merits, and righteousness, how many lambs, goats, bulls, rams, turtledoves, or pigeons do you own? By the way, because of Jesus's work, you might as well barbeque em' up because they are no longer acceptable to God. Jesus's death on His cross *was* the perfect sacrifice! Now, *what are you going to do?*

There is a Definite Difference

The statement "I am" sorry or "I" apologize is about removing the bad feeling "I" have. Once someone says "I'm sorry" or "I apologize," they now can release the "bad" feeling they have because of their sinful act. Since one uses the term "I am" sorry, now the burden is on the other person and it is no longer "my" problem. It's theirs, because "I" did "my part." When someone makes these statements, they can move on and no longer care, since they no longer feel bad. You see, it is all about you. It must be, as the first word out of one's mouth is "I." The key here is "*I am*" sorry.

Asking for forgiveness, on the other hand, is about the other person and the pain you have caused them. Therefore, you will hear, "Please forgive me for the sin I committed against you."

The key here is "you," the *other* person. It is focused on the hurting person rather than on oneself! That's biblical. We must consider others more important than ourselves. Philippians 2:3 says, "Do nothing from selfishness or empty conceit, but with humility of mind regard one another as more important than yourselves." This tears down the barrier of pride, and through the act of forgiveness, it removes strife and relationships develop, be it between family members, or the community of disciples of Jesus. One should not expect unbelievers to freely forgive, because as mentioned, it will take the love of God to initiate true and complete forgiveness. Only Jesus's disciples live to testify about this marvelous work of God in their lives and the lives of others!

Here is the difference: when a disciple of Jesus sins against another, regardless of who they may be, a saint or an unbeliever, asking for forgiveness is an immediate action and an expectation of Jesus for all His disciples. Repentance is instantaneous when asking for forgiveness. When sin is present, rest assured, you will know by the Holy Spirit's conviction those actions, whether in thought, word, or deed were sinful, repentance and seeking forgiveness *is* commanded.

The request for forgiveness specifically addresses the sin committed. This confirms you are acknowledging exactly what your sin was and how your sin caused them to hurt. "Please forgive me for the _____ (sin) I committed against you." This ensures they are fully aware that you know exactly what you have done and the pain you caused.

Forgiveness will remove the vengeance, but the hurt and pain is in the healing. And when one truly forgives another, the healing process begins immediately. However, it requires time to heal. Even the smallest cut takes time to heal, and emotional wounds are no different; they also take time to heal, just like the body. If the sinner continues to carry the hurt for the sin caused even when forgiveness is granted, then they should surrender it to God. And if you become anxious, uneasy, or worried from it, then know 1 Peter 5:7 is available to you.

How one acts after they sin against another will either confirm or contradict one's authenticity as one of Jesus's disciples. And you must believe and understand that God expects if we proclaim to be His disciple, then our lives, every fragment of them, must be a reflection of His, especially when it comes to loving one another. A disciple of Jesus asks and seeks forgiveness regardless of their own feelings.

More times than not, through the action of forgiveness, relationships can grow even stronger because the love of God is at the heart of the hurt, pain, and forgiveness. A deeper understanding and *the application of God's unconditional love produces growth through the amazing power of forgiveness.*

His Healing Power Is Working and Unmistakably

I know I am not the only one who has been sinned against by someone else. Mine may not be the most extreme, nor is it the least either. I understand that when someone sins against another, it's personal to them, as it should be. We all should recognize the significance of sin toward another, regardless of how it may appear to us. And where compassion is needed, then we are called to be compassionate, just like God. Lamentations 3:22 says, "The Lord's lovingkindnesses indeed never cease, for His compassions never fail." As disciples of Jesus, we must imitate Him.

Many say they can forgive, but forgetting transgressions is out of the question, as they need to remember, to ensure it does not happen to them again by anybody. I am so thankful God forgives and forgets. I could not imagine God taking into account every sin I committed my entire life. But He does for those not in Christ. So what would be in the books? First, if you doubt there are books, here is the evidence. You and I and myriads of others will be standing before God. Daniel 7:10 says,

> A river of fire was flowing
> And coming out from before Him;
> Thousands upon thousands were attending Him,
> And myriads upon myriads were standing before Him;
> The court sat,
> And the books were opened.

Revelation 20:12 says, "And I saw the dead, the great and the small, standing before the throne, and books were opened; and another book was opened, which is the *book* of life; and the dead were judged from the things which were written in the books, according to their deeds."

I believe when the books are opened for Jesus's disciples, the first entry is "Born of the Spirit." Then you will see half page, full page, empty page, quarter page, full page, empty page, eighth page, full page, full page, and on and on for all the books. What could this represent? It could be all the good works you completed by the power of the Holy Spirit. These good works fill the pages, and the blank spaces would have contained the sin. In Jesus, none are written anywhere, because "Therefore there is now no condemnation for those who are in Christ Jesus" (Romans 8:1).

God only sees the good works through love as you are conformed to the image of His Son, and His light shines through your life into the lives of others. The evidence or proof of you walking by His Spirit and living according to His Word is what is written in Ephesians 2:10: "For we are His workmanship, created in Christ Jesus for good works, which God prepared beforehand so that we would walk in them."

So, therefore, those who are not in Christ Jesus will be condemned, their every sin recorded, believe me.

But when I do sin against God, He forgives as if it were the first time, and He does not have the human-like mindset of "Here we go again!" Forgiveness from God is a wonderful blessing because He removes my sin from His sight in Christ. I do not go on living and thinking about them. It is not like God is keeping track and saying, "Here's David again with the same sin over and over again." God knows I have a sin nature that wants to control me. But in Christ, I can conquer it, and the more I do, my sin decreases as my love and faithfulness for Jesus increases.

To possess a mindset of constantly remembering, or saying "I cannot forget," is really keeping or harboring the thoughts of sin of any kind, yours or anyone else's, which is an extremely dangerous deed to live out. *It is like the cry, whimper, or yelp of an injured prey, and the prowling lion comes in to devour.* Scripture says, in 1 Peter 5:8, "Be of sober spirit, be on the alert. Your adversary, the devil, prowls around like a roaring lion, seeking someone to devour." And as injured prey, you are still, fixed in the mind. You become motionless as you choose to call to mind sin and dwell on it, and you could easily become the devil's next meal.

Here is an amazing contrast to remembering the sins committed against you. Most say they cannot help but remember. You know the interesting thing about this? It is really a choice to remember. Here is why. When you were in second grade, what color shirt did you wear on Tuesday of the second week of school? If you had to wear a uniform, you are excluded. When you were in ninth grade, who was the first person you talked to when you entered your second period class on the first Thursday in October? Can you name all your classmates, barring the home school students and those with less than ten in their graduating class? As an athlete, do you remember every pitch and hit since T-ball through college?

Are you seeing my point? God has given us this ability to forget as well. We just choose to rewire when it is suitable. If not, then all the above questions, and every event, conversation, and image would be retained and constantly on our mind. But why are they not? You did not forget it, did you? Hmmm. Yes, we can forget some things, so why not all? I am so thankful God has given me the ability to forget those images and all those sinful acts—mine, and those committed against me. But I must tell you, it takes the renewing and saturating of my mind with His Word and the mighty work of God the Holy Spirit. Thank You, Jesus!

This is where you must look to God and His Word for help in this time of need. Yes, it's true, and I am one to be very thankful of this, as He places our sin as far as the East is from the West, and so must I. Have you ever tried? If not, freedom from bondage is closer than you know. But most say, "He's God and I am a human being." Well, I just want to remind you, *Jesus is also a human being, and He knows what the flesh and the spirit are truly and fully capable of doing and accomplishing.*

We are called to imitate God. I have mentioned Ephesians 5:1 several times in this book, and rest assured, I mention it often when talking with a disciple face to face. It is critically important to keep this command in the forefront of our minds as a disciple of Jesus because He expects we will be a faithful imitation of Him. We are to "remain, stand, stay, and exist in the character and attributes of God." You are right—no, you cannot forget in your own strength. I agree! I lived it continuously for over thirty years. I needed God's strength, power, and might to live a life where forgetting becomes like Him. Why would you want so many other characteristics and attributes of God but not think you can obtain the same with forgetting. Paul tells us to "forget" what lies behind. I guess many would say, "I can't. *I cannot forget the bondage and captivity because the freedom I have in Jesus is not wonderful enough to erase the pain and anguish I lived through when I was in sin's clutches." Then I will tell you that you have yet to live the true freedom found in Jesus Christ!*

Contemplate this. We say we need to be healed, right? Well, have you noticed that when you get a cut, bruise, or broken bone, it *heals*! We already have healing properties in our bodies, so why would these be missing from our minds? Believe it, God has provided us with those same properties in our minds. What if this was Satan's way of trapping or deceiving you from fully experiencing the depths of God's attributes and healing? What if Satan is stopping you from using your life as a living example of God's grace and healing? The truth is Satan is keeping the hurt in the forefront of your mind so that you continue to dwell on it!

There must be something said about Philippians 4:8. You see it mentioned above; go back and read it and truly meditate on it! What does it tell us? We must dwell on the things of God, and forgiveness brings the healing we truly need and desire. So why keep picking at the scab? Unless you like to watch it bleed, leave it alone and *let it heal*! Stop being deceived, and live with the freedom forgiveness brings, as it also is a gift from God.

Know this, you are correct if you think you cannot forgive and forget in your own strength. This would be like Jesus looking at His hands, body and feet, and reliving the crucifixion ... repeatedly! No! He looks at the Father, knowing how pleasing His sacrifice was to Him! We know His sacrifice made us free and we have peace with God. Our lives now have His Spirit and we live out His commands and spread the *Good News*!

Can you now see Philippians 4:8 being lived out by Jesus? Therefore, "fixing our eyes on Jesus" is so essential, as it says in Hebrews 12:2. He knows what and how to do it. Just imitate Him! This gives our minds a rest from the constant dwelling on hurt, pain, sadness, disappointment, and most importantly sin. Your mind begins to heal and be renewed.

Do you remember what Romans 12:2 says should happen to the minds of Jesus's disciple? Are you working at renewing your mind, or are you letting the clutter get in the way of healing and healthiness?

Unbelievers say, "I cannot forget," or "I'll remember what you did for the rest of my life!" Yet some state, "I cannot forget," or "I'll remember," and proclaim they are a disciple of Jesus and say to the unbeliever, "Amen, brother! I do the exact same thing, as I am no different than you. And you know the amazing thing, unbelieving person? You do not have the Spirit of God living in you, and I am supposed to ... hmmm." As disciples of Jesus, we get to prove to the unbelieving world the will of God, and His will for our lives as we live out His truths and promises every day and everywhere. And if you do, how is your forgetting going today?

> And do not be conformed to this world, but be transformed by the renewing of your mind, so that you may prove what the will of God is, that which is good and acceptable and perfect.
>
> Romans 12:2

Mentioned Repeatedly, Means Something

As mentioned, I love researching God's Word to find the nuggets of truth and the application of it in my life. If God places emphasis on it, so should I. It is a great exercise to see where God continually emphasizes to make His point and get our attention. It also must be the focus of our lives, and Jesus expects we will live by it. If you are paying close attention when reading God's Word, you will see it, and when you do, go research, and it will amaze you how many times God makes a point for a particular word or action throughout His Holy Scripture.

For example, this segment is on forgiveness, so I looked at the words "forgive," "forgiveness," and "forgiven." God mentions forgive, forgiveness, or forgiven collectively over 114 times! I guess you would have to confess, it is important to God, and it must be to us as well. Those words are mentioned from Genesis 50 to 1 John 2. It must be something important, as it is also a part of the Lord's Prayer, revealed in Matthew 6. Look at the following examples of forgiveness.

First, consider how God forgives. God's forgiveness comes through his Son, Jesus Christ. It says in 1 John 1:9, "If we confess our sins,

He is faithful and righteous to forgive us our sins and to cleanse us from all unrighteousness." It is especially important not to deceive ourselves about the presence and practice of the sin of unforgiveness. Explanations will have no effect on God at all. The more we recognize sin, the more we confess and repent, and God in His infinite love, forgives us unconditionally.

Second, with God's forgiveness, we are delivered from the guilt of sin. And with this assurance we can continue in our calling as Jesus's disciple. Forgiveness is included in our testimony and confirms it is the work and power of God in our life. The act of true forgiveness could speak specifically to the unbeliever's struggle or sin.

Finally, there is the power and work of the Holy Spirit. His work confirms God's faithfulness to His promises and Word. This truly means, all sin is forgiven in Jesus Christ. We are thereby justified in Christ and become the righteousness of God in Him.

These actions are present in the life of the disciple. We know He is faithful to forgive, and we, as disciples, must imitate Him and forgive as we have been forgiven. Colossians 3:13 instructs us to ensure we are "bearing with one another, and forgiving each other, whoever has a complaint against anyone; just as the Lord forgave you, so also should you."

Jesus, on the cross dying for the sin of the world, asks the Father to forgive those who were crucifying Him (Luke 23:34)! Okay, some would say He was God and was able to have a loving heart during His persecution. However, please understand, Jesus was fully man, and can fully relate to the challenges of humanity.

If you love God with all your heart, soul, mind, and strength, fully understanding God's love for you, and the work of God the Father, God the Son, and God the Holy Spirit in your life, *then* you will lovingly forgive, just as Jesus has lovingly forgiven you. Are you living as a faithful disciple of Jesus and forgiving without any reservation or hesitation?

You must forgive others as God has forgiven you. Do you need to ask for forgiveness? Are you willing to forgive those who sinned against you, regardless of the sin committed? Do you need to ask God for forgiveness for the sins you committed against Him? Through the forgiveness you receive from God, you will be empowered to freely forgive others.

Romans 4:7 is a wonderful promise to claim. It says, "Blessed are those whose lawless deeds have been forgiven, and whose sins have been covered." I would hope and pray you are someone who sees the significance of God's promise of forgiveness. Repent for your sins, ask for forgiveness, and you will be eternally grateful you did!

A Prayer for You:

ABBA, I love You and thank You for today. This is the day the Lord has made; let us rejoice and be glad in it. ABBA, I am truly humbled by Your love and the forgiveness You have given to me. I love how Your Spirit is working in and through my life. I thank You for freeing me from the bondage and captivity of sin, bitterness, hatred, and anger. Giving me the ability to freely forgive those who have sinned against me. I ask for forgiveness this day for my evil thoughts, words, and deeds.

I pray You lead someone to this book who is struggling with forgiveness. Whether it's Your forgiveness, forgiveness for themselves, or forgiveness toward others. When they open this book and review the Table of Contents, they will see the segment on forgiveness. And once they have read it, make it known to them, You will forgive, and they can overcome their struggle and forgive themselves, seek forgiveness for their sin committed, and forgive anyone who has committed sin against them. Free them from the bondage of the sin of unforgiveness.

I pray to You God the Holy Spirit, please move in their lives, bringing conviction of their sin committed against our holy and righteous God. Lord, we know we can come to You because Your Word is truth and life, and a broken and contrite heart You will not despise. I know forgiveness is a wonderful expression of love, and it is Your love flowing through us to the lives of those we encounter.

I pray they will learn the truth of who You are, and come to You with a repentant heart, and You will make Yourself known to them, as You have done to me. I know You love them. Demonstrate Your power, give them a new heart and Your Spirit. Through Your love, make them a disciple so that they become useful vessels, preaching the good news of Jesus Christ by sharing the gospel and doing the will of the Father. I pray and ask these things in Jesus's name, AMEN!

Reflections

WORK

"Do not work for the food which perishes …" (John 6:27)
"This is the work of God, that you believe in Him whom He has sent."
(John 6:29)

HOW YOU VIEW WORK MATTERS

Man, did I have a very shallow perspective of the total significance of work as God had in mind. My view was a far cry from God's, and what He intends for work to be in the lives of His disciples. I thought it was all the things requiring physical effort, like mowing the lawn, fixing stuff, my honey-do's, and of course what I do to earn a living. But I made what I do for a living an idol in my life. My primary drive was way off center, and I missed the mark by miles!

In my career before Jesus saved me, it did not matter how much I did yesterday, there was always a demand for today. "I gotta get to work" was a common mantra out of my mouth. God made it clear, it was my perspective of work; my position and pay, giving me identity and status. Work was just as important as my personal life, and most of the time, it was more. The more effort I put in at work, the less I put into my marriage and family. Yet, the demand to do more at work continued to increase, and my role as husband and father decreased. Boy, I was deceiving myself.

This may explain why so many dads feel disjointed, disconnected and disappointed, in their family dynamic, not fully understanding they are the culprit. When Dad is not responding to God the Holy Spirit in his family, it becomes deficient of the nutrients provided by a disciple who's a husband and dad, *which is crucial for spiritual guidance, strength, and enrichment of the family.* This absence of spiritual leadership inhibits the growth of true loving intimacy, and relationships just revolve versus develop, grow, and flourish as God intended them to do!

After all, what I do for work sets the tone for the lifestyle I want to live and my indulgence in the pleasures of the world. This was a shallow outlook I had about work. I was using work to elevate myself, and I would do anything to make it to what I perceived was the top, because the top had the two P's: pay and power. And most of the time, they come as a package. If you were in my way, I did not care who you were—either push, pull, or GIT OUTTA MY WAY, and that meant anybody!

We should be incredibly careful of making success, recognition, power, and money the aim of our labor. All of it is fleeting, yet we put more effort and energy into the temporal than we do with relationships which are eternal. And you know the amazing thing? You cannot take success, recognition, power, and money with you when you die, but you do take relationships with you. Interesting perspective, isn't it? And more times than not, these are the driving forces for so many, and the reason why they go to work each day. These can easily become a type of god or idol in their lives, and will become a tremendous distraction, and impair their ability to work effectively as a disciple of Jesus, because focus on their purpose has begun to change right before their eyes.

There is one common denominator relating to accomplishments, recognition, power, and money: it's *you*. This is not to say work performed biblically and the achievement from such work is wrong. What I am saying is that when accomplishments, recognition, power, and money become more to you than God Himself, and the work God intended for you to carry out where He placed you, then expect temptation to enter. Soon the desire to get *more* recognition, success, power, and money, begins to grow into an idol. When this happens sin slowly begins to slither into your life, and before you realize it, you have begun to move away from God because of this distortion caused by evil cravings. The amazing thing, it appears to be good, right?

It would be normal to think an idol is an object, and it is, depending on what we are talking about. In the Old Testament, it was a golden calf, an object. But what was really happening was that their hearts had moved away from God. Therefore, they needed an image to take the place of Him, since they chose to move. Today, it could be your car or home that is an object and could become an idol. But what I am referencing is status, success, money, and comfort. These become an obsessive pursuit and the aim of your work efforts. Your eyes have been moved from God onto self, shifting God from the center or rock in your life onto yourself.

Idols vary in form, and they could be what we call "good" things," like hobbies, recreation, and entertainment. We can see them as good things, and they are in and of themselves. But the more we pursue them they begin to consume, taking us away from those given to us and our relationship with God. Then it becomes an idol. Be mindful of addictions as well, like drugs, alcohol, pornography, and gambling. This also includes career, stuff, and relationships of all kinds. It does not matter—anything taking the place of God in your heart is an idol. These false gods cause us to submit ourselves to it, as we bow down to them. We begin to distance ourselves from the very source, God, the holder of every good thing we could ever acquire.

Do you want to know why? When success, recognition, power, and money define one's identity, idolatry is now ruling, as it consumes your heart. On the other hand, Jesus's disciples find their identity in Him. How many times have you heard someone introduce themselves by stating their position right after their name? For example, "Hello, I am so and so, and I'm owner, chairman, CEO, president, VP, director, manager, and pastor ... I have my BA, BS, MBA, PhD, JD, and I graduated from— blah, blah, blah. In other words, know who I am, see my title, power, and income. The saddest is when their title precedes their own name. That should scream volumes about what defines them, and how they find their identity in their position. Their position is the idol.

What you possess and get to do, and how others view you, should not be your motivation to work. If anyone peers below the surface, they will see selfishness, greed, and pride consuming the heart, *and the idol is you*. It will surely convey to others what you truly treasure. Jesus says, "where your treasure is, there your heart will be also" (Luke 12:34). If these areas are your primary focus of work, then when your success, accomplishments, recognition, power, and money vanish—and at some point, they will—all of your worth placed in them will be lost, and it will shake you to the core of your existence. And then the question will become: "What's next?" On the other hand, if that day comes far quicker than you think or expect, what will you do when Jesus reveals that your heart was consumed with self and full of idolatry, because your true heart's desire was for the large home, expensive cars, and your place at the lake. You were really trying to impress your family, friends, neighbors, and coworkers with your financial success instead of using the blessing of income to bless the unfortunate in your midst. No, it was consumed by me, myself, and I, Lord, and I stand before you, convicted of my sin of selfishness and greed. I saw what I had as "mine" because it was the sweat of my brow, and never considered You were the provider of it all. Nor did I ever consider the blessings and joy I could have received from You.

If one's motivation is to be esteemed by man, and one lives for the applause, *one has missed the mark by miles.* We must know whose we are; then the driving force becomes carrying out our work in our mission as a disciple, and the "applause" goes to God not man. Working unto God confirms you are serving and living faithfully to Him and His commands. When we are faithful workers to God, our labor is never in vain, none of it! Colossians 3:24 says, "knowing that from the Lord you will receive the reward of the inheritance. It is the Lord Christ whom you serve." This is the heart and mindset of a disciple of Jesus, to be a servant leader, and put others before oneself.

As Jesus's disciple the quality of my work produced from my efforts should be at or above the employer's expectations always, and not just during the evaluation period of my performance. The manner and method by which I work, and my interactions with everyone, confirms my testimony. Then when the gospel proceeds from my mouth to their eyes and ears, they are able to witness the authenticity of my walk, talk, and the totality of discipleship which *is* my life. And at the right time, when God the Holy Spirit is working and preparing hearts for the receipt of the gospel, there will be no surprises or hypocrisy when the conversation turns to their spirituality and mine.

What I learned in my *new life* as a disciple of Jesus is that work is intricately involved in all aspects of my life, and not just the job I go to every day. God requires us to work in discipling, parenting, marriage, and relationships of all kind, which includes family, friends, co-workers, and those we do not know intimately. Work is a calling from God, and if God is working, we must work also, as we imitate Him. As I looked around in my career over the past thirty years, I saw a lot of people who proclaimed to be Jesus's disciples and an imitation of Him in the workplace. However, when it came to work, and their work was supposed to be projecting God's image, attributes, and characteristics, they gave the impression to the unbelieving world that God must not be working up to His potential, because their work product was well below the standard of the employer and, of course God.

What God has in mind is for us to be like Jesus and work like Him. Our journey to eternal life goes through the people and places everywhere the Spirit of God leads us. We are called to do kingdom work, as there are so many who are living in spiritual blindness, roaming around aimlessly, who need the light of Jesus to be rescued from the domain of darkness, just like me. God desires for us to work by preaching and living out the gospel daily. Jesus lived out the gospel in His life on earth daily, and I would expect, He expects the same from His disciples. Each disciple has different work to carry out on their journey along the narrow way. Why would it be necessary for a true disciple of Jesus to be motivated to love others as God loves them? Do you not realize that in loving others, your work as a disciple continues to grow and thrive? If Jesus looks at the harvest field where you have been assigned, what does He see, and what does it reveal about you and your work ethic related to your calling to be and make disciples?

How we work as a disciple of Jesus must be the *fulcrum* in our lives, as we live faithfully by doing (work) the will of the Father every time, every day, and everywhere! I do not know about you, but even the earthly owner of the vineyard will only tolerate excuses for the lack of work for so long. If your employer expects you to work, I expect, Jesus is no different. Where do you think the owner of the vineyard got it from? Him! Jesus was clear in His instruction about what should drive our desire to work. John 6:27 says, in its entirety, "Do not work for the food which perishes, but for the food which endures to eternal life, which the Son of Man will give to you, for on Him the Father, God, has set His seal." As a disciple of Jesus; our perspective must be an honest day's work for an honest day's pay. But just the pay must not be our primary motivation, nor should it be the accumulation of the things the world says we must have to confirm our success meets its standard.

We work according to His Word, as it says in Colossians 3:23: "Whatever you do, do your work heartily, as for the Lord rather than for men," Jesus's disciples work in obedience to His Word and example. As we work faithfully unto the Lord, man reaps the benefit of our labor when our work effort is devoted entirely unto God. Yes, we must complete our tasks and responsibilities as good stewards of where the Lord has placed us; however, we also must be ever mindful of our calling for kingdom work.

Our life is to consist of more than just waiting for the Lord to call, and then our life on this earth is over and we spend eternity with Him. We are *called* to carry out His work as His disciples every day we get to open our eyes here on this planet!

We must ask the Lord each day, expecting He will be faithful to bring a life into your path or yours into theirs, as we must be always ready to be a useful vessel for Him. How many times have you asked Him? If you have not, when will you begin? Be expectant He will respond, because *the harvest is overflowing, but the laborers are few.*

God the Holy Spirit equips the disciple to share the *Good News* of Jesus Christ where they spend more time than they do at home or anywhere else; work! The latter part of John 6:27 says, "but for the food which endures to eternal life." Jesus has the only food capable of supplying life, instruction, knowledge, wisdom, and understanding, as He is "the bread of life" (John 6:35). Does your day consist of any purposeful spiritual conversations, or, do you just head in, do your job, and head home, counting your money all the way?

If you would only realize it's God who placed you where you are. Without His will, you would not be, so do not go pulling too hard on those suspenders, thinking it's you. It's not you; it's God. And this applies from the lowliest worker to the king or president. Here is the proof since we see the role of king or president as the most powerful position in government. Romans 13:1 states, "Every person is to be in subjection to the governing authorities. For there is no authority except from God, and those which exist are established by God." So *everyone* who is in authority, believe me, *is placed there by God!*

The Creator Worked

Work has been going on even before the creation of this world. Many are deceived to believe the creation of earth and everything above it, which stretches far beyond where we can even aspire to reach, happened by chance or some other man-made hypothesis. But the truth, God created it. One day by the grace of God, you will come to a full understanding of creation. This was like so many others who have stood in your exact place in unbelief. Then when they stood before God, it was too late to change, for their fate was sealed in unbelief. While others who believe and are Jesus's disciples marvel at the wonders and works of God in all creation, and in themselves! Just watch one of the telecasts on nature, and marvel at God's work that goes unnoticed by the masses.

God did actually work Himself. And since God works, and has been working since creation, including this day as you are reading this, everyone who proclaims they love and follow Him must also follow His example *to work*. Genesis 2:2 confirms the truth of God's work. It says, "By the seventh day God completed His work which He had done, and He rested on the seventh day from all His work which He had done." Jesus, "the image of the invisible God," as it says in Colossians 1:15, worked as well. When you read the Gospels—Matthew, Mark, Luke, and John—you will be like so many of Jesus's disciples, living in awe and wonder of the work Jesus performed in the lives of His disciples and all the others. I pray you will ask God in humility to have Jesus do His mighty work in you. And if He has not yet, then ask Him!

Jesus is very specific about His claim for work. Read "The Healing at Bethesda" (John 5:1–17). Jesus says in verse 17, "My Father is working until now, and I Myself am working." So, without question, Jesus *is* working.

It would only be prudent on my behalf to mention the Holy Spirit's work. You read the segment on Him. It should explain the work He has done throughout time and in humanity. In relation to this point, John 16:13 says, "But when He, the Spirit of truth, comes, He will guide you into all the truth." If the Spirit's guiding, then He is working. Would you agree with me that the Spirit needs to do a lot of guiding? Amen? Then we all *need* His work to be done in us!

Thus, a lot of work is going on by them! And based on God's Word, there is only one way to work for God, and that is like Jesus. This becomes the way of life as a "worker" for Jesus.

When you consider the work product they created, there surely is something to be said for what they did. *They made the dead come to life.* I do not know about you, but God's work is matchless to any work performed by anybody. New life is one of the most phenomenal works performed by God. If you are one who has been born of the Spirit, you know in your heart, mind, and soul, it is! And if not, know that it will be the most incredible phenomenon to happen in you on this earth and in your life, ever! When you are standing before Him, you will then know why, and how extremely wonderful it really is, and it will be that way forever! You will be like the myriads of so many of us, declaring over and over a hundred million times, THANK YOU, JESUS, for Your mighty work in me!

Then Work Was Passed On

The first person to complete the work example of the Trinity was Adam. Genesis 2:15 tells us, "Then the Lord God took the man and put him into the Garden of Eden to cultivate and keep it." Adam was commanded to cultivate (plant, plow, tend, and harvest,); in other words ... work! It was astounding to think God had every plant and tree sprout from just His Word, but it is work, working in unison with Him for it to continue to produce and flourish. And Adam was the man for the job.

I imagine Adam loved to work. He enjoyed the beautiful trees, flowers, and growing plants of every kind—some for beauty, others for food, but all serving God's purpose. When Adam worked the perfect soil, it would not have taken a tremendous amount of effort to prepare, for the seed generated from the first vegetation. What God provided in creation was perfect. I bet he only had to use his hand to make a row, as no John Deere equipment was available or needed.

The soil was rich and did not have one weed. There was work needed to prune, harvest, and plant so it could produce more crops, and he worked to produce food for their nutrition and nourishment, as God created trees, vegetation and plants yielding seed. Genesis 1:11–12 says, "Then God said, 'Let the earth sprout vegetation, plants yielding seed, *and* fruit trees on the earth bearing fruit after their kind with seed in them'; and it was so. The earth brought forth vegetation, plants yielding seed after their kind, and trees bearing fruit with seed in them, after their kind; and God saw that it was good."

As God instructed Adam to cultivate, so it is with His disciples. The work in Adam has been passed on to us, as God instructs us to cultivate and keep the soil (hearts) where we work, as we respond in obedience and faithfulness to His command to make disciples. It is a *narrow* perspective to think disciples are only made in church. Disciple making encompasses everywhere we go. Did you ever wonder why God *planted* you in the place where you work? He planted you there to grow and blossom in the work He has planned for you to do as His disciple. Have you ever asked God to assign you someone to disciple at work?

We do not know whom or when God will choose to open their ears and heart to receive His gospel. It is by these acts of obedience that the disciple lives out their calling. Paul explains Timothy's calling in 2 Timothy 1:9; "who has saved us and called us with a holy calling, not according to our works, but according to His own purpose and grace granted to us in Christ Jesus from all eternity."

Our work as a disciple reflects the work of God in our lives and we proclaim the *Good News*. Our gratitude for His saving grace is on display for those all around us in the workplace to see and experience. The way we live is in full anticipation of every opportunity to *sow the seed*. We sow the Word of God to co-workers as we live out God's truths in our lives.

It is been said a picture is worth a thousand words. How many words are being spoken about the picture of your workmanship as a disciple in your workplace? What is being seen by how you conduct yourself when facing challenges, conflict, and problems? What you say and how you act speaks volumes about you to those seeing, both unbelievers and disciples alike. I hope and pray it is millions! You can be certain that if it's not, there are thousands of words being spoken about how your life contradicts what you are professing. And the word "hypocrite" is floating around the atmosphere.

Our work life must be consistent with the truth of God's Word. What future disciples should see, is the mind, eyes, ears, hands, and feet of Jesus where they work. And then when they, like so many others in Jesus's day on earth, come to Him, they will come to you asking, "You have a minute to talk?" If co-workers are not seeing Christlikeness in you, that may explain why they don't approach you, because you look, talk, and handle work just like they do.

Life Sprouts Everywhere

It is easy to just go to the supermarket for our fruits and veggies, and most of us who have been born and raised in the city may not fully appreciate the wonder of vegetation growth. Anyone who has lived in a rural area and grow their own crops for their primary source of food can tell you, *it is an amazing work to see*. The city person goes to the supermarket to buy the produce picked and cleaned, and the only labor is to pick it up from the shelf and place it in the cart. Some never see or experience the growth cycle of vegetation from seed to harvest.

I had a wonderful opportunity to attend college in the Midwest. It was an agricultural area and the college had corn fields on multiple sides that went on for miles. Some fields I could see right out of my dorm window. It was strange at first to move from the city where there were trees, although they were sparse, to where there were corn fields everywhere you went.

I was able to see the growth cycle of corn. It was incredible to see the small rows of tiny corn plants break through the soil. It seemed like in only a few days the black dirt went to tiny indications of green, as they began to form the rows. I was amazed how straight the rows were, and the millions of plants, especially later in the year when it was time for harvest.

I saw large plants with ears of corn, row after row, and field after field. One day I was traveling in an eastwardly direction, and the sun was just above the horizon, when I saw a combine offloading corn into a transport wagon alongside the roadway. The sun was beaming on the corn, giving it the appearance of gold. I then began to understand the significance of the harvest and how anxiety could overwhelm a farmer whenever there was mention of inclement weather. Hail and excessive rain could destroy the crop, and potentially mean no yield.

When inclement weather happens, and destroys the crop, all the toil from last winter, the plowing of the ground in spring and getting it ready for seed, is lost. The idea of putting forth so much labor, for so many hours, and investing so much money, only to have one bad storm hit leaving you with

"and he goes to bed at night and gets up by day, and the seed sprouts and grows—how, he himself does not know."

Mark 4:27

nothing to show or take to market was an overwhelming thought. There must be a tremendous amount of faith in the field of farming since there are so many things beyond the farmer's control. And you know, that's biblical. Mark 4:26-29, tells of the parable of the seed. Verse 27 points to the *wonder, power, and work of God.* That wonder, power, and work was present in the garden, and is still actively working today. The farmer does not know how the seed grows. Likewise, when the disciple sows the seed, the Word of God, only God knows how the seed implants, takes root, and begins to grow.

It was only when I was able to have a garden of my own that I truly was able to appreciate and marvel at what can be produced from a single seed, all a blessing from God! From the initial garden and even to today, as the Word of God says, we see seed after their kind: peppers from pepper seed, cucumber from cucumber seed. So it makes perfect sense that we get man from man's seed, and monkey from monkey's seed. *If you believe anything other than this biblical truth, "seed, each according to its kind," know that, you are being deceived.*

A Lasagna Garden

We have a small area in our backyard where we built a lasagna garden. I would suggest you investigate it, build a small one, plant some seed, and watch the works of God! The plant growth from nothingness will remind you of what happened in creation.

Lasagna garden

A lasagna garden is designed to be all above ground. It has four sides of wood and layers of dirt, hay, leaves, and manure, one layer on top of the other and tilled together. Prepare the box and soil and sow the seed and water it. The same holds true to the heart of the new convert. God the Holy Spirit prepares the heart for the implanting of God's Word, the Word is sown and takes root, and then they grow!

That's biblical: one plants, then another waters, and God causes the growth. First Corinthians 3:7 supports this work of God: "So then neither the one who plants nor the one who waters is anything, but God who causes the growth." But it does take both planting and watering for the plant to grow. The same holds true for new disciples. Disciples teach as disciples of Jesus. This parallels watering the soil. The sower shows up in one place along the journey of life. The disciple who waters comes at a later time, and both assist in the growth of the disciple.

Water plays a significant role in the growth of vegetation. It helps transport the nutrients through the plant, and without proper water, there is no fruit. Water helps the new disciple to move along in spiritual knowledge and growth. Both the sower and the one who waters work unto Jesus. They are both working in unison, as the Spirit works in unison with the Father and the Son. Everyone has the same interest in the growth of new disciples. The waterer and the sower are different processes, and so are His disciples. Knowing each other is not important, but the growth in the disciple *is* most important.

You know something else amazing? This year we had a few plants spring up from a seed we did not plant! In the gardening world, this would be a volunteer plant. Imagine that! A seed planted last year in a different place grew without any effort on my own part. I cannot tell you how, except that God is AMAZING! As a disciple of Jesus, I could either be the sower or the one who waters. In either task, I am called to complete my work, and God will cause the growth! AMAZING!

Sowers of the "Seed"

There are several Bible passages in which Jesus references the sower, seed, and soil. They explain the different responses to the gospel. All three applied to our garden, sower, seed and soil. Jesus mentions all three in Luke 8:4–15, where He tells the parable of the sower. In Luke 8:11, Jesus confirms *"the seed is the word of God."* (*emphasis* added) As disciples of Jesus, we must be sowers of the Word of God. In Matthew 13:18–23, Jesus describes the different types of soil receiving His Word. He also addresses the outcome for each.

This is an interesting concept about the soils, sower, seed, and the relationship to discipleship. The disciple is the sower, the seed is the Word of God, and the soil is the unbelieving heart receiving the Word. Meditate on this. The sower (disciple) sows to all four soils. The four soils consisted of: beside the road, on rocky ground, in the thorns, and in the good soil. Our mission is to sow everywhere. We are to be faithful to Jesus, to sow wherever we work. You will notice that in the parable, no soil is left unsown. So, regardless of the person's demeanor or attitude, we are to sow! Based on Jesus's plan for sowing, His disciples sow the Word of God in the world, everywhere, and there will be no heart left unsown.

All four soils are people in the world who hear God's Word preached (Mark 4:13–20). All soils receive the seed sown. As with gardening, there is always hope the soil is good for the seed to take root, grow into a plant, and produce a yield. It is fascinating to see seed growing in some of the most surprising places. Have you ever seen a tree or vegetation growing out of the side of a mountain? One would expect it not to grow there, but with God all things are possible. This would be the same as God's Word planted in the heart of a person who by the world's standards is a lost cause. BUT GOD implants His Word, and growth occurs! The growth of the plant is only a part of it. It truly depends upon the condition of the soil, and the amount of sun and water, all working together to complete a successful growing process. That's also biblical!

You may get a plant to grow, but the plant or tree may not produce the desired vegetable or fruit, hence no future seed and no ability to replant. The consequence is no replication, which is also biblical. Look at what happens to 3/4 of the soils mentioned in Mark 4. Only 1/4 of the soils are good. Think of it this way: based on what Jesus was saying, the soils are the people in the world, and only 1/4 is good soil which "bears and brings forth yield." The responsibility of sowing, which Jesus gives to His disciples, must be taken very seriously, as even the production of fruit and bringing forth varies. Jesus said, "some a hundredfold, some sixty, and some thirty." So only a 1/4 produce, and they do not all produce the same, but there is production, and although it varies, they *all produce a yield for God*. What is Jesus yielding from the seed you are sowing?

Judicious Pruning

When I sent the first manuscript, the editor required me to complete the process of judicious pruning. I said, "Okay, that's biblical!" So I must be about my pruning work, and my work must be thoughtful, using good judgment, based on the content and context by which I am attempting to communicate what God has done in my life to you. Neither I nor God would just carelessly start hacking away without careful consideration of the fruit. Pruning does have a practical and divine purpose. It is designed to remove what inhibits growth. God prunes away sin, and I prune what detracts from the message. I am watching Him as He prunes, and He is watching as I do. We are both pruning with the utmost care.

What do you do if a plant does not produce vegetables, nor a tree bear fruit? Since we are comparing it to scripture, what does Jesus say about the lack of yield? Read John 15:2, which states, "Every branch in Me that does not bear fruit, He takes away; and every *branch* that bears fruit, He prunes it so that it may bear more fruit." You might ask, why? Jesus is referencing the significant difference between true disciples and their work, and those simply professing to be disciples. In the lives of those who are simply professing, there is no evidence of work for Him by living out His command to "Go and make disciples." So He prunes.

It is wonderful to know that God will lovingly tend to the branches, to ensure they produce yield. God desires spiritual growth in His disciples so that they can produce even more fruit. He prunes away the sin in our lives that prevents usefulness to Him. Matthew 13 explains why the Word of God is not received. The amazing thing is the same holds true for the physical garden as well. Is the garden overgrown and requiring pruning? It would be foolish to wait until the harvest if during the growing season there's no sign of crop growth, especially if the garden were the only source for your food.

In order to recognize changes in the garden, the gardener must continually and carefully examine the vegetation. This ensures that he will take any action needed for the plants pertaining to water, fertilizer, or insects wreaking havoc. All can affect the growth and production of the garden and must be acted upon immediately. I prune away the words that detract from the message, regardless of whether I thought they were good or not. If they are taking away from the message, then prune I must. In my due diligence to prune my work, my pruning shears started out the size of a first grader's scissors. Now they are as large as hedge trimmers. When pruning, you must cut deep into the plant to ensure the other branches get the nutrients to grow. This will ensure a bountiful crop.

Working as a faithful disciple is the same. When discipling another, there should be evidence of a continuous and growing intimate relationship. They are attentive to edify, reprove, teach, rebuke, pray, or any other action needed to ensure spiritual growth is continuous in their work. They are also pruning, when they recognize sin is preventing the spiritual growth that could be occurring had it not started to gnaw away at the fruit which was beginning to develop.

The disciple, as the gardener, looks for the first indicator of yield—blooms. The gardener must know their plants and trees, as the disciple should know those they are discipling. When plants produce blooms, this is a sure sign the root is taking hold and receiving nourishment from the soil.

Discipleship is no different: we know those we are discipling. We grow in understanding of them through an intimate relationship. You begin to see the implanted seed taking root (love) and they begin to show signs of spiritual growth (fruit – obedience). You begin to recognize the same Christlike characteristics of prayer, reading, studying, memorizing, and obedience to live out God's Word. There is confidence in sharing the gospel, encouraging others, dying to self, and forgiveness. Love is intrinsic, and creates a heart of joy in both when the evidence of God the Holy Spirit's work comes alive in them!

However, we must be very vigilant of blooms as the only indicator of growth and production. In our garden, we had two huge tomato plants with blooms everywhere. With the numerous blooms, we expected loads of tomatoes. Unfortunately, little fruit was produced. Makes one ask if the soil, plant, amount of sun, water, lack of pollination or all the above were to blame.

The same could be said about discipleship. You see quiet-time, devotionals, reading, prayer, and the like, which are parallel to the blooms in the garden. This must be why Jesus explains the soils in Mark 4:13–19. There is immediate receipt of the seed, and they respond. There are indicators (blooms), but only temporary. When difficulty, hardship, the worries of the world, or the deceitfulness of riches come into their life, they immediately fall away with no yield. The blooms also were temporary on the tomato plant. Initially, the appearance provided excitement and hope, only to turn to discouragement later when there were only a few tomatoes, yet hundreds of blooms. We must continue to work, by being actively involved in the lives of those we are discipling, when Jesus puts them into our care as the Gardener.

God is attentive and gives special attention to those disciples who are not producing the expected yield. He prunes away the sin and behavior prohibiting spiritual growth. The disciple is to grow in understanding of His Word and His will for their lives as they grow into useful laborers for Him in humanity. The same applies to the disciples making disciples.

They are to serve as a mentor as the new disciple begins to live out and speak of Jesus Christ and His truths. Their testimony of how God has changed their life is important. They walk with the new disciple as they begin their journey as another of Jesus's disciples. They teach the new disciple as they become more equipped. They grow in the knowledge of God and complete the work Jesus commands of His disciples.

They speak the truth in love, as they imitate Jesus by the power of the Holy Spirit. They identify and communicate to the discipled, just as God in His workmanship prunes all as the Master Gardener.

Replication Is a Command

When I was looking at the bell pepper when it was ripe for harvest, I cut one open to see the amount of seed it produced for replanting. I was in awe of the wonder of God! Although the seed amount is limited, and the amazing thing is that not all the peppers had the same number of seeds. Sound familiar, some a hundred, some sixty and thirty? Yet, a yield nonetheless! I am in awe of how the pepper by producing seed, is

Peppers from pepper seed

obeying the command of Jesus by *still* making peppers. When Jesus says, "plants yielding seed according to their kinds," nature, without fail, follows the command of His voice. And if we love Him, we will respond the same as nature and without fail, *follow the commands of His voice.*

Take some time and observe a picture of an orchid seed pod. It is INCREDIBLE the amount of seed it produces! It's said this plant contains the most seed of any plant created by God. So in creation, God only needed to make one! Adam had a lot of work to do, when He opened the seed pod of the orchid. I imagine he said, like we do with plants, "Place some by the tree. They will look beautiful there." There must have been orchids everywhere!

Can you imagine when all disciples are working faithfully to accomplish Jesus's command to "go and make disciples"? I would expect it would be the same as the orchid seed pod: millions. There must be a need, or Jesus would not have told us, "The harvest is plentiful, but the workers are few." Agreed? I anticipate Jesus expects His disciples to be as faithful to make disciples, as the orchid is faithful to make seed.

I continue to be delighted at the production of our little garden with so few plants and the limited space. Again, it's biblical. The Word of God spreads wherever it is planted in good soil (Mark 4:20). The sown seed goes into the soil, grows, and produces a yield. This is applicable today, as the seed (Word of God) is sown (sower) into a person's heart (soil), the Word is received and takes root, and produces a yield (disciple). Read the entire passage on the sower in Mark 4:1–20. It's God giving life to plants, and in doing so, they replicate. Humanity is identical, God gives life and replication occurs—the giving of life to another by the *work* of His disciples.

Eternally Grateful

Consider this: there was a man standing before Jesus at judgment. He was a bit anxious as he stood there and Jesus opened the books before Him. His mind was racing. The contents confirmed his thoughts, words, and deeds. He knew his life was far from perfection, and he knew God in His mercy had saved him on a clear October day. His trust was in the promises of God. God's faithfulness was evident, and his mind went to the many opportunities he'd missed. It was all during his journey as Jesus's disciple. The longer Jesus read, the longer the man held his breath.

At a moment's notice, Jesus told him to turn around, so He could see what he deserved. As the man turned around, he saw a great chasm separating heaven from hell. After peering at the chasm for several moments, he lifted his eyes and saw hell. Immediately, the reality of all God's truths came rushing into his mind. There was no longer speculation. It was real, with his eyes fixed upon hell. The sight and sounds of it horrified him to the core of his existence. His body frozen and rigid as a board, and his mouth and eyes gaped wide open in shock. Not only did he see the horror of hell, but he also saw those he knew. Standing on the edge of the chasm in hell, their eyes met. It was the most devastating thing he had ever seen in his entire life.

In a breathless and speechless state, he was powerless to do anything. He knew those in hell would be experiencing the wrath of God forever. What a horrific sight to see if you were this person. How do you think you would react? In the man's mind were the words of Jesus, saying, "This is what you deserved, and not deserve." Instantly, Jesus turned him around toward Himself. Jesus, with love in His eyes and a smile on His face, told him He would show him where he would spend eternity. The man wiped the tears from His eyes, and when he did, he saw heaven and the glory of God! He knew in his heart this meant spending eternal life with God! He would be in the presence of His Lord and Savior Jesus Christ, forever!

The man immediately collapsed to his knees and grabbed hold of Jesus's legs. As he cried, gratitude flowed out of His soul for Jesus's saving grace. He repeated continuously, "THANK YOU, JESUS! THANK YOU, JESUS!" Jesus helped him to his feet and explained what was next. Immediately, they stood before the Father. The man saw cup after cup full of joy. These were cups of joy God the Father would have poured into this man's soul, had he been as grateful on earth as he was at Jesus's feet! I pray you understand the joy God pours into your life when you are one of His disciples. I pray you live out discipleship with love, gratitude, and devotion to Jesus.

The disciple's life must possess a tremendous amount of gratitude for what God has, is, and will be doing (work) in your life! You should know whose you are and what He has made of you. This should create an eternal gratitude in the heart of the person chosen by God and who has been saved by His grace! Most are not fully aware of what they are saved from and saved to, and *the full magnitude of what it really means to be saved.* Possessing a shallow perspective of salvation lessens one's effectiveness for the work one should be accomplishing as Jesus's disciple. The disciple who understands the faithfulness of God's truth and promises would respond daily with a heart full of gratitude, love, and adoration, and would see more work being performed in their lives by the Holy Spirit.

The Harvest Is Plenty

This past season we were blessed to have a crop of jalapeno, poblano, bell peppers, cucumber, lettuce, broccoli, tomatoes (a few), and cabbage. Some to keep and more to share. It was amazing to see the yield from a few plants. The same could be said for making disciples. One must look to the seasons of a disciple as well. This also confirms if a disciple is as faithful as the vegetation is faithful to the commands of God. The Lord planted His Word in the hearts of the initial disciples, and by their faithful work, discipleship continues to produce a harvest. As a result of their work, by the power of the Holy Spirit and preaching the gospel, look at the harvest throughout history and today! Through the faithfulness of the initial converts, who became disciples, you know the saying, "even as we speak ..." I would say that even as these words are being written, disciples are being made by disciples and are faithfully living out Jesus's command. PRAISE GOD! If it was not for Jesus's saving power, and the disciples He placed in my life sowing and watering, there would not be a disciple authoring this book today. *BUT GOD* caused the growth is all I can say!

Believe me, my heart is full of gratitude because I was walking as a dead man in darkness. In God's love, mercy and grace, He placed several men in my life to disciple me. Based on their work, this disciple is producing fruit and making disciples. I am eternally grateful and will continue in His Word, being obedient to the promptings of God the Holy Spirit walking with those disciples who are walking alongside of me! Who is walking alongside of you? Are you walking alongside someone, or just moseying along by yourself along the path of life?

Jesus references Himself in John 12:24 when He describes a grain of wheat dying and producing yield. Without His death, we never learn to live. It was necessary for Him to give His life so there would be a yield, eternal life for all disciples following Him. Because of Him, we love and are obedient to His Word and commands. He demands His disciples to die to self, crucify one's own sinful desires, to produce a yield, other disciples, coming because of their faithful work to God.

The Time Is Now, SOW!

Discipleship is like planting; it's hard and demanding work. Life as a disciple requires sacrifice. Depending on where Jesus places them, their life could be a life full of famine and persecution, compared to a life of comfort and entitlement as life is for most in the United States.

You are interacting with human beings who are or may be dealing with the same or similar circumstances, events, etc. in their lives as you. It could be those same distractions you are struggling with. Is it possible the work of the enemy is deceiving you which is inhibiting you from doing the Lord Jesus's work, or you yourself, the flesh, could also be restricting you as well? Do you allow those distractions to inhibit you? You could be leaving or missing those plants needing tilling, watering, pruning, and nurturing. *Are you being obedient and attentive to your calling?*

The thing about gardening is that you just do not plant the seed and walk away, and then presto, yield! You must tend to the garden. It's the same with making disciples. You don't just preach the gospel walk away, and presto, a disciple is now making disciples. It takes work! For Jesus, it was a three-year period of work with the initial converts.

The present-day United States does not compare to the early days of discipleship. The initial disciples and Paul faced hostility, beatings and imprisonment, just like some parts of the world today. All of the initial disciples and Paul were martyred, except John.

Can you imagine total isolation from everybody? I hope you are beginning to see how so many conveniences can hinder or distract a person when a disciple is desiring to share the *Good News.*

Could you be missing out on the blessings of God by not completing your work as His disciple? By blessings I mean strength in times of weakness, wisdom in times of ignorance, courage in times of fear, faith in times of doubt, prayer in times of need, rest in times of weariness, peace in times of conflict, love in times of bitterness, and self-control in times of unrestraint. How many people do you think would be able to accomplish this task, never mind survive? So goes it with the disciple. How many people could hear the gospel if all disciples were about preaching it? Would it be like the orchid?

Throughout your reading thus far, can you see how the gardening analogy fits and applies to the life of the disciple? Discipleship is a journey, not an event. A journey has a beginning, midpoint, and end. Each phase has depth and width. The beginning is when the gospel is preached, the midpoint is the relationship building and training, and the end is designed for those being discipled to "GO" and make disciples as they grow. The one discipling should see growth in the discipled, and the yield ought to be evident, just like it is for the gardener. This discipling often creates eternal relationships.

In our life while on earth, we experience distinct types of relationships. There are those we encounter who are just acquaintances, passing through our lives for a brief period. Even with acquaintances, we must be ready to live out 1 Peter 3:15 as disciples. There are others whose relationship continues to grow year after year, leading to eternity. You find these types of relationships in making disciples. Have you ever experienced an acquaintance who became a friend, which grew into a relationship? What do you think is the mechanism for this kind of growth? One would have to think God ordained it. He did, and Psalm 139:16 proves it.

Welcome to the Fishbowl

Could it be possible to make disciples without even trying? Let me explain. Have you ever considered people who may not have been approached directly by you and could be observing you? They could be in proximity or could even be at a distance. Yes, they are watching everything you do, your words, and deeds. Consider some of the places you frequent: restaurants near your job or home, workout facility, supermarket, movies, shopping mall, or traveling, would anyone know you are a disciple of Jesus Christ, or would they think you are just another person along the way?

Would they be surprised if they found out? How would you feel and answer, if someone asked you is there a difference between a Christian and a disciple? Is there a difference? I would say in today's culture, there is one. There are many *proclaiming* to be a Christian. And when Jesus demands all, as discipleship *is* costly, many return from whence they came. Just like the ones mentioned in John 6. This is where apostasy occurs and brings a surprise to *many*, as they were convinced, they would surely be a disciple. Know, if you are paying close attention to one's testimony, there are but a *few* saying they are a *disciple* of Jesus. I guess the appropriate question here is: "What would someone see if they were watching you?" Would your actions and interactions with others indicate something different about your character, or would you resemble everyone else around you?

Do you walk with a purpose as a disciple of Jesus, or are you just getting something to eat, working out to stay healthy, picking up some groceries, catching the latest flick, picking up a gift or something to wear? Do they see Jesus working and walking in their midst, as He was working and walking along the roads to Cana, Samaria, Capernaum, Bethsaida, Emmaus, and Jerusalem?

How would you feel if you knew what Jesus thought and felt about your words and work as His disciple? Would He be pleased by what He heard and saw? Remember what Jesus says in Revelation 22:12: "Behold, I am coming quickly, and My reward *is* with Me, to render to every man according to what he has done [work]."

Please understand, this is not about justifying salvation by working! Read James 2:14–18 regarding faith and works, primarily verses 17 and 18:

> Even so faith, if it has no works, is dead, *being* by itself.

> But someone may *well* say, "You have faith and I have works; show me your faith without the works, and I will show you my faith by my works."

In other words, I can see what a disciple is by how they work. If they know who Jesus is, would they say your work resembles His, and you must have been with Jesus? But if they do not know Jesus and what He's done, and there is no evidence of Him present in your life, they may believe that the gospel is just a story. The Bible says He lives in you, yet they see no evidence of it, so it must be fiction versus fact, right?

What wonderful words to hear from another about you? I heard these lyrics in a song: "they think about my Lord when they mention me." This is how a disciple should live. Read Acts 4:13. Could they say *that* about you? Could they say—after they have read the gospels, and find out all the wonderful characteristics of God—that your life exhibits His walk, talk, love, forgiveness, mercy, grace, compassion, faithfulness to the Father, responsiveness to the Spirit, and determining to live by every Word proceeding out of the mouth of God?

When salvation comes into our life, you become children of the only true God in the Bible. Therefore, we obtain aspects of His character, and the more the disciple grows, they become more like Him. Even though the disciple does not yet fully mirror Jesus, they do possess qualities and attributes of His divine nature—the physical and spiritual form that separates His disciples from the world.

Take 'Em to Jesus

Discipleship is truly diverse work and encompasses so much effort and action. Look at Jesus. The morning He was out walking, and John the Baptist saw Him, He was en route to "choosing" His disciples. Read "Jesus' Public Ministry, First Converts" (John 1:35–50) and notice what happened. First, the disciple follows Jesus. Next, the disciple stays with Jesus. Then the disciple goes, which immediately sets into action "the Great Commission" BEFORE Jesus ever formally gives the command written in Matthew 28:19. As you can see, the power of God the Holy Spirit was at work; even the Spirit is WORKING!

The primary work of discipleship is to "just bring them to Jesus." I believe this would change the perspective and boost confidence in sharing the gospel, knowing it is Jesus who ensures salvation. The work of the disciple is to preach the gospel to the unbelieving. No, my friend, just do what Andrew did; *he went to get his brother and brought him to Jesus*! And the amazing thing? Andrew had only been with Jesus a short time, so a great wealth of knowledge and training are not needed before one is able to "bring someone to Jesus."

They had Jesus and the Holy Spirit. There must be something said about God the Holy Spirit and the work He completes in and through God's disciples. I believe there is more, much more, the disciple could accomplish if they depended more on God the Holy Spirit versus all the man-made tools! Besides, what tools did the initial disciples have? Jesus told them not to take anything! My friend, there is something to be said about full reliance on the Spirit of God! How the disciples share their heart and the testimony of God's saving power would have a greater influence on the heart of the hearer as *God opens their heart to receive the gospel.* Andrew's was simple: "We have found the Messiah!" I wonder how converts would respond if the testimony of the disciple was as simple as "I found Jesus" or "Jesus saved me!" What they would see in the face and voice of the disciple is the excitement and joy of finding the "treasure" (Matthew 13:44). Do you think the response could be, "Can you take me to Him?" "Where is He?" or "Why do I need to be saved by Him?"

Jesus's disciples are not disciples when He calls them, and neither was Abraham. Abraham did not become a believer until he "believed in the LORD;" (Genesis 15:6). Abraham's belief is mentioned three times in the New Testament: Romans 4:3, Galatians 3:6, and James 2:23. To believe is one of the most important confessions a convert can make. A person either believes or they don't.

It makes me want to ask the person proclaiming that they have accepted Jesus as Savior, "How did you accept Him, and where did you put Him when you did, especially if you are dead in your trespass and sin?" I understand the importance of making salvation a simplistic message, and easy to understand, but sometimes simplicity can be very misleading and, based on true salvation, extremely dangerous. If one says one accepts Him, then salvation truly becomes the work of man. *Being saved is truly the work of God.* And when you read throughout Scripture, it is always God doing the work in His people.[5]

Consider the gift of eternal life. When a person receives it, where do they put it, since it's something you must receive? Here's another question: Can you receive something, and not believe in it? I would expect

5   Romans 10:9 if you "confess" with your mouth.

the answer would be yes. But how? I met with a couple of young men who were Mormons. I desired to have dialogue with them at my home. They handed me the Book of Mormon for discussion. I received it, but I did not believe in it. What I truly desired was to talk to them about their beliefs, and why they believed them.

You may be able to accept Jesus as Savior because you acknowledge the facts. But simply recognizing Him does not confirm that you believe in Him at all. This philosophy places your focus on the gift and not the giver. *Justification and sanctification for your salvation becomes what you did versus what Jesus did.*

This could result in a false sense of salvation. Could it be, even though it would be done in true sincerity, that it's really a deception? One could still be spiritually dead, deficient of the work of God, and going through one's life expecting to be the recipient of eternal life, only to find out one was living a life of unbelief and was never really saved. And finally, what do you believe if you do, and why do you believe it? Why are there statements made like: *I... but never... I... but didn't... Let me assure you, when God does the work of salvation in a person's life, the statements are God did... and I responded... God moved... and I moved... I repented... and God saved...* Believe that!

If He Was There, so Must You

There seems to be a tendency to want to hang out with other disciples, and that is important for accountability, but it is *the unbelieving who are the focus of our work.* Most importantly, it is the interaction with those who are unbelievers of Jesus Christ, those who need Him that should concern us. How did you get saved? There must have been a disciple in your life, because if there wasn't, you would still be living a life of unbelief. It makes sense, especially since the book of Romans talks about the mission of disciples. Romans 10:14–15 says, "How then will they call on Him in whom they have not believed? How will they believe in Him whom they have not heard? And how will they hear without a preacher? How will they preach unless they are sent? Just as it is written, 'How beautiful are the feet of those who bring good news of good things!'" Can I say it in a few words? The disciple is a preacher, preaching the gospel to the unbelieving, sent by Jesus! So how do you make disciples? By *PREACHING to the unbelieving!*

So the conflict is, with so *many* proclaiming to be a "Christian" there are so *few* who are truly walking the way of Jesus. Many fail to look for discipling opportunities, because if the truth be known, they are only concerned about themselves and their own salvation. The true work of a disciple of Jesus is to help others who do not know of the love and saving power of God. Please understand this conflict between this internal and external perspective because it is more prevalent than one imagines. It's easy to think "unbelievers" are only the people in the "other than the Christian" category. Have you ever considered that an unbeliever could be sitting right next to you at church, even though they are professing that they are a Christian?

In Matthew 7, Jesus refers to the "*many*" and the "*few*," specifically in the passage titled "The Narrow and Wide Gate." Matthew 7:13–14 says, "Enter through the narrow gate; for the gate is wide and the way is broad that leads to destruction, and there are **many** who enter through it. For the gate is small and the way is narrow that leads to life, and there are *few* who find it" (emphasis added). In this message, Jesus uses the words "many" and "few." Many will be on the way leading to destruction, and few will be on the way leading to eternal life. But in today's ecumenical community, you would think it's the opposite—few are heading to destruction and many to life. How could it be? It could be easy to say, "Oh, we are much better than they were!" But I must caution you if you have this perspective. Jesus's words are living and eternal; if they applied then, they apply now. Can you see the conflict?

Every disciple was once an unbeliever. Jesus preached the gospel, and made them a disciple. Jesus is the perfect model of how to make disciples. Read Luke 9:1–6. The key points here are take nothing with you and stay where you are accepted. They, like us, must completely depend on Jesus. Our total dependence will cause us to rely fully on the power and work of God the Holy Spirit! God knows those who are to receive Him and His teaching. What do you suppose they were preaching, if they were not fully aware of Jesus's death on the cross? What should be the gospel today? Should it be any different? If it worked then, it would work now! And once His death occurred, it was really a powerful message! Does your speaking, preaching, and teaching possess any power, or is it just mere words?

I heard someone say: "we are specifically made, deliberately purposed, and lovingly placed; bloom where you are planted!" So if we are specifically made that would mean no two people are identical. Even identical twins are not really identical. Deliberately purposed, we all have a different role in the kingdom of God. That's biblical, as seen in Ephesians 4:11–12: "And He gave some *as* apostles, and some *as* prophets, and some *as* evangelists, and some *as* pastors and teachers, for the equipping of the saints for the work of service, to the building up of the body of Christ." Ask anyone who served in the military, they all have distinct roles and they work in unison. Disciples of Jesus do the same. All working together for the advancement of the gospel. Romans 12:6–8 says, "Since we have gifts that differ according to the grace given to us, *each of us is to exercise them accordingly*: if prophecy, according to the proportion of his faith; if service, in his serving; or he who teaches, in his teaching; or he who exhorts, in his exhortation; he who gives, with liberality; he who leads, with diligence; he who shows mercy, with cheerfulness." Can you see that not everybody is doing the same work, although every member is *working* as one body in Christ? Look at your heart, hands, and feet, is there evidence of discipleship work?

Lovingly placed, everyone is not working at the same place. We all are sent to various places to bloom and show all the characteristics of a Christlike nature where He plants us. How does it apply? There is a tendency to separate our personal, work, and spiritual lives. The spiritual life only applies on Sunday, when or if one gathers with other believers. But in reality, spiritual life is 24/7, and work is forty plus hours per week. How much more useful would we be if we did not separate work, our personal lives from our belief in Jesus, but instead demonstrated a spirit–filled life working for the kingdom of God? What would the atmosphere and our lives really be like?

It is Easier Than You Think

I understand employers are careful about "religion" in the workplace. Being selective or showing any kind of favoritism could put the organization into a precarious situation. One would expect this position to be taken when someone attempts to force their religion on the masses. However, as relationships are developed in the workplace, and the disciple is walking by the Spirit, the light of Christ shines brightly in them, and those living in darkness, as well as other disciples who may be in a trial, will be drawn to His light in you. Remember, it's "God who is at work in you, both to will and to work for *His* good pleasure" (Philippians 2:13).

God develops the opportunities when and wherever they are to be completed in and through you. Psalm 139:16 refers to, ... all "The days ordained *for me.*" Remember I keep saying, "you know that's biblical." Read Psalm 77:11–12. God calls us to continuously remember His marvelous work in our lives. It's truly about God's incredible work of faith, believing, conviction, salvation, deliverance, a new heart, a renewed mind, and placing His Spirit in you.

> "I shall remember the deeds of the Lord;
> Surely I will remember Your wonders of old.
> I will meditate on all Your work
> And muse on Your deeds."
>
> Psalm 77:11–12

God brings gratitude and joy into your life as His love pours into you and through you to others. Jesus says in Matthew 5:15, "nor does *anyone* light a lamp and put it under a basket, but on the lampstand, and it gives light to all who are in the house." Have confidence that those in your midst will be drawn to you as people were drawn to Jesus when He was *Walking, The Way.* Remember what Scripture says in John 6:44 and John 14:23. The Father draws all to Jesus and God's Spirit is living in you!

Many times, in my workplace, spiritual conversations and prayer resulted from simply saying, "That's biblical!" More times than not, the person responds with, "How's that biblical?" I must warn you; this requires you to know God's Word in order to explain how the situation or occurrence is biblical and applies to their lives. Believe me, you will be amazed how the Holy Spirit works in you and them! And you know the amazing thing? They eagerly listen and respond. This is not to say you must know God's Word in its entirety; remember, God the Holy Spirit *is working*, and He will bring to remembrance all what Jesus has said then and now. His promises applied then, and they do now. Remember, everything is BIBLICAL! *The Word of God is vital and must be used in our daily lives.*

God's Word, will, and love lived out in His disciple's lives is a mark of true discipleship. This is why *Walking, The Way* has been amazing to me, because I can see the work of God in my life wherever I tread. Praise God! Imagine the impact you will have daily for the kingdom of God when all aspects of your life are Christ-centered. You live out God's Word, will, and work wherever you go! You will desire to share the gospel and communicate God's work completed in your heart, the world, and in the hearts of unbelievers.

We must imitate a heart like Jesus, who said, "It is not the healthy who need a physician..." Mark 2:17. If so, then it's those sick that need Him. Again, I can only speak for myself, but if you had asked me if I was sick, I would have told you no. *Only after God made me well did I realize the extent of my sickness.* You should desire to be a light in darkness, faithful to God and doing the work of His Son by proclaiming the *Good News* of Jesus Christ. Start *working* by being His ambassador on earth as you await the coming of the master, bridegroom, and our king!

Here are two great passages. One was written to the Corinthian Church, and the other to the twelve tribes. Both are good reminders on which to end the work segment. I know some standing on both sides of the aisle of the faith and works discussion (the naysayers will call it an argument, but disciples call it a discussion).

You decide if your life as a disciple of Jesus requires any *work*. Read 1 Corinthians 15:58. It says, "Therefore, my beloved brethren, be steadfast, immovable, always abounding in the work of the Lord, knowing your toil is not in vain in the Lord."

Consider the words "work" and "toil." Both are required to be carried out "of" and "in the Lord." As Jesus's disciples we *work* and *toil* holding fast to the truth of Jesus, knowing our labor will never be in vain. God has entrusted His disciples with the most precious truth anyone could ever possess. So my fellow disciple … *WORK ON!*

The apostle James confirms a great truth: "For just as the body without the spirit is dead, so also faith without works is dead" (James 2:26). Look at your feet, where are you standing? What will Jesus receive from your *labor* (*work*) in the harvest?

A Prayer for You:

ABBA, I love You and thank You for today. This is the day the Lord has made. Let us rejoice and be glad in it. You have ordained work from the foundation of the world because You work Yourself. The work of Your hands is marvelous and amazing. You promise to work in Your disciples faithfully and lovingly until the day of our last breath here on earth, or until You appear in the sky, coming in power and great glory. And when that happens, we will come to know Your plan for our eternal work, as Your work through us will go on forever! You have Your magnificent work of creating new creatures in Christ leaves us breathless, full of joy and gratitude and with a heart full of thankfulness. You are truly an amazing God!

You have made it very obvious in Your living Word the importance of being faithful disciples and doing the will of the Father in our lives every day. I thank You for the faithfulness of the initial disciples because it was by Your Spirit, they worked to preach the gospel, which is still being spread today. I pray for all of those who You will lead to this book and who will read this segment on what You expect of them, as faithfully working for You is what You desire for them. You promise to give us the desires of our heart when what we desire is what You desire for us. Create this desire in them.

I pray they respond in obedience to Your commands, ordinances, and statutes. ABBA make it known to them the importance of stopping and looking at their lives and the way they work in comparison to how You are working in their lives and the lives of those around them. Their lives and the work they do will be a reflection of You to the world, as they imitate Jesus.

God, make known to each one of them that there is more work to do in the workplace, and all shall see and know that our labor, speech, and love come as a result of You living in us. The job where they work is Your harvest field, and I beseech You to send workers into Your harvest. Please provide wisdom and discernment so that their tasks and responsibilities will exceed the expectations of their employer, and their focus will be on You versus the job. You've said that "if any of you lacks wisdom, let him ask of God." I ask You God the Holy Spirit to create a desire in each disciple to ask for wisdom. Wisdom for family situations; work issues and troubles; and most importantly when they are discipling and being discipled.

God, make it known to them that their job must go beyond just earning an income to live. I pray Your work in them will cause them to seek first Your kingdom and Your righteousness.

Father, You know there are so many people in this world who are hurting, and do not have hope. You know there are so many blinded by the god of this world who cannot find their way. Bring Your light to the unbelieving through Your disciples, making a way for them to hear Your gospel. Open their hearts to receive Your truth through the words of Your disciples.

I pray You inspire them all, enlightened them all, empowering them to be the disciples You have called and made them to be. You have made apparent to me how easy it is to be consumed by the demands of my job—so much so, it can be a distraction and inhibit my usefulness to You. Thank You for freeing me from this bondage. Help them to see and realize You have placed them there, and there are many Psalm 139:16 moments written for them, awaiting their steps to fulfil them. Make known to them that there are those all around whom You have ordained to hear the gospel. Create a faithfulness in them, to respond to Your calling and the promptings of the Holy Spirit. Give them the ability to act in faithfulness, courage, and truth.

I pray they will walk, bear fruit, and increase in the knowledge of Your Word and truths. ABBA, please strengthen them with all power, according to Your might. Make them steadfast and patient when they encounter those who oppose You. Let Your love flow freely through them to others as they respond in love as they imitate You. Let their worship and thanksgiving be solely to You. ABBA, who rescued them and gave them life so they can imitate You as your instrument of redemption for humanity. And all will see they are Your saints in the light of Christ. I pray and ask in Jesus's name, amen.

Reflections

THE SCARIEST THING I EVER READ OR HEARD...

———

"Not everyone who says to me, 'Lord, Lord'" (Matthew 7:21)

EVERYONE'S INCLUDED

Can you imagine a time when everyone is all together? I enjoy it when all the faces, voices, and hearts are in one place. The kitchen is our common gathering spot. I enjoy any individual time I get with each of our children, especially my grandchildren Lily and Tate! As with everyone, it seems, everyone cannot be with everyone at the same time, all the time. Life change guarantees absence. But there are times when everyone can be in the same place at the same time, and when we are, it's wonderful!

Do you have family reunions when everyone shows up? The stories would begin, and laughter fills the air. As time passes by, some of the old faces fade away, and by the blessings of God, new ones appear by births or marriage—either way, the many new faces joining into the festive occasion. I enjoy the buzz in the air from the interaction, and it is awesome to hear. There can be multiple conversations, with multiple people, discussing assorted topics, all going on simultaneously.

The same air of the family reunion will be present when all of Jesus's disciples are together. Joy will fill the air when that day finally comes and you actually meet Jesus's eyes as He gazes into yours. His arms will open to embrace you with the warmth and love of God as He whispers in your ear, *"Well done, good and faithful servant, enter into the joy of Your Master!"* Oh to think! FINALLY, to see Him, touch Him, hear His voice

273

directly into my ears! I hope you have the same assurance and live with the same conviction and anticipation when it comes to Jesus.

How do the love, characteristics, attributes, faithfulness, promises, and truth He has demonstrated and continues to demonstrate impact you today? It would be foolishness to believe that everyone believes in the only true God, because they don't, and Jesus said they wouldn't. The saddest part, though, is that not all of those who profess to be Christ-followers believe the same about Him.

I am so thankful Jesus is the same as He always has been. His Word confirms this fact in Hebrews 13:8, where it says, "Jesus Christ is the same yesterday and today and forever." Neither culture, rhetoric, religion, socioeconomic status, race, gender, nor any other thing swayed Jesus. He knows the truth because He is truth. I am confident that what Jesus says, He means, and He will do what He says He will do; you can trust Him! It is only on His truth of who He says He is that we can have faith and trust in Him alone.

Throughout time, everything and everyone changes. Nothing, and no one, remains the same. I get great comfort knowing nobody will escape the judgment seat of Christ. When you believe, this truth will bring you comfort too. Regardless of what anyone does to you, they will face Christ. Can you live with complete faith, trust, and confidence Jesus will judge righteously? Everyone will stand before God to answer to Him for their actions. Everyone is accountable to God for their lives, decisions, and works. In other words, your thoughts, words, and deeds will be before you, as God opens the Book of Life and it tells the story of you. It would only make perfect sense Jesus would say "Not everyone," because everyone has their own opinion, beliefs, ideas, concerns, and interests. Everyone plays a role in God's plan, from the beginning of humanity until the last day of it. But not everyone will end up in the same place, believe it or not. You may believe something different, as you have your own opinion; however, you must know that everyone will end up somewhere, and nobody will be left out.

Not Everyone

Jesus says in John 14:6, "I am the way, and the truth, and the life; no one comes to the Father but through Me." Even though Jesus tells us the way, many religions and cults claim there is a way to eternal life apart from Jesus. There seems to be a conflict, as everyone is on the path to glory. How can everyone reach the same point with all the different belief systems? Surely not everyone is correct, are they?

Think of things everyone does, and no matter what the thing is, you find *not everyone* will be doing it. We tend to think everyone drives ... well, *not everyone*. Everyone walks ... well, *not everyone*. Everyone talks, but *not everyone*! We can go on and on about it and get the same answer: *not everyone*. At first we think yes, but then immediately information and memories come flooding into our minds about people we know, or have seen, and then we must answer, *not everyone*.

Why would living eternally be any different? Imagine everyone gathered in one place, and I mean everyone, no one left out. There is conversation, laughter, and an air of anticipation for Jesus's arrival. Then the Lord appears before the myriads and myriads of people. As He speaks, the first words spoken to everyone are, "Not everyone!"

A hush falls, and you think of that the line you have always heard, "It was so quiet, you could hear a pin drop." It was, for everyone. At that moment, everyone begins to look around at each other in total silence. There are many who were expecting that it was time to celebrate eternal life with God. They discover that this is a gathering of the great and small, every tribe, nation, and tongue. The collection of all, and it is not for entrance into the kingdom. It is the great white throne, which is the judgment seat of Christ.

What do you think the immediate thought will be for all in attendance? It will be the same question asked at the Passover supper. Mark 14:19 identifies the question asked by Jesus's disciples. "They began to be grieved and to say to Him one by one, 'Surely not I?'" The many start thinking, *I did what I needed to do. God isn't talking to me, or is He?* Everyone's expecting Jesus to raise His hands, waving everyone forward. And when He does, everyone enters His kingdom.

His words "not everyone" create an immediate examination of one's own heart. This examination reveals stubbornness and unrepentant hearts in many. At this very moment, their hearts actually condemn them. Romans 2:5 says, "But because of your stubbornness and unrepentant heart you are storing up wrath for yourself in the day of wrath and revelation of the righteous judgment of God." First John 3:20-21 says, "in whatever our heart condemns us; for God is greater than our heart and knows all things. Beloved, if our heart does not condemn us, we have confidence before God."

The few examine their hearts and confirm they have a heart that believed which resulted in righteousness. They were confessing with their mouth, which resulted in their salvation. Romans 10:10 says, "for with the heart a person believes, resulting in righteousness, and with the mouth he confesses, resulting in salvation."

God knows, and now through the power of the Holy Spirit, everyone knows for certain their own heart. Conviction and guilt become overwhelming for the many. This creates the need to justify themselves by the religious works they performed. Jesus began to separate everyone. The Shepherd then begins to separate the sheep to His right and the goats to the left.

There are so many different belief systems, opinions, and religions. How does one know the way to eternal life? Everyone desires to live beyond this physical life. This must be true, or no one would be proclaiming the way to eternal life, and so many would not be searching for *the Way*.

We must have an absolute authority, one supreme answer. How else will one know the truth about God's kingdom and eternal life? It is God's kingdom, and He is the *grantor* of eternal life. Then we must look to God since there are so many perspectives and beliefs. Everyone cannot be right, can they? No, not everyone!

What We Think Is Scary Ain't

There are many situations I could mention to create a scary mindset for you. I do not think it is necessary to mention them all. Have you experienced one or several scary situations in your life? Have you seen a few, or even heard about others? Are you someone who likes to read scary books or see scary movies?

You could be someone who likes scary things in general, because of how your mind perceives it, triggering your flight or fight acute stress response.

Of course, *not everyone* perceives all events as scary. This would depend on their psychological makeup. Something may be scary to one person, and exciting to another. Before salvation came to my tent, there were several scary events in my life. I will mention a few of them because they were breath-taking and heart-pounding. And you know what I learned? I could have avoided them, yet, I chose to do them. I never once seriously considered the consequence of injury or death. And you know something? Both were lurking at my door. Before I proceed, do you want to know what I know now, which I did not know then? Why I escaped the danger and tragedy? Believe me, they were near-death experiences, and I lived through them to testify to you about it.

It makes total sense today. It was by God's hand, preserving this life to accomplish His will and work today! Philippians 2:13 is a passage explaining it all. It is God, at work in me. Do I thank Him for His saving power now, then, and beyond?

> "for it is God who is at work in you, both to will and to work for His good pleasure."
> Philippians 2:13

ABSOLUTELY! His saving grace brings significant joy, thankfulness, and gratitude to my life. Please know, I am not deserving of it, BELIEVE ME! For without it, I am not only physically dead, but also spiritually dead in my sin. And because of what would have been unbelief, I would be eternally separated from God, FOREVER!

The truth? We live according to God's will. Philippians 2:13 goes on to say, "both to will and to work for *His* good pleasure." I have been asked, "Can I do things outside of the will of God?" Absolutely, but even when I do, BUT GOD, "can cause all things to work together for good," Romans 8:28—even my foolishness. He can even turn what I've made a disaster for the good, and THAT'S BIBLICAL! If God did not intervene and preserve my life in the following events, I would have no life ... dead ... and you do not hear a sound from me.

As a fourth grader, I was passing by a five-story building, and a friend and I wanted to climb the fire escape to the roof. We were, may I say, adventurous. We dropped our book-bags and proceeded to climb the fire escape to the roof. I expected to climb to the top, and then down. There was a pipe on the outside of the building from the roof to the ground. My friend went first, hopped from the roof to the pipe, and down he went to the ground. I followed him, not thinking for one second I could have fallen from the roof. I stuck my foot behind the pipe, wrapped my arms and legs around it and let gravity take over.

Fearful, I clenched the pipe with my arms and legs. As I passed the fifth and then fourth floor, it seemed like fun. Passed the fourth floor, the pipe was closer to the wall than it was when I jumped onto it. My leg became wedged between the pipe and the wall! I was stuck and could not pull myself up, nor could I go down any farther. Believe me, I tried to yank my leg out, but I couldn't! My leg was stuck. The pipe could have broken away from the wall, dropping me forty-five feet to the ground. I yelled as loud as I could. A window opened and a man looked down at me. He disappeared and shortly after I heard the sirens.

The fire and police arrived. They had a fireman on the roof who rappelled down and wrapped a rope around me to "keep me from falling!" Imagine that! Once secured, another fireman lifted me up out of the crevice and I was free! He lowered me to the ground right into the face of the policeman. My friend was long gone by then! I faced judgment alone. The officer saw my face and my damaged pants and knew he was the least of my worries. He secured my name and address and let me go. I looked back over my shoulder at the pipe thinking, *WHAT A BLOCKHEAD! I could have fallen*! Death was waiting, but for the grace of God, I escaped.

By sixth grade, I was being chased by a friend on a downhill sidewalk. If you do not know, when you run downhill, as fast as you can, stopping is not an option. I approached the intersection and tried to stop. When I couldn't, I ran right out into the street. A car I did not see entered, and I ran right into the passenger side fender. At impact, I rolled down the side of the car. Had I not tried to stop; I would have been right in front of the car and run over for sure. The driver immediately got out of the car and ran back and yelled, "Are you OK?" I must have spun around a million times between the front and rear of the car. As I crossed the street, I couldn't believe I had escaped death by a car. You must know, God preserves life, even when we have no idea He's working.

When I was an adolescent; the state was constructing a new road across the Garden State Parkway. The construction was in the beginning stages. Steel I beams passed over the parkway. If you look at the construction of a bridge, those are them! A friend wanted to walk across the beams. I stepped onto the beam and began to walk across. As I got out over the parkway, I looked down and at the cars whizzing by in a blur. I began to lose my balance and immediately dropped down onto the beam to keep from falling. I do not have to tell you, falling would have been certain death either from falling or being run over by a car or several cars driving at sixty miles per hour. I clutched the beam with my arms, legs, and feet. My heart was racing a thousand beats per minute! I bet you could see my fingernail marks and prints in the beam. Immediately, the pipe event shot into my mind, and I held even tighter. I inched my way backwards to the side where I had started and ran home, shaking like a leaf in a storm. Again, all I can say is, BUT GOD!

I do have another story to share, but I suspect you are wondering why I am sharing these events with you. You may have ones like it, or even much scarier, especially if you were in the military and had bullets whizzing by your head or were actually shot. Any event which is out of the norm can be scary. I imagine in those times you may have told someone your story, and added the comment, "Boy, was I lucky!" You will now realize it's not luck ... it's God who is at work.

I was working as a senior in high school at a facility because I'd left home and was living on my own. One of my responsibilities was to supervise the recreation area at the center. One day, there was a conversation floating around about a need for a handgun. I knew of someone who had handguns, and I was pretty certain he could secure one. I'd seen them in his possession. There was money in it for anyone able to make the arrangement and sale. This was enticing, as I was living on my own, working, and going to high school. Any extra funds were always welcomed, especially if it did not need any real labor to get it! I made my way over to those asking and mentioned I knew someone. They showed immediate interest. I was a trustworthy friend, and my friend confirmed it. I made the call, we talked, and he stated he could make it happen. I notified the interested party and let them know the price. They needed to know, if the gun was shown, they better buy!

The seller did not live in the same city, and the buyer did not want to drive to another city. There needed to be a place in the middle where both parties felt comfortable with the exchange. Here I was, a broker in the illegal sale of a handgun, and right in the middle of two villains.

The date, time, and location were set. A few hours before the transaction, I got a message passed to me to contact the seller. I made the call. After a few minutes of talking, he notified me he had no interest in selling the gun. He was setting up a double-cross and would rob them when they came to the buy. I told him, "No! These are people who know me, where I work and where I live!" My plea seemed to fall on deaf ears. He continued with his plan. I needed to be there, to play a part in the diversion to rob these men. I couldn't believe it! He wanted me to duck down when were guns drawn, and they would shoot over my head, rob them, and leave.

That way it would not appear like I was a villain involved in the double-cross. Immediately, all I could see was myself ending up a corpse! I told him, "I won't be coming. The deal's off!" I returned to the buyer, communicated the change, and went on about my work. As the day progressed, I put this event in the "unbelievable" category and never gave it another thought. About four hours later, one of my friends came up to me and said, "Hey, you're wanted outside!" The thought never crossed my mind that it was related to what had happened earlier in the day.

I walked outside to the car parked by the curb. I walked up, and someone said, "Come closer," so I leaned into the window on the passenger side of the car. Immediately, a man grabbed me by the collar of my shirt and stuck .45 caliber handgun right in the center of my forehead! I could feel the cold barrel pressing into my skull. He yelled, "Don't you ever do this again. I should blow your head off right now! What were you trying to do?" I tried to explain, but he was not hearing it. He yelled, "Shut up. I should kill you right now!" He had to have seen the terror on my face, because he let me go, shoved me from the window, and the car sped off. Terrified, I could not even return to work. Scared to death, I needed to go home and change my pants. When I looked in the mirror, I saw the barrel mark in my forehead. I remembered the feeling from the barrel and seeing his finger on the trigger. I thought I was dead. Could you agree with me, BUT GOD applies here, as well as to the other events?

Sure I could say, "Man, I was lucky, walking away from those events unscathed." But when you have a true knowledge and understanding of who God is, and how He works, it is not luck, my friend, it's God who is at work. I tell you the truth, Philippians 2:13 is one of my life memory verses! In Jesus's sermon on the mount, He mentions one of the scariest passages I have ever heard or read in the Bible, Matthew 7:21. Up until God the Holy Spirit provided understanding of this passage, the events mentioned *were* the scariest in my life!

So many people expect to live eternally; however, based on God's Word, nothing faced on this earth will be scarier than hearing Jesus say, "*Not everyone*" and knowing that you are the person He is talking to. That my friend, *is a scary thought.*

He Will Get Your Attention

Matthew 7:21 says, "Not everyone who says to Me, 'Lord, Lord,' will enter the kingdom of heaven, but he who does the *will* of My Father who is in heaven *will enter.* Many will say to Me on that day, 'Lord, Lord, did we not prophesy in Your name, and in Your name cast out demons, and in Your name perform many miracles?' And then I will declare to them, 'I never knew you; depart from Me, you who practice lawlessness.'"

Believe me, I was fixed on His words and thinking, *No more chances, no reconsidering, nor pleading to a higher court!* I went "Whew" when I escaped unscathed from the events I shared with you, but I now know that there's no escaping or avoiding the judgment seat of Christ. Jesus's words are judgment and final.

I meditated on His Word and asked myself, *Why would He say this? After all, these are phenomenal works done in His name, right.* Imagine being able to prophesy, cast out demons, and perform many miracles. Those types of works confirm and make us believers. We are doing the work of God, right? You would not question if person involved were a Christian, believer, follower, or disciple of Jesus, would you?

When I read this, I was thinking that Jesus must be speaking to unbelievers, since He said, "I never knew you." In John 10:27, Jesus says, "My sheep hear My voice, and I know them, and they follow Me." If Jesus knows His sheep, it must be unbelievers, right? Can you see how this passage could be misunderstood?

I studied and meditated on it, and the Holy Spirit revealed understanding and clarity. Jesus was talking to those who call Him "Lord." Unbelievers do not call Him Lord. They refuse to accept His deity. He is speaking to those proclaiming to follow Him and calling Him their Lord.

Oh my, Jesus is talking to all who proclaim they are "Christians!" Jesus is denouncing those professing to be Christian. I do not know about you, but this passage is scary; in fact, real scary! Especially since there is life after this physical death. The difficulty with some people is that they do not believe. Failing to believe, they dismiss or ignore what God says is truth.

One must believe the Word of God. In John 1, the Word of God is Jesus! If Jesus says, heaven and hell exist, then they do. It is either heaven, eternal life, or hell, "the second death" (Revelation 20:14). Based on God's Word, hell and the second death are real. Jesus is the one making the decision. Those who thought the life of Jesus was just a story in the Bible, or those who believe He's only a great prophet and teacher, will find out the truth of who He is! Once they discover the truth, devastation immediately follows. What's expected is now different, especially for those who do not believe. Now everybody knows that Jesus is all the Bible says He is—God!

Some people think they are going to spend eternity with God, but they will hear the shocking response from Jesus: *"not everyone."* This "everyone" refers to those who proclaim to be a Christian, believer, follower, and disciple. This would be *everyone* SURELY going to spend eternity with God in His kingdom, right? Does this not stop you in your tracks? Or are you *so* confident or prideful, you could say, "**Surely, He's not talking to me!**"

Matthew 7:21 is so profound. It caused me to stop and ask myself, *Could I be one Jesus is speaking about? Am I performing religious activities so that I can check the box and claim salvation?* I expect to spend eternity with God when in reality, those "religious" activities serve no purpose in what Jesus commands of me.

Remember, Jesus says, "but he who does the will of the Father will enter." This removes the asking. It is obvious that false followers do not do the will of the Father. Their lives lack obedience to Jesus's commands. I want you to know that the judgment seat is well before the entrance. Jesus's judgment determines *entrance* into His kingdom.

Please understand, the ticket you got punched does not get you past Jesus's judgment seat. Everyone must take everything Jesus says *very seriously*! After all, He's the judge and the standard. I recommend you consider all the intentions and motivations of your heart. Ask yourself, *Is how I am living, all aspects of my life, aligned with Jesus's words? Are the "things" I am doing a disguise, and my life is hypocrisy?* Are you are walking by the Holy Spirit, and there is *evidence* of His work, and your life is a *reflection* of Jesus's image?

I know many want to believe that "all you gotta do is..." But based on the *decision maker* and *His words*, it sounds like it is *His decision* and not what one just *does* determining access into *His kingdom*! Believe that! What initially appeared to be unclear becomes very obvious. Jesus uses the parable of the tares among wheat, mentioned in Matthew 13:24–30, to explain and confirm this truth. Jesus will command the hypocrites to depart from His presence. Matthew 7:21–23, calls for an immediate, serious, and comprehensive self-examination. That's biblical. Read 2 Corinthians 13:5 carefully, because of the risk, danger, and what's at stake. It's your

> "Test yourselves to see if you are in the faith; examine yourselves! Or do you not recognize this about yourselves, that Jesus Christ is in you—unless indeed you fail the test?"
>
> 2 Corinthians 13:5

eternal destination. It's tragic if one ignores the need for self-examination and continues to live life on assumptions. They will overlook the practice of sin and fail to do the will of the Father, which could have an eternal consequence far beyond the outcome one expected.

When completing the examination, you must be truthful with yourself. However, I am not the guide for the truth, as it could be so easy to dismiss or ignore sinful behavior, and the presence of sinful patterns. I could easily blame someone else for this sinful life, like parents, siblings, or my environment—because of them I act this way! Jesus looks at the heart, and when He does, He makes the truth known to you. And the truth is that there is either the love of God or the practice of sin. There is no gray area here, either. I had to understand who Jesus was referencing when He made this statement. Could I be one of those He was referencing? To think, you could live your life, believing you are saved, and you're not! My life was not pleasing and honoring to God, nor did I live out His Word or commands.

He would not allow me into His presence. He did not know me, and finally, He commanded me to depart from His presence forever. I don't think the word *scary* even comes close to how horrific it would be to find out you are not one of His and are being cast into hell! I cannot comprehend the only true God saying, "I never knew you" and "Depart from Me." This makes those scary events in my life very insignificant. To think that the last words, you will hear from God, echoing forever are "Depart from Me." His words would be hell in itself. I hope this section got your attention like He did mine and you stop ... whatever it is. You need to STOP!

You Need an Advocate

Here's a story about a self-confident person and how they lived their life. He possessed the mindset that he could stand before God on his own merits. He lived what he considered a good life, and felt he had a good heart. He did attend church, and especially on Christmas and Easter. He gave to the poor when he could afford it, and he read his Bible when time permitted.

He was first to apologize when he hurt anyone. His life was not in any way like some murderer, adulterer, thief, or liar ... although he did lust from time to time, and there was fornication before marriage. He even admitted there were times of some drunkenness, but his drinking was far from being habitual. He's sporadically active in what the church called community. These were community groups, home teams, or life groups where other disciples of Jesus gathered to love and encourage each other. No doubt in his mind, he was a Christian. He had no real involvement or intimacy in relationships with others. No devotional time with God to speak of. He would pray, but rarely, but he definitely did if something went wrong.

There are many who live like this man. Their belief and hope of eternal life rests on the spiritual things, actions or works they perform. They believe this confirms they're a Christian and they would call themselves a disciple of Jesus. These spiritual things, actions, or works justify their salvation.

As with all, death was approaching, and a recommendation was made for him to see the Advocate. He was very confident in his works, as well as his accomplishments in life. Plenty of good deeds. These deeds outweighed the not so good ones, from his perspective. He never murdered, committed adultery, or stole, so he did not feel there was any need for an Advocate. He felt confident he could face any of his accusers and was willing to stand in judgment alone. So he did, and immediately the gavel sounded and "guilty of the law" was the verdict. Because he was not a student of God's Word, he was not aware of James 2:10. It says, "For whoever keeps the whole law and yet stumbles in one point, he has become guilty of all."

Immediately, he pleaded for the Advocate. Because the wages of sin are death, death is eternal separation from God. He went to the Advocate, only to discover the Advocate had a new role and would not be his Advocate any longer. He was irritated by this announcement and blurted out, "New role?" The response he received was as shocking as the verdict. "I AM the judge, and you're My first case!" In other words, today Jesus is and can be your Advocate. You may still have time. Read Job 16:19 and 1 John 2; both proclaim Christ is our Advocate. Be mindful, no one knows the time of their last breath ... no one, that is, except God!

The Holy Spirit brought to mind a live example of how life can end without warning. Bonnie and I journeyed to the supermarket. We pulled into the parking lot, got out of the car, and the brightest light I've ever seen flashed in a split second. Being blinded by the light, like it was for Paul! Immediately following the flash we heard the loudest boom of thunder I've ever heard in my entire life. I was frozen, and Bonnie bolted into the store like a shot out of a gun. I never saw her move so fast in all our years together!

I realized then that death could come in an instant, and there would be no time for anything, not even a breath. No time to think, and no time to confess the sins I committed my entire life. No time to quote Romans 10:9, and no time to ask for forgiveness from everyone I sinned against and especially God. *There is no time.*

But if you are reading this, it may be your time, the only time you may have. I pray God uses this to get your attention. God is the only One who knows your heart. In love, I hope you see Him as your Advocate. He's the only One from whom you can receive grace, mercy, a new heart, new birth, forgiveness, and eternal life!

You are reading this, and I am thinking about you as I write. I pray that you would be one of *many* the Holy Spirit leads to this book. Jesus can and will save the lost! Do you need saving, or do you think you can stand on your *own* merits before Jesus; claiming a right to His kingdom based on what you've done? Remember, you may not have as much time as you think ...

There Must Be More

Consider the above-mentioned works from a different perspective. In Matthew 7:22, the works included prophesying, casting out demons, and performing many miracles. When one is convicted in the heart at the White Throne Judgment, Jesus might hear, "*I* attended and served at church regularly," "*I* was involved in community." "*I* did quiet time and journaled." "*I* got baptized after *I* said a prayer and *I* walked the aisle," "*I* gave my life to You," or "*I* accepted You." And may also say—"Based on what "*I*" was told these works "*I*" performed made me a Christian—and "*I*" have earned my way into Your kingdom!

Can you see it? "*I*" did versus *what Jesus has done*? And just a reminder— "*we*" is a whole bunch of "*I's*" ... If you don't believe me, ask my fellow disciple Danny D.

Is professing to be religious or spiritual enough to enter the kingdom of God? According to Jesus, no. Is going through the motions, or doing the religious things while sin is prevalent in the heart, really being a Christian? I would hope you would agree that the answer is also no. Many want to believe being a disciple is as easy as punching your ticket. But expect if it was this easy, the rich young ruler would be a disciple today. You can read about his decision to follow Jesus in Mark 10. So, my friend, it takes the work of God to become a disciple of Jesus.

Obvious signs of religious actions are not a guarantee of eternal life. Partial obedience fails to demonstrate the work of God, and the needed heart transplant. The self-motivated attempts at righteousness cannot match up to the righteousness in Jesus. There is no character change, no believing, and no repentance. This life lacks the belief in Jesus as Savior. It is a life void of belief and faith in the only true God. God knows them, as He is all knowing. He is saying that those who profess to be disciples, yet who have no evidence of the Spirit's work, are those who will not receive the promised inheritance. There is no evidence of believing, repentance, living, loving, or an intimate personal relationship with Jesus. These are really the tares resembling wheat.

Based on all that has been communicated thus far, Ephesians 2:8–9 comes to mind, as this passage addresses salvation. "For **by grace** you have been **saved through faith**; and that *not of yourselves, it is* **the gift of God; not** as a result of **works**, so that *no one* **may boast**" (emphasis added). Can you see it? *No one* can boast about their own salvation, because if salvation was dependent on man's decision, then no one would be saved. Therefore the "I" accepted, gave, or turned my life over to Him makes salvation a work of man.

Those in Matthew 7:22 stated over and over, "we" did these works in Your name. They were saying, "I did Your work, and I should enter." You have read Jesus's response to their plea. Today, because of how the phenomenal gift of salvation from God is communicated, it takes man's work (*accept, gave, turn*) to set salvation in motion, and that, my friend, is not biblical. Man does not set salvation in motion, God does. Because on the last breath of life on this planet, your life ends up in a box or a pile of ash. God makes it truly clear: you will not be able to stand before Him and say, "I accepted You, and I deserve ..."

Based on these teachings, one's testimony must default to "I," because the focus is on one's action and not on the work and power of God for the transformation of life. God is not waiting at the foot of the cross, hoping someone will "accept Him," "give their life," or "turn their life" to Him. No, *God moves into the darkness with His marvelous light, SAVING the soul of the dead*. This mighty work of God creates a heart full of gratitude for His saving power, and with a new heart and spirit, one begins the journey to everlasting life, because one realizes that without the work of God, one remains in darkness, separated from Him forever. I understand that many want to display their accomplishments of God's work in their ministry, and this is a means to accomplish this outward evidence of life change. But true life change will be evident, and when the love of God is flowing through the lives of His people, and God will add to the number, day by day, those who are being *saved*.

This creates a newfound HOPE for everyone God saves, and this hope and faith can only be found in Jesus! *If* there is hope for me, *then* there is hope for you! In other words, FAITH alone, in CHRIST alone! I looked at the words jumping off the page in Ephesians 2:8–9, **GRACE, SAVED, FAITH, NOT OF YOU, GIFT, GOD, NO WORKS, NO ONE.** It's all the work of God, and my boasting is in Him alone! You must be confident that when true life change does occur in one saved by God, you *will see* the evidence (fruit) and work of God being carried out. And the first words out of the mouths of the saved are, "God saved me; thank You, Jesus!"

I must put complete faith and trust in Christ alone! I could not save myself on the pipe, down the hill, on the beam, or at the car!

The amazing thing? I was lost and spiritually blind. I thought I was a Christian and did not know I wasn't. I was not saved. I was practicing sin and had a heart of stone. I was far from God, yet by His love and grace, He was near to me! Grace was saving me—a grace I was not aware of at the time. It would be His grace saving me some thirty years later, PRAISE GOD!

Without Jesus's saving grace, hell and eternal separation from God was my destination. Had I continued living a life of sin, "Depart from Me" would have been the last words I heard forever. BUT GOD! Based on what Jesus is saying about the professors in Matthew 7:22, there is no heart change. They are not born again and have not received the new life He promises to give. Matthew 7:22 states that amazing "actions or works" were performed, yet none of those "saying Lord, Lord" were known by Jesus.

Jesus is the same. I hope you read Hebrews 13:8. Why would anyone think, if they believe God's Word, that the standard has been lowered? Believe me, it has not! Jesus has the same expectations as He always has. Therefore, one must be very careful in determining if a life is saved, and if baptism by the Spirit and conversion has truly occurred! One could develop a false sense of salvation, only to hear Jesus say, "I never knew you." I hope you have the same question after reading Matthew 7:21–23 and the echo of "*not everyone*" resounds loudly in your mind.

The disciples ask an important question in Matthew 19:25. Even though Jesus was addressing something different—wealth and its clutches—this question applies here also in Matthew 7:21–23! "Then who can be saved?" Jesus is saying not everyone calling Him Lord will enter the kingdom. Although in Matthew 19:25, the context is different, it has the same consequence: they will not inherit the kingdom! Could the following be statements people would make today? I have been faithful to You, look at the actions or works I performed. I've done all the things I was told and taught. These works confirm to myself and others that I have a right to enter Your kingdom. In my mind, salvation is guaranteed, right? They are doing those things and are supposed to be the evidence or proof life change has occurred, right? They were not doing any of those things before going to church and performing these religious deeds.

I could not save myself then nor later in life. God must do the saving work through the power of God the Holy Spirit! The important work is what Jesus says, in John 6:28–29: "Therefore they said to Him, "What shall we do, so that we may work the works of God?" Jesus answered and said to them, "*This is the work of God*, that you believe in Him whom He has sent" (*emphasis added*). Even then, there is the thought that something I do, will bring about salvation. The truth is, it's the work of God bringing about believing and salvation. Do you believe?

Do You Call Him Lord?

Can you relate to why this is such a *terrifying* passage, for one who expects to inherit the kingdom but is forbidden to enter? God commands His Word to be continually on His people's minds and hearts. God states what we should do with His commandments in Proverbs 7:2–3: "Keep my commandments and live, and my teaching as the apple of your eye. Bind them on your fingers; Write them on the tablet of your heart." God desires to write them on the hearts of His people, so He makes a new covenant providing the power through God the Holy Spirit, giving the disciple the ability to remain faithful.

Hebrews 8:10 confirms this marvelous work of God. It says, "For this is the covenant that I will make with the house of Israel After those days, says the Lord: I will put My laws into their minds, And I will write them on their hearts. And I will be their God, and they shall be My people." The difference? God wrote His law and gave it to His people. Now, as people of the only true God, God writes His law in us! We then grow in understanding to know and believe. Without His inscription, we would not have the ability to remember, love, and live out His truths. Oh, the vastness and depth of His Word! It requires constant review and study, day and night, as the human mind cannot fully comprehend all contained in it!

What is the will of the Father? Jesus said this was why they could not enter. The will of God is for us to know and have faith in the only true God of the Bible and in Jesus Christ whom He sent. We are to be conformed to the image of His Son, and as we are, we preach the gospel to the unbelieving.

God prefers to be made known, versus being made famous. One could be famous and yet not known. Therefore, as Jesus's disciple, you must make known God's love for the world by testifying of His Son, Spirit, love, attributes, characteristics, grace, mercy, omnipotence, omniscience, and omnipresence.

You must believe Jesus Christ is the Son of God. As one grows in love and adoration for God the Father, one's mind and heart is saturated with His Word. We begin to love one another, seek and extend forgiveness, and live a life which models Jesus's. We will do the will of God the Father. If anyone lacks obedience to God's will, they mock Jesus by calling Him Lord!

Remember, if you are going to say Jesus is Lord, then He must be Lord of your life. As Lord, He has total say, and we must conform to His will and ways. We are to serve Him for the interests of His kingdom. We must deny our flesh and the way of our own eyes and hearts. We cannot call Him Lord in prayer and not obey His commands! Obedience and love for our Lord go far beyond hearing His sayings, even more so than professing to be His follower. Just professing will not guarantee entrance into His kingdom! Jesus's disciples live out God's truths, and the Lord's work is being carried out in and through their lives. This is the *evidence* of His Lordship.

Chapter 7 concludes Jesus's Sermon on the Mount. If you want to read one of the most powerful sermons given to humanity, read Matthew chapters 5–7.

It is a wonderful collection of Jesus's teachings on the Kingdom of God. Jesus addresses God's commandments, statutes, and ordinances. He explains love, how to pray, truth, money, and mourning for one's own sinfulness, to name a few. Read and meditate on it. With the Holy Spirit's power, you'll get a clearer understanding of how we are to live as Jesus's disciples.

It would bless your life to read, meditate, live it out, and pass it on! Jesus touches all aspects of life for His disciples. Live out His Word in your life, daily! It's my prayer; God opens your heart to see the truth of Who He is!

Ready or Not ...

When the game of hide and go seek was played, being caught or making it back to base determined if one won or lost. It was loads of fun, because of one's ability to hide and not be found, and sometimes hiding in the most obvious places was the best. It also required speed to outrun the seeker back to base and win! This is a game... *but life is lived at game speed!*

As we all know, the end of one's life does come, whether we are ready or not. Believe it, it's true, and it's biblical! Yes, there are times when illness has one lying on one's death bed and it is just a matter of time for the end to arrive. But there are so many others for whom their final day comes when they least expect it. This applies to both the end of life on this earth and the coming of Jesus. In either case, each person must be ready, because ready or not, here He comes!

Jesus tells us how we are to live in anticipation of the final day. In Luke 12:35–48, Jesus says we are to "be in readiness." It seems natural to lock your doors and windows in your home, because if the thief does come, he will meet with at least some resistance, allowing time for a response to the intrusion. If someone was fully aware of when the thief was coming, surely they would be prepared to defend all they own. But what about your life? How will someone defend their life when it comes to the question of being a disciple or unbeliever in Jesus Christ, on that day? In Matthew 24:42–51, God's Word tells us we are to *Be Ready for His Coming.* So how does one get ready for the coming of Jesus, be it when He calls or when He comes in person? Both passages deal with being "alert" and "ready" for both days. That day, you will either spiritually wake up before the judgment seat of Jesus, or you will be among those who see Him coming on the clouds. Either day, you must be "prepared" and "watchful" for its arrival!

Many seem to be just going through life with no anticipation of Jesus's call or arrival. There is so much focus on self, pleasures, desires, and the accumulation of wealth, and little, if any focus on Jesus. Jesus warned them when He was preaching the gospel, and His words apply in our day as well. Remember Hebrews 4:12, which says, "For the word of God is living," and because it's living, it applies to everyone, everywhere, in all times of humanity. That means it applies to you, me, and everyone else; no one is excluded. Please be aware, Jesus is coming, and He makes it obvious in Luke 12:40: "You too, be ready; for the Son of Man is coming at an hour that you do not expect." He also talked about it in conversation with the rich man in Luke 12:20, titled "Covetousness Denounced." He said, "But God said to him, 'You fool! This very night your soul is required of you; and now who will own what you have prepared?'"

Life as one knows it can end without warning when God deems it to end. Are you ready, prepared and alert? Are you doing the will of the Father? Jesus's coming is not a game, for it's about where your spirit and soul will be living forever. It will be either in God's presence or not. Because His words apply to everyone, no one's excluded. Where are you going to spend eternity? If you are reading this, know God in His patience allowed for it. *The time for you is now*!

A Prayer for You:

ABBA I love You and thank You for today. This is the day the Lord has made. Let us rejoice and be glad in it. You desire for all people to heed the truth of Your Words. You have given Your life so that we could have life. There will be many who read this segment, and I pray You give them the ability to look at their lives as You would and see as You see. Make known to them the truth and understanding of Your warning in Matthew 7 about the narrow and wide gates. You already know how horrific life can be away from the Father. And we claim and live by Your promise to never leave us as orphans, thank You, Jesus!

I know You will save, but give us the courage to speak the truth to those who are held in the clutches and bondage of Satan. Allow us to be the light of Jesus, so we can be seen by those living in spiritual darkness. Empower all Your disciples to move. Incline Your ears to hear the prayers through our petitions and supplications. Receive our prayers as I know You will respond according to Your will.

I know You are a loving God, forgiving, and merciful. You desire to have your children spend eternity in Your presence. I know there are many who believe salvation is an easy way to eternity. It took Your life to satisfy Your wrath. I know there are many distractions and deceptions in the world, which are designed to keep them from the truth of Your existence and the knowledge of You. ABBA, make Yourself known to them this day, and on the day they will be reading this prayer for them.

You are a patient God, who will allow time for repentance; if it was not so, You would have told us. But Your words clearly say, "but is patient with you." ABBA, You continue to demonstrate patience through Your loving heart for those who need to hear Your voice through the gospel. Be merciful and create a clean heart in them so they can faithfully live out Your commands and do the will of the Father.

I AM so thankful for Your saving grace. I know I was not deserving of it, yet, in love You freely gave it to me. I now know that by Your hand, I am alive today to proclaim the wonders of Your will and work in my life. I should have been dead numerous times, yet through Your agape love You hand reached out and saved me; thank You, Jesus! I pray that as they reach out their hand to You, You touch their lives so they can feel the warmth of Your unfailing agape love.

Give them the ability to see. Allow Your Spirit to move. Remove the veil causing spiritual blindness. Identify the sin preventing them from seeing You and the truth of who You are. Open their hearts to hear Your voice and the truth of Your Word.

Thank You for listening and responding, and I ask this in Jesus's name, amen.

Reflections

DISCIPLESHIP ...

———

"If you continue in My word, then you are truly disciples of Mine"
(John 8:31)

HOW YOU MUST LIVE

I wonder if people really look at discipleship as a calling from God, versus just another deed to perform as a Christian. Based on how discipleship is presented to the ecumenical community today, in general, it seems that many may perceive discipleship as just another role they need to add to their lives.

Discipling another does lead to one's own spiritual growth and maturity. Continuous reading, studying, and meditating on God's Word leads to a renewed mind, a deeper understanding, and growing in the knowledge of God. Biblical knowledge and understanding allows you to begin applying God's truths to your life and live it out more consistently. The work of God the Holy Spirit through His leading, teaching, wisdom, and promptings ensures you will answer God's call as a faithful disciple.

The quality of the healthiness, intimacy, trust, and authenticity in each individual relationship is crucial to the effectiveness of their work and influence as a disciple. Discipleship is either a genuine focus, or it could be just another fragment to add, in an already crowded life. And if one perceives discipleship as something devouring the valuable commodity of time, then it will become like any tool—only used when needed, if you can find it.

Here is a visual I hope brings clarity to what I am attempting to communicate to you. This is what an attempt at discipleship may look like if it is just something one needs to add because an emphasis has been placed on it by the church you attend. And this may be because discipleship is not a way of life. There seems to be a habit to see one's life in totality, versus directionally. There are days when some of the circles have little interaction, if any. Yet, they are attached to our lives.

The person (me) is at the center, and this person is actually *you*. I am using it as me, because as you look at this example, as well as the one below, you should personalize it. I hope you understand. The circles are the lives intertwined within one's life. Sure, the lives indicated here could vary, because some may not be married, and some may not have children, but it is the concept I would like to address with you. As you can see, with this *added*

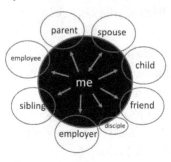

Discipleship is more than just another thing added to our lives

to my life concept, discipleship becomes a small fraction. However, it was added so one can now say, "I am doing what the church says I need to do." This added work to my life should confirm to myself and others, I am a Christian, and living in obedience to the "church," right?

The arrows represent the relational flow, which involves me and my time. I wish this diagram could be automated, so that you would see the work, spouse, and parent circles continuously change in size. As they do, the others reduce considerably. For most, work could be as large as the circle containing the word "me." When it happens, all the circles shrivel up to the size of a dot. And some wonder why their spouse and family feel they have lost touch and involvement in their lives and play an absent role more frequently than not. Can you see how the meaningful relationships in one's life suffer because of me, myself, and I? How idolatry moves in as one attempts to satisfy selfishness, pride, and greed, which is hiding under the cloak of "job."

The portion identified as me indicates the allotted attention to each circle. Most of the time, it is me being poured out to others. And it seems at times that there is truly little, if any, being poured back into me. This way of living could be extremely draining, and the other meaningful people in one's life are just left to fend for themselves, because there is not enough of me to spread around. Each circle does require me to play some role in others' lives. One attempts to spread themselves out based on the supply and demand philosophy. If there is no need or demand, the circle will naturally shrink. And when there's a plea for my attention and time, the circle enlarges, as there is a need for supply.

So the written circle would look like this: I am David, who is a husband, dad, employee, child, sibling, and friend, who is a disciple of Jesus.

However, I believe Jesus's design for discipleship is totally the opposite than what many view discipleship to be. That's biblical. Second Corinthians 5:17 says, "Therefore if anyone is in Christ, *he is* a new creature; the old things passed away; behold, new things have come." This involves a *new identity as a disciple of Jesus!* As Jesus's disciple, discipling now becomes *the Way* of life to live.

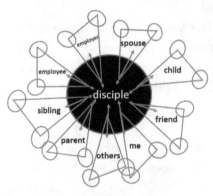

Disciple of Jesus is our
NEW IDENTITY

In other words, you become a disciple who's a husband, dad, employee or employer, child, sibling, and friend. Your focus is now on how you live as a disciple in the lives of those who are in your life. The diagram looks like this.

As a result of your discipling, you disciple as you interact with them. Now, you are responding with discipleship as your primary focus, and not yourself. You are living a Christ-centered life and not a me-centered one. In other words, there are days when your interaction will not involve every person in the circle. And as you disciple others in their lives—the circles attached to the triangle represent your work in making disciples—they begin to live out discipleship because of your work as Jesus's disciple! Your life becomes multi-directional, versus singularly focused. *You then begin to see and realize spiritual growth* in them and you!

I would hope you recognize the change from where "me" was in the center to where "me" is now located. It's because if *you* are going to disciple others, you *must* make certain you are discipling yourself, and being discipled as well. This is accomplished by and through the power of the Holy Spirit, reading, studying, and meditating on the Word of God every day, and having a disciple(s) of Jesus active in your life. Then discipleship is actively working as Jesus planned, and all are growing in the knowledge of God, sowing the word, serving the body, and being faithful to do the will of the Father.

Reading, studying, and meditating on the Word of God is biblical. Joshua 1:8 says, "This book of the law shall not depart from your mouth, but you shall meditate on it day and night, so that you may be careful to do according to all that is written in it; for then you will make your way prosperous, and then you will have success." You will be prosperous in your work as a disciple, making disciples. I do not know any other way to do it.

You will need to renew your mind, as before this new life you have been conditioned to respond and live the way the world indicates you should. Romans 12:2 tells us what is required to change your world view from on yourself to a biblical one, onto God and others. It says, "And do not be conformed to this world, but be transformed by the renewing of your mind, so that you may prove what the will of God is, that which is good and acceptable and perfect." God is telling us He knows what we need. *We need a renewed mind.* A renewed mind changes the way we live as faithful disciples of Jesus! The only means to a renewed mind is with God's Word and the work of His Spirit. If one is to be faithful in doing the will of the Father, godly wisdom is one's best resource!

Jesus calls us to disciple. Sometimes there is a tendency to look past those who are closest to us. Each circle contains a different person, and each person has a unique relationship. All impact our lives differently. For instance, you disciple yourself differently than your spouse. Yes, I said it. You, as a disciple of Jesus, must disciple your spouse. God commands husbands to live with their wives in an understanding way.

Husbands, know that you are accountable to God for your discipling of your spouse. Discipleship involving your spouse is best centered around your time together in God's Word. You both will experience God the Holy Spirit's work. He will sharpen and encourage as you encourage and sharpen each other.

Discipling your children is also important, and this looks different than how you disciple your spouse. You are to disciple at work. It differs from discipling a relative or friend. Even when discipling an unbeliever, the Holy Spirit will guide you. What you will find is you are discipling wherever the Spirit leads you. As His vessel, you will touch lives as someone did yours. Remember, "no one "comes to Jesus, unless the Father draws them John 6:44 says. And when you are faithfully living out the command to "*Go and make disciples*," you will find Jesus through the Holy Spirit will lead others to you.

As a disciple of Jesus, you will need Wisdom! Proverbs 8 is a great chapter to read *continuously*, because Wisdom contains the guidebook for all disciples. She has the answers for morality and explains the essentials for success in life. Wisdom communicates where she was, and what she saw in creation. Everlasting was the beginning of Wisdom's way.

How 'bout this for a tongue twister: Wisdom's wisdom is inexhaustible! She can assist and providing all one may need when seeking wisdom. And God knows that as His disciples, we need it. Wisdom has seen, heard, and knows! She expresses the essence for the basis of life in Proverbs 8:32–36, and it is her plea to all disciples to seek her to live!

"I love those who love me; And those who diligently seek me will find me."

Proverbs 8:17

Proverbs 8:17 is a verse you must commit to memory: "I love those who love me; And those who diligently seek me will find me." What a promise! If you seek, you will find. Doesn't this sound familiar? If not, read Deuteronomy 4:29; Jeremiah 29:13; and Matthew 7:7. As a disciple of Jesus, you must be purposeful in seeking wisdom. Because as a disciple, you will be faced with more than you may have experience or knowledge to address. Have faith, believe, and be confident. When you find her, she will supply you with the wisdom you will need to do your work!

300

Jesus in speaking with the Jews who believed, so we should expect that what He said then will apply to every disciple now: "If you continue in My word, *then* you are truly disciples of Mine" (John 8:31). Jesus is making it clear that His disciples are those who continue in His teaching and instruction. It is hard to believe there are religions that do not encourage reading God's word, as they are instructed to depend of the clergyman for the truth of God. We have His Spirit living in us, we must be faithful learners and be students of His Word. Devotion and perseverance to continue in His Word is the evidence of true faith and obedience to Jesus. Jesus's life, sacrifice and teachings unchain us from the captivity and bondage of sin, spiritual blindness, and death. How could you be a useful vessel to God, if you ignore His Words, which is one of the greatest gifts given by Jesus to His disciples?

Who Are These Men?

"Disciple" and "apostle" are interchangeable, although there is a difference. Disciple, as mentioned, means "learner," or a person who is learning *from* the teacher. Apostle means to be "sent out." This is a person who is sent *by* the teacher. I would be remiss not to mention all of the first disciples of Jesus, in case you do not know their names: "The first, Simon, who is called **Peter,** and **Andrew** his brother; and **James** the son of Zebedee, and **John** his brother; **Philip** and **Bartholomew**; **Thomas** and **Matthew** the tax collector; **James** the son of Alphaeus, and **Thaddaeus**; **Simon** the Zealot, and **Judas** Iscariot, the one who betrayed Him" (Matthew 10:2, **emphasis** added bold). And shortly after **Matthias, and Paul** who was converted later. They gave their lives for the furtherance of the gospel, so it would be alive, as it is today. You can do the research to find the manner of death for each if you desire to do so. *This will confirm for you their understanding, heart, passion, and love for Jesus, His gospel, and you!*

This is the point I would like to make: They all willingly and freely, like Jesus, gave their lives for the gospel that *you and I have heard as a result of their work!* Who are going to be the ones who hear the gospel later in time from the work you do as a disciple today? What are you willing to give for the gospel? I would expect all of Jesus's disciples to say, "My life, of course." If freely and willingly giving your life is your answer, then you must freely and willingly give of your time. And not having the "margin" will be unacceptable.

Do you see your calling as Jesus's disciple with the same purpose and fervor as Jesus did when he made the first converts disciples? I would expect their lives were not much different from ours today. They had families and work; some were employees, while others were employers. I am certain they had friends and the normal challenges of everyday life. Of course, it would make sense that they may not have had the distractions plaguing us today. And I do not think it is necessary to list them, because everyone has different ones. I would suspect they were hard workers, and something must be said about their character. It's no different than today, Jesus chooses all who will faithfully perform the duty as His disciple, and you can be something other than a seminary graduate.

I have often wondered why God chose these men. The answer became obvious to me with the writing of *Walking, The Way*. It was about love. We know God is omniscient and knows all things, so He would know the hearts of these men before they were born. Therefore, He knew they would love people like He loves people. I expect Jesus will choose the rest of His disciples with the same thought in mind; *they all will love people like I love people*. And that's biblical. Jesus says in John 13:35, "By this all men will know that you are My disciples, if you have love for one another." How would those in your circles respond to the question: How do you love them?

It was the work of God the Holy Spirit, and the obedience and faithfulness of these men to their calling to "*Go and make disciples*." As a result of this magnificent work of God, there are disciples today, over two thousand years later! Today's disciple must be obedient and faithful to do the Lord's work in making disciples and doing the will of the Father. Even when it seems growth is lacking, there is no dispute. God the Holy Spirit continues to make disciples, as Jesus continues to save!

One day when writing "The Scariest Thing" segment, I was pondering on what it would look like as the myriads of people were standing before the judgment seat of Christ. In the midst of it, the Holy Spirit interrupted that thought and brought this thought to my mind.

Jesus was standing in an exceptionally large lush green field. Over in the distance there was a rise, like a small hill. The original disciples, including Paul, were facing Jesus with their backs to the rise. Jesus was speaking and they were listening with their eyes and hearts fixed on His every word. Jesus was telling them that the work He entrusted them to do did reap the harvest He planned and expected.

He wanted them to know that although they lost their lives, the gospel spread throughout time and to the ends of the earth. He reassured them that their lives and work were not in vain. Jesus raised His arms. The apostles turned around. This picture is the best way I could explain what they saw.

Millions and millions of disciples came walking toward Jesus. PRAISE GOD! The question I have for you today is: Would any of the millions coming over the rise be from your work as a disciple, making disciples?

Millions of disciples

So their lives, like ours, should have the same desire, passion, faithfulness, and evidence. Would you like to know a great passage you can use as your mission statement? I hope you already know it, and if you don't, it's Colossians 1:28–29, which says, "We proclaim Him, admonishing every man and teaching every man with all wisdom, so that we may present every man complete in Christ. For this purpose also I labor, striving according to His power, which mightily works within me." Amen?

How It Should Look in Your Life

It truly takes *life change* to make a disciple of Jesus Christ. He requires His disciples to give all; heart, mind, spirit, and body! Does that sound like Him? Just because you go buy a uniform of your favorite team, your purchase doesn't make you a teammate. The same applies to discipleship. It's more than attending church, associating with Christians, and carrying a Bible. These actions are a far cry from being a disciple of Jesus. *Being made a disciple truly takes the power and work of God making you a new creature, giving you a new heart, and placing His Spirit in you.* You respond by giving it *all* back to Him!

As Jesus's disciple, He creates a desire in you to learn about the truths of the only true God. As you are learning, you begin to follow Jesus's teachings and commands. Being a disciple today would be the same as the initial disciples in our calling to *preach the gospel!* They were following Jesus so closely, the dust of His feet as He walked landed on them. Reading and studying His Word will be the same as walking with Him, and the "dust" from His sandals should fall on us.

As you grow in the knowledge of God, you become a reproducer, and you reproduce what you have learned so that others learn from you by the power of the Holy Spirit, and they, in turn, teach others. In other words, if we were to see the actual footprints from where all of Jesus's disciples walked, there should be countless sets of prints going the same way, all on top of the foundational steps made by Jesus. Then the replication process continues and Matthew 28:19 comes to life in you!

Where is discipleship carried out? It's carried out wherever a disciple of Jesus walks. These days we would have to say where we travel. It is at school, work, home, exercise facilities, parks, sporting events, community, church, supermarkets, hospitals, doctor's offices, hair salons, airports, airplanes, trains, and bus stations. Are you getting the concept? It's EVERYWHERE! How do you know where you will encounter an opportunity to proclaim the *Good News*? Where are all the nations? EVERYWHERE! So if everything is biblical, then the gospel is to be preached everywhere by the disciples, so "Go!" And the first place you should start is with you then your family and those you interact with every day. Just imagine the impact of discipleship if each disciple discipled right where they were! And then those who were discipled went on to disciple, and on and on it goes!

There is a main ingredient in the disciple's "spice bag," so to speak: it is love. It is vital how the disciple loves God and others. A disciple of Jesus loves God the way Jesus loves the Father. He tells us *the Way* to love God in Deuteronomy 6:5. It says, "You shall love the Lord your God with all your heart and with all your soul and with all your might." Why is loving a person so important as a disciple of Jesus? In the segment titled "Love," you read the explanation of how God loves. The passage I am referencing is 1 Corinthians 13:4–8a. When you are discipling, you will need to *love* versus condemn, ridicule, slander, insult, humiliate, or judge ... do you get the message?

When you get hurt, forgive. Discipling requires patience. Those who do not understand and who are walking in spiritual blindness will not believe as you do. You need to exercise kind-heartedness, endurance, and perseverance as you walk with them. When you encounter people, who do not believe in what you are preaching, trust God. It is His light and Word breaking into their darkness.

So you rejoice in the truth of who God is and what He can do in the lives of people. God does love them, and so should you. Remember, Jesus doesn't say, "You can tell my disciples by how often or long they pray." Nor is it by the amount of our biblical knowledge, or how often one reads their Bible. It doesn't matter your amount of quiet time, or how often you go to church. No, He says, "My disciples are known by how they love one another" (John 13:34–35). Believe me, it is not only other disciples, it is one another.

Discipleship is not seasonal. It is a continuous work for the rest of our lives on this earth. This is how faithful disciples of Jesus live! It begins at salvation when the disciple is baptized with the Holy Spirit. He teaches us while we continue to work, and this work continues into eternity! John 14:16 confirms this truth: "I will ask the Father, and He will give you another Helper that He may be with you forever." This sounds like ongoing to me! I wonder why we would need a helper in eternity. I guess there must be work to do, and we will need a helper, forever.

There's another indication confirming a disciple of Jesus Christ. It is mentioned in 2 Corinthians 5:20, which says, "Therefore, we are ambassadors for Christ, as though God were making an appeal through us, we beg you on behalf of Christ, be reconciled to God." Why would someone need reconciliation to God? Remember Adam and Eve and original sin? This sin is in every human being. As a result of sin, there is unbelief. As Jesus's disciples, we approach the unbelieving in Jesus's name. We act on His behalf. We communicate (preach) to the needs of the unbelieving. They have a need to repent of their sin. It is their unbelief making them hostile toward God and causing them to live in spiritual darkness.

Discussions with unbelievers seem to gravitate to sin. Addressing only the sins or the deeds of the flesh is just scratching the surface. In Galatians 5:19–21, it is evident the sins are lived out. When these sins are ruling their life, you could say they are living out the judgment of the sin of unbelief. As a result of unbelief, they will not enter the kingdom of God. This includes those who profess they are not a believer in Jesus, and those who proclaim they are but whose lives are lacking the work of God the Holy Spirit. You can find the truth and the danger of unbelief in "The Peril of Unbelief," Hebrews 3:12–19. There is hope when one is reconciled to God. They receive grace through saving faith. They become the recipients of His atonement, Spirit, attributes, provision, and promises. And they, like so many others before them, become heirs according to His promise. And they now receive the promise of eternal life.

Do you ever wonder why people seem to seek you out? This could confirm why it "seems" others are drawn to you. God tells us in John 14:23, "... If anyone loves Me, he will keep My word; and My Father will love him, and We will come to him and make Our abode with him." The disciple of Jesus is the dwelling place for the Father, Son, and Spirit. What is occurring? God is performing the reconciliation process through you, His vessel. Reconciliation is a process of restoring what was broken. I do not know about you, but I was a broken person ... heck, shattered! My relationship with God—and I AM telling you the truth—was no relationship at all. I needed Jesus, and I needed to be reconciled to God. All people on this earth need to be reconciled to God. *Do you need to be reconciled to God?*

Everyone—yes, I said everyone—born into this world is born of the seed of Adam into sin, spiritually dead and separated from God. Romans 5:12 confirms this truth, saying, "Therefore, just as through one man sin entered into the world, and death through sin, and so death spread to all men, because all sinned." However, I would like to circle back to the "Not everyone," as it applies here as well. You want to know how? Well, here's how. Jesus was born in this world, but He was not born of the seed of Adam. *So not everyone.*

The fall of man in Genesis 3 confirms why all must repent of sin and be reconciled to God. Romans 5:10 says, "For if while we were enemies we were reconciled to God through the death of His Son, much more, having been reconciled, we shall be saved by His life." With repentance there is forgiveness and you are redeemed by the blood of Jesus. You're declared righteous before God and justified by Jesus's blood. The gospel is the only effective way to talk about Jesus's saving power! *The disciple must speak the truth in love.* Address sin and repentance head on. Scripture makes it clear about why Jesus died. His death, burial, and resurrection were the catalyst for moving us from darkness into His light. Without the shed blood of a perfect sacrifice, we perish in our sin.

There are times in our lives when relationships become stressed to the point of damage. In my life, I surely damaged my relationship with Bonnie. If you were to ask her, she would say, "there was pain, heartache, disappointment, deception, and loss of trust. It would take more than just and "apology" to fix it!" It would require reconciliation to repair and restore it. It takes a forgiving heart to go through the reconciliation process and come out as one on the other side. Jesus is the perfect example of reconciliation. Because of Jesus giving His life, those who believe in Him are reconciled to God.

The most important question a disciple must always answer is, "Who is Jesus?" The answer they must hear out of your mouth with true conviction is, "Jesus is God!" How they respond to your answer will quickly confirm their spiritual state, belief or unbelief. The disciple responds to the inquirer as Peter wrote in 1 Peter 3:15: "but sanctify Christ as Lord in your hearts, always *being* ready to make a defense to everyone who asks you to give an account for the hope that is in you, yet with gentleness and reverence." Then you will discern if there is a need for the gospel to be preached. As a disciple of Jesus, you live out 2 Timothy 4:2: "preach the word; be ready in season *and* out of season; reprove, rebuke, exhort, with great patience and instruction."

And while you are preaching the gospel, you are praying and asking God to give them the Holy Spirit. Have you ever prayed and asked God to give them His Spirit, or do you just talk? Salvation testimony and the gospel go well beyond mere words. The fervent prayer of a disciple of Jesus demonstrates faith. This asking in faith causes Jesus to respond to His promises to do what He says He would do. Do you know what He will do if you would ask in faith? Here's what He said He would do.

John 14:14 says, "If you ask Me anything in My name, I will do *it*." He reiterates this in John 16:23–24, "Truly, truly, I say to you, if you ask the Father for anything in My name, He will give it to you. Until now you have asked for nothing in My name; ask and you will receive, so your joy may be made full." Do you believe? So, when you are preaching to a person who does not believe, then live out Acts 8:15 and pray "… for them that they might receive the Holy Spirit." And live your life as you believe God will do EVERTHING He says He will do! The initial disciples and Paul did, and *you know what happened—God moved and that's why there are disciples TODAY!*

And as for Me ...

I would be foolish if I did not testify of the works of God in my life as His disciple and gave you any indication, I had anything to do with it. Please understand, the love and gratitude I have for Him for ALL He has done, is doing, and will be doing in my life from now until eternity, has me on fire, and I AM telling you the truth! The work of God the Holy Spirit in my life has been more than I could have ever imagined, or even planned for a matter of fact. I am spiritually alive, with eyes to see, and I'm free, making known God the Father, proclaiming the *Good News* of Jesus Christ, loving others, and making disciples who desire to follow me, as I follow Him.

If you only knew me personally and intimately, you would know that what I am saying is the truth. So you will have to believe the loving words from Bonnie, as she is the most reliable witness you can trust … that is, except for God. They both know me intimately, and as God did the work, Bonnie watched His workmanship, day in and day out for over sixteen years now. I trust and believe that if you asked either, their answers would be the same, and I praise God for His faithfulness and work!

Therefore, as I imitate Jesus in my thoughts, words, and deeds, I must say what He said in John 10:37–38: "If I do not do the works of My Father, do not believe Me; but if I do them, though you do not believe Me, believe the works, so that you may know and understand that the Father is in Me, and I in the Father." If I do not do the work of Jesus, do not believe me. But if I do them, though you may not believe me, believe the work of this book so you may know and understand Jesus is in me, and I AM in Him. You want to know the most magnificent, incredible, and phenomenal thing? It can happen to you as well! But you must *believe* in the work and saving power of Jesus Christ!

His work did begin with me. It had to I was sick, desperately wicked, and dead. And when He begins His work, you will know it. The same applies with every disciple of Jesus. And although we all have worked differently, in various places, with different people, at various times, every one of us will all say the same thing about God! His miraculous work began with me, and as His Spirit worked and moved in me, I moved and worked! As you learn and grow, you begin to touch the lives of others and you begin to make disciples, *The Way* Jesus touched your life and made you one. And again, Matthew 28:19 comes alive in you!

Our testimony of sanctification, which is a life set apart from sin unto God, confirms the work of the Spirit in and through our lives. And this is one way you will know for certain salvation has come to your house, as you immediately begin to live totally different than you lived even from yesterday! I've heard many say, "Oh, it takes time when it comes to spiritual development." But they never explain themselves so that a new disciple, or even an unbelieving person, can fully understand what they mean. *What it means is that the saving work of Jesus is immediate, and life change from old to new is also immediate!* Jesus confirmed this truth when He made the cripple walk, blind see, and dead rise. They all were immediate works for everyone! And the saving work He does today is no different, believe that! If it were not true, we would have no example of what His saving work would look like, and we all would have to be physically crippled, blind, and dead. You can find the reference to this truth in Mark 2:1—12 titled, "The Paralytic Healed." But because we are spiritually dead, we must be made alive to live out His truths in this world full of spiritual darkness, disease, and death.

The process taking the most time is sanctification. Sanctification has three phases: positional, progressive, and ultimate. When God grants sanctification, you are set apart from the world, who are not sanctified. When Ephesians 2:8–9 comes alive in your life, this is positional sanctification. The Holy Spirit performs the mighty work of making you born again! Positional sanctification causes all the hosts of heaven to rejoice for God's immediate work! Some argue positional sanctification is the most important phase. Without positional, there can be no progressive or ultimate, believe that!

The positional state confirms sin has lost its power. We understand sin's bondage and captivity. We know it was God who saved us, and my own "good" works fall short of His glory. We need Jesus to be our Savior and to bring us out of the darkness of sin and unbelief into His marvelous light!

Progressive sanctification is the ongoing process many reference in their discussions. This is the most amazing process of the three, because the power and practice of sin has been BROKEN, PRAISE GOD! The lure and beckoning call from sin can FINALLY be ignored, whereas before salvation, we answered its crafty call every time! In your progressive state of sanctification, you will grow by the work of the Holy Spirit. You will have a desire to love, serve, worship, and honor God with your life. You move in unison with and by God the Holy Spirit as you respond in obedience to His promptings and commands. Progressive sanctification is designed to conform you into the image of Jesus. This also is an area to truly test and examine yourself, as mentioned in 1 Corinthians 13:5. So if you are going to perform the test, look, read, and scour the Word of God for how Jesus looks, lives, and acts like, and if you see the same work of God in you. If so, then you passed that is, as God says, unless, indeed you fail the test.

And finally, there is ultimate sanctification. This is the phase of all phases! First, we are saved from the practice of sin. I guess it would depend on one's perspective of sin. Not all see their sin as opposed to God. But it is, all of it. And if you are walking on this planet, you will sin and have sinned because the flesh is still alive. Can you imagine never again having an evil thought, word, or deed? I do not know about you, but I get extremely disappointed at myself when I do sin. But as I grow and learn, I have a great High Priest who can sympathize with my weakness. Therefore, the progressive phase is so important as you read, study, and meditate on God's Word. Our great High Priest is mentioned in Hebrews 4:14–16. When I sin, I can go to Him, because "He is faithful and righteous to forgive" me. That's biblical and found in, 1 John 1:9. Most importantly, in ultimate sanctification, we will see Him as He is, face to face! And we will be just like Him! And, the presence of sin is GONE forever! Hallelujah to the Lamb!

As you disciple; there will be more times than not when you must be an active listener as you interact with others. How else will you know their thoughts, concerns, challenges, or beliefs if you are always talking? I understand the excitement coming from this new-found faith, and the joy of sharing the *Good News*! However, there is an important characteristic and desire needed by the disciple of Jesus. It is the ability to listen to God and others. It is no wonder unbelievers question the testimony of those who *profess* to be Christian. The unbeliever observes with an analytical eye. They look at the "Christian's" habits, demeanor, speech, and attitude. They see no real difference in their walk than they do with their own. Then they ask, "So why do I need your Jesus? Hmmm." Know this: you will be held *accountable* to Jesus for your work as His disciple, wherever the Spirit leads.

Discipleship is not an additional fragment you add to your life. Possessing this mindset, we tend to only divvy out a portion to those in our lives, and the true focus remains on self. This perspective is self-serving, to say the least, and only when those in the circles need something does one deem to let them have, or let them into one's life. This is displayed in the direction of the arrows; as you saw in the first example, most arrows point one way, as one just attaches being Jesus's disciple into the limited space of their life.

I would like to be clear; you are a disciple first and foremost, and because of your life as Jesus's disciple, you are a disciple who's a child, sibling, spouse, parent, employee, and friend. This life as a disciple of

Jesus becomes the core of how you live and love others, and it sets the tone for all the work you perform with a heart which is faithful to God in all areas of your life, equally. And now, discipleship becomes how you live your life, and not just a fragment added to it!

Therefore, I am a disciple, who's a husband, dad, employee, child, sibling, and friend.

In conclusion, if you are someone who does not believe in Jesus Christ, and God the Holy Spirit has led you to read this book, *my prayer is God will renew your mind with truth, you will believe, and His Spirit will come upon you, and do His mighty work in you!* Perhaps you are asking the question, "What must I do to be saved?" I will quote Peter in Acts 2:38, where he says, "Repent, and each of you be baptized in the name of Jesus Christ for the forgiveness of your sins; and you will receive the gift of the Holy Spirit!" If this is you, PRAISE GOD!

For the disciple needing encouragement. Read and meditate on John 17. It is Jesus's prayer for us! It is sincere and immensely powerful! It moved my heart to know how Jesus feels and the love He has for His disciples. It was not only for the first eleven disciples; it's for all of us! Be thankful our Lord, Master, Rabbi, and Savior loves us the way He does. My prayer for you as a believer is Colossians 1:9–14:

> "For this reason also, since the day we heard *of it*, we have not ceased to pray for you and ask that you may be filled with the knowledge of His will in all spiritual wisdom and understanding, so that you will walk in a manner worthy of the Lord, to please *Him* in all respects, bearing fruit in every good work and increasing in the knowledge of God; strengthened with all power according to His glorious might, for obtaining of all steadfastness and patience; joyously giving thanks to the Father, who qualified us to share in the inheritance of the saints and light.
>
> For He rescued us from the domain of darkness, and transferred us to the kingdom of His beloved Son, in whom we have redemption, the forgiveness of sins."

I was lost and now found, was blind and now see, was old and became new, dead and now alive in Christ! HALLELUJAH!

My Prayer for You:

ABBA I love You and thank You for today. I know I've said and thought for all other segments of the book that this is an important segment and work as Your disciple. But all segments, working in conjunction with each other, all culminate in this segment. You have made it known to me the fragments are a portion of the segment and all the segments make up the whole. By Your Word You call us to be disciples. You entrust us with Your truth and bring it to the world so those who desire to know You can hear. Lord, give them ears to hear. I ask You to speak to all of those You have ordained to hear Your loving voice. I know it's by Your work, God the Holy Spirit that new life is imparted. Impart life to all who are holding this book and reading, studying, and meditating on Your Word. I pray You give them wisdom, discernment, and under-standing so that they will understand Your love for them.

There are so many who desire to know and have a disciple to walk alongside of them as they go forth on their journey to share the *Good News* of Jesus! Please respond by moving a faithful disciple into their lives to receive the training and make them a passionate learner of Your truths, so they can go on and make disciples.

Create a burning desire in them to be baptized by water, as You baptize them in the Spirit. Make them fully aware of their need for salvation because there is room on the front line for more disciples to preach the gospel and make disciples.

You have demonstrated Your faithfulness throughout the history of the world. Please continue to demonstrate the same faithfulness now in the lives of those who are reading this prayer. I thank You for Your work in me, for providing me with the ability to remain faithful all these days required to complete this task. I know in my heart I could not have accomplished this work without Your Spirit.

You know I have kept Your Word in my heart, and I know You have come from God, and we are here to do the will of the Father. You have kept every promise You have made, and there are so many lives changed by Your loving words. Fill their hearts with joy and their minds with Your truth. Open their hearts to receive the teachings of this book, so You will again be glorified in the work of Your disciple as it has been done so many times before.

I love You, ABBA, and I ask this in Jesus's name, amen.

Reflections

CONSIDERATION...

"For consider your calling..." (1 Corinthians 1:26)

A GENUINE THANK YOU!

I am thankful to God for His saving grace, love, and mercy demonstrated to a wretch like me. God, if He chose, could have easily left me in darkness. But again, all I can say is, BUT GOD!

Also, I thank God for all the men *He placed* in my life and *He used* as *His disciples!* To you, Keith G., Mike D., David A., Mitch M., David C., Kyle T., Todd W., Blake H., Freddie M., Danny D., Curtis S., Geoffrey O., Dale T., Robert F., Regan E., Eddie G., Hugh V., John D., Kevin G., Quentin L., and Mark C. for your insight, time, and encouragement. I so look forward to how our relationship grows intimately in each other and in Jesus!

I AM eternally grateful for your love for God, and how His love flowed through you to me. How you encouraged me in your own ways, and you always encouraged me, right when it was needed! Thank you, and thank You, Jesus!

Additionally, I am thankful for Jack, Alistair, and John, for their radio broadcasts of *PowerPoint, Truth for Life,* and *Grace to You.* God also used you in the hours of driving hundreds of miles. The saturation of my mind with His truth from your preaching has helped me understand God's Word so much more. And to my current pastor, Pete C.—when I heard your sermon for the first time, I knew it was the dwelling place God had led us to, and I was to set my tent here. I thank the Lord for your passion and love for God, and your commitment to study and teach His Word to God's people.

One of the most difficult segments to write was the Preface. Most would think it would be easy, and I guess it would be, if it did not cover the full extent of someone's sin and depravity. But I am here to tell you that it was EXTREMELY hard and painful. It was a life full of so much sin, disappointment, hurt, and pain, because how I live now was years away from all of it, and I did not want to go there for nothing. But this too also glorifies God for His saving power. It confirmed how far I have journeyed from the captivity of sin. I remember sitting in the chair where so much inspiration came flowing through my pencil, and now it was dried up, like the lead turned into tar. It was not the pencil; it was me. It was the fear of all the images and having to relive all of it! And now to have to focus on it, to communicate to you? Ahhhhh, I hated it!

One day in my whining to God about the Preface, God the Holy Spirit made it perfectly clear that my dealing with the images was not about "living it again"—it was about telling the story. I was delivered and free by the love and work of Jesus. It was necessary for me to explain it so that others may know there is hope, regardless of where they are, have come from, or what they may be struggling with now. They must look to Jesus! I want you to know, hope, and understand, Jesus continues to SAVE! He can and will DELIVER you from the bondage of sin!

Looking back in my life, if I was to describe it in a few words, it would be this: I look through the light, and I can see the end of darkness. It is where the darkness ends and the light begins. So, the end of darkness is the last day of spiritual death. The beginning of the light in my life was the day of my salvation! The moment of salvation is biblical. Genesis 1:3 says, "Then God said, 'Let there be light'; and there was light." This is the day Jesus rescued me from the domain of darkness! He must have said, "Let there be light," and I was born again! PRAISE GOD!

What You Must Bear in Mind

This segment is the conclusion, but I am inspired to call it "consideration." There will be a conclusion one day, as all will be standing before the judgment seat of Christ. Revelation 20:11–13 describes the day when all of humanity will be standing in judgment at the throne of God. At this time, the books are opened, and another is as well; it is called "the book of life" (Revelation 20:12). And judgment will be rendered for everything written in it for every person "according to their deeds" (Revelation 20:13).

Walking, The Way is an echo of John 1:23, which says, "I am a voice of one crying in the wilderness, 'Make straight the way of the Lord,' as Isaiah the prophet said." God's Word requires *all* to *consider all* segments of their lives, even down to the fragments. Fragments, if ignored, will affect the entire part! There are times when one may overlook a fragment or two, and if they do, they create cracks and weaken the integrity. Cracks eventually create vulnerability, exposure, and distress.

We are called to live faithfully and be obedient to *God's Word, will, and commands*. Our life must be an imitation of His! Ephesians 5:1 says, "Therefore be imitators of God, as beloved children." The life of the disciple of Jesus, even down to the fragments, exhibits a readiness to live out the gospel daily. I pray *Walking, The Way* compels you to stop and consider how you are living your everyday life. Does your life possess the evidence you are living by His "*every* Word?" Matthew 4:4 says, "But He answered and said, 'It is written, "MAN SHALL NOT LIVE ON BREAD ALONE, BUT ON EVERY WORD THAT PROCEEDS OUT OF THE MOUTH OF GOD."'" Jesus lived by *every word* proceeding out of the mouth of God the Father, and He has the same standard and expectation for His disciples.

Consider means to reflect, contemplate, cogitate, ponder, think, mull over, and study. There are scores of passages in the Word of God creating the need for consideration. I will mention a few, and they are:[6]

James 1:2, "***Consider*** it all joy, my brethren, when you encounter various trials;"

Haggai 1:7, "Thus says the Lord of hosts, "***Consider*** your ways!"";

Hosea 7:2, "And they do not ***consider*** in their hearts that I remember all their wickedness. Now their deeds are all around them; They are before My face.";

---

6   emphasis added italicized consider

2 Timothy 2:7, "*Consider* what I say, for the Lord will give you understanding in everything;"

Romans 6:11, "Even so *consider* yourselves to be dead to sin, but alive to God in Christ Jesus."

You must fully *consider* the magnificent gift of eternal life, being *born again*, made *new*, and being made *alive* in Jesus Christ! As John 3:3 says, "Jesus answered and said to him, 'Truly, truly, I say to you, unless one is born again, he cannot see the kingdom of God.'"

Each segment of this book touches on some important attribute of our life as a disciple of Jesus. Without going back to the Table of Contents to locate them, they are Love, Bible, Faith, God the Holy Spirit, Regeneration, Prayer, Testimony, Trials, Forgiveness, Work, and Discipleship. We're commanded to have growth and maturity in each. As we grow and mature, we begin to see the continuous work of sanctification in our lives.

When we began our occupation, we had little experience, if any at all. The basics got us started. We must continue to educate ourselves. In doing so, improvement and effectiveness are realized. Continuing education (CE) is a must these days. Things are moving and changing. CE is a two-way street. Both the employer and the employee share in the benefits. It is the motivator to cause one to strive. The goal for the employer is accurate and sustained production. For the employee, it results in compensation and recognition.

Why would discipleship be any different than one's occupation? When Jesus saves and new life begins, He expects His disciples to grow in the knowledge and truth of the only true God. By the work of the Holy Spirit, each disciple gets cultivated, developed, and thus matures.

Have you ever considered what happens to you after salvation comes to your tent? There's a newfound love for God and others. A desire is created in you, a desire you never had before. You begin to read, meditate, and understand the truth of God and His Word. You start living out, and then passing on everything discovered and learned from God. Your faith and trust in God mature. The evidence of the workings of

God the Holy Spirit are real. Being born again becomes evident. *You follow Jesus's teachings, prompts, and commands.* This regeneration into a new creature causes our life and walk to change forever!

Our life contains unceasing and effectual *prayer* to God, seeking His wisdom, discernment, and understanding for every challenge and event we encounter in our journey. Our life becomes our *testimony* to others, and we face the various *trials* of life with confidence, knowing it is God Who is at work conforming us into Jesus's image. We freely *forgive* others because we know God has forgiven us. And because of these attributes developing in our life—in depth, width, and height—we *work* as His disciple continuously and everywhere. And our *discipleship* begins to produce the fruit for the expected harvest. Development of these attributes should produce tangible results in our walk. It is the evidence of life in Jesus, and His life in you. You will do the will of the Father, as you are truly one of His disciples. God brings and leads others to His faithful disciples so the Father's will can be accomplished in your life and theirs.

The reward is the joy from God directly to you as you work as His disciple. You are the vessel of God, touching the lives of those who are in need of salvation. And you live in anticipation of being in the presence of God for all eternity. This is something never to be taken away, destroyed, or stolen, because your treasure and citizenship are not on earth, it is in heaven! How do these segments look in your life today? Are you just leaning on what you have done, or are you fully trusting in the saving power and work of God the Father, God the Son, and God the Holy Spirit?

Consider all what God is accomplishing through everything He's done from the foundation of the world until eternity. Believe me, it is true if you are not reading His Word, you will never know His heart, love, and what He's communicating. I believe ignorance will not be a defense for anyone standing at the judgment seat of Christ. Believe it or not, when you reflect, cogitate, ponder, and think, you are taking steps toward decisions you make. Those everyday decisions impact your life in one way or another. But your decision to live according to God's Word, will, and commands will have a greater impact on your life today and forever. You can count on that! I pray God draws you to Him so that you can see, know, and understand what Jesus is calling you to be as His disciple.

You must decide if you are going to believe every word God says about Himself: love, Word, Spirit, truth, and work. You must know and understand you are dead apart from God and need to be made alive by the power of the Holy Spirit. It will not matter to God how many good things you *try* to do or attempting to live a good life—your efforts and deeds will be fruitless and could never make you good enough or satisfy the wrath of God. BUT GOD! Who is rich in love and mercy, gives a new heart, renewed mind, and most importantly His Spirit! This new creature begins to live the life God intended!

Some believe and live as though eternal life with God is as easy as getting your fire insurance. It prevents spending eternity in hell. Pick up your free ticket, and you will live forever! Get your card punched, show it, and you are in! And many will say, "Just say a simple prayer," then heaven and eternal life are yours, and God is awaiting your arrival. You know the shocking thing about these approaches? You are told those things are "*all 'you' have to do,*" yet, what Jesus commands of His disciples is nonexistent in any of those practices. Please consider this: it will be obedience to the Father's will being carried out in your life determining and confirming your entrance into the kingdom of God or not. And *the judgment seat of Christ comes well before even seeing the entrance to His kingdom*; you can believe that.

Jesus told them in John 14:6, "I am the way, and the truth, and the life; no one comes to the Father but through Me." His words applied then and they apply today. We live as His disciples with the same conviction as all the other disciples before us because Jesus's disciples believe, have faith in, know, and understand Jesus is the only path, only truth, and the only life to God the Father. Jesus reveals Himself—love, truth, and commands—to His disciples.

I know there are many different belief systems, false professors, and false prophets in the world today. God said there are—and we must believe what He says, and what the false professors and prophets are attempting to do to you. Therefore, it will not be those actions mentioned above bringing about eternal life. It will be by grace through faith in Jesus Christ, and the power of the Holy Spirit, *bringing* salvation to you. You must believe deception is all around you, attempting to prevent you from knowing the truth of God, His will, love, and plan for your life. Do not be deceived. God is not like us. We must be like Him. Anyone who desires to live the way they want and sow to the flesh will not reap eternal life.

As you stop, test, and consider your life, remember it is all about Jesus Christ and Him crucified; the rest is error. Jesus's life is the only way to satisfy the wrath of God. Humanity is flawed, God the Father only accepts perfection, and Jesus is the only perfect One. And as a disciple of Jesus, we find our identity, life, and righteousness are in Him alone. Remember, faith alone, in Christ alone.

Essentials to Understand, and Then Press On

The work of God is to believe in the only true God and Jesus Christ, His Son. God's inspiration led you to this book. Believe me, it's not a replacement for God's Word, as nothing can ever replace or take the place of God and His truths. BUT GOD has inspired me to be a voice crying out to you. Please see *Walking, The Way* as a means to point you to Jesus, and as His disciple, I am being faithful to His calling to make disciples. At the moment of my salvation, it became clear to me,

> "Seek the Lord while He may be found;
> Call upon Him while He is near.
> Let the wicked forsake his way
> And the unrighteous man his thoughts;
> And let him return to the Lord,
> And He will have compassion on him,
> And to our God,
> For He will abundantly pardon." (Isaiah 55:6–7)

I did not have life, and my head knowledge, traditions, and rituals were not enough for me to enter the kingdom of God.

You are reading this book as an answer to my prayer, and the purposeful and effectual prayers of others for you, and God is moving in response to those prayers. In His grace and patience, God is allowing you the opportunity to see and reach out to Him. You've just read Isaiah 55:6: "Seek the Lord while He may be found; Call upon Him while He is near." You can freely reach out to God, asking Him to bring His light into your darkness and transform your life. He is near, so move, as He will not always be available as your Savior. One day, He will be your judge. Know this promise of God from, 2 Corinthians 6:2: "for He says, "'At the acceptable time I listened to you, And on the day of salvation I helped you."' Behold, now is "the acceptable time," behold, now is "the day of salvation"— I pray these passages cause you to think. I pray they created an interest in your heart to know more about the only true God, to have an intimate relationship with Him, and to become another one of His disciples.

You have seen His Words, and you will be without excuse. Jesus will hold you accountable for every decision you've made in your entire life. I know in my heart that if you genuinely want to know, all you need to do is ask. Please believe, *Jesus is alive*! I know because I have asked and He has answered. I AM sure you know, based on what you have experienced in your natural life, that dead men do not speak! It all takes faith, a genuine faith believing in Jesus Christ.

I'll ask you again. Stop and look at your life. You must be honest with yourself if you can. If you need help, ask God. He will help you see the parts or whole of your life opposed to Him. Psalm 139:23 confirms that God, in His

"Search me, O God, and know my heart; Try me and know my anxious thoughts;"

Psalm 139:23

omniscience, will reveal it to you. Once He does, and you see that it's sin, you must decide if you will repent. You must seek forgiveness from God, and all others, if necessary.

God is loving and forgiving and will always welcome you with open arms. He desires to impart life to you. It is so easy to move about life without considering all that's at stake. Look to Jesus to lead you in the way of everlasting life! Amen?

Remember the line, "there is no gray area with God?" You will either love God or hate Him, be obedient or disobedient, believe or live in unbelief, and have His Spirit or not. You will remain spiritually dead or be made alive. So, what side of the aisle do you find yourself on?

God can make you a new creature by the power of the Holy Spirit, but it will take the power of God for you to believe. God desires for you to know Him so that you can live an abundant life as His disciple, making disciples. Jesus has provided life throughout the history of humanity, and there's nowhere else where you can find this true life. True life can only be found in Jesus, and your life must be an imitation of His. I have mentioned several times throughout the book of being saved for over sixteen years. My, how the time flies, and that too is biblical! Ecclesiastes 5:20 says, "For he will not often *consider* the years of his life, because God keeps him occupied with the gladness of his heart" (emphasis added). Salvation has been a wonderful gift from God. His blessing, provision, trials, work, and inspiration have caused spiritual growth I could have never achieved on my own, no matter how hard I tried.

I continue to marvel at the power and work of God the Holy Spirit in my life, and *Walking, The Way* is the evidence of His work in my life. He was always there; but it took God the Father's work to draw me closer to Him. I look forward to how much more our relationship will grow over the remaining time He wills for my life on this planet. My entire life has changed, and I never want to be the same again. I can see why the initial disciples felt the way they did when He ascended, but I know in my heart He will be with me forever, and I will be with Him. His power working in me as a husband, father, papa to grandchildren, father-in-law to sons, serving and leading in church, being and making disciples, minister, encourager, evangelist, friend, and mentor has truly humbled me.

There was a time when my focus was only on me, myself, and I. Now I find myself meeting other men and getting to know them, since we pass each other most days in the same place, at the same times. I feel more purpose in being led to do so. I respond in love to God for any opportunity to share the *Good News* of Jesus Christ. You know the amazing thing? It has led to spiritual conversations, prayer, and relationships. I am so thankful for the Holy Spirit prompting me to speak to

Mark, Big Joe B., Fred, Tony, Richard, John, Chris, Brian, John, Mark, Matt, Lawrence, Mathias, Heath, Michael, Alexander, Brandon, Jerry, Nolan, Greg, Todd, and Jay, every time we see each other. Praise God! These would be people many would just walk by and say or do nothing. God only knows why these relationships have formed. And whenever God desires to use me for a specific task, I will respond in faithfulness, trusting God will fulfill His purpose in me, and them.

How can one ever get to know someone if they never introduce themselves to a stranger? Believe it or not, everyone starts out as strangers. Bonnie was a stranger at one point in my life. It is the work of God that makes the stranger into a friend. A living example in our lives today is Bonnie's fellow disciple, Heather.

They started out as strangers going to the same church. God's providential will brought them together. They began to meet and study the Word of God. Jesus was at the center and foundation of their relationship. Faithfulness to God and each other was being lived out. I have watched them grow over the past three years!

Heather and her husband Cutter are in community with us today, PRAISE GOD! Now, Cutter and I have a growing relationship. We started off as strangers. GOD is AMAZING! How we love one another is a key to the work of God in our lives. As a result of being set apart by God, we live as the chosen people of the only true God. Would this help you look at the strangers in your life differently?

As disciples of Jesus, we are "A CHOSEN RACE, A royal PRIESTHOOD, A HOLY NATION, A PEOPLE FOR *God's* OWN POSSESSION [...] who has called you out of darkness into His marvelous light;" as it says in 1 Peter 2:9. We must live our lives as we know and believe this biblical truth! God placed you into His nation and calls you His own. Jesus commands us to live out 1 Peter 2:9 in this world. We are to be His royal priesthood, preaching the gospel everywhere! Our message is proclaiming God's will and work in our lives. It was God who called us out of the darkness of this world into His marvelous light! Thank You, Jesus! Do you see yourself as 1 Peter 2:9 defines you in Christ?

I suggest you MOVE and watch how the Spirit of God works in your life! This new life created in Jesus does have me asking God from time to time, "Jesus, why did you wait so long to save me?" I've learned though, that all things are in God's timing, and that's biblical! Ecclesiastes 3:1 says, "There is an appointed time for everything. And there is a time for every event under heaven." So in His perfect timing, He saved me, and I am eternally grateful He did, when He did it. So even though I may have thought I could have been of more use to Him being saved as a younger man, I've learned God knows better than I! Isaiah 55:9 says, "For as the heavens are higher than the earth, So are My ways higher than your ways, and My thoughts than your thoughts." So, if He knew, and knows, I will just trust in Him!

A Passionate Spark

People have said numerous times about Monday, "What a way to spend 1/7 of your life!" And you know, this may be true for some, but I sure love Fridays, because it is closer to Sabbath! God willing, we will go to His house with other disciples, praising and worshiping the only true God, our Lord, King, and Savior, Jesus Christ! I love to hear His Word being preached and taught! From time to time, I get the honor to read God's Word to the body of Christ! My heart is filled with unspeakable joy when I do! Can you imagine a person whose mouth was continuously full of a language opposed to God? That was me, but now God's Words are proceeding out of my mouth. AMAZING GRACE!

Think of it this way: When Jesus came to Nazareth, led by the power of the Spirit, He entered the synagogue and stood up to read. He was handed the Word of God and read from the book of Isaiah. You can find this referenced in Luke 4:14–20a. Just think, God, in His mercy and love for me, would have me do exactly what Jesus did in His ministry—get up and read from His Word. All I can say is, BUT GOD!

I pray that if you've been stagnant, lethargic, or hesitant, lacking the fire or desire burning within you, this book will help you see and respond to God's calling on your life. His flame ignited within me and inspired me to author a poem titled "Burning Ember." I hope you can see the work of God the Holy Spirit in the words of my favorite poem. The Spirit is working in my life being the light of Christ to the world, and before the presence of God. His light illuminates my path as I walk as

His disciple in this world of darkness. His light and power will always burn in me forever. God's Spirit produces His fruits in me. When I pray and ask; the Spirit carries my petitions and supplications as a sweet aroma to His holy nostrils. God responds in love, faithfully answering according to His will.

When you hear songs like "Amazing Grace," "How Great Thou Art," "In Christ Alone," "Here I am to Worship," "Where Would I be without my Savior," "Resurrecting," "Blessed Assurance," "Always," and the plethora of others, you should sing with gratitude and thankfulness in your heart to God! Keep on singing, praising, and worshiping Him—that's biblical! First Chronicles 16:9 says, "Sing to Him, sing praises to Him; Speak of all His wonders." Keep *going, making* disciples, and faithfully *doing* the will of the Father. May the Lord bless and keep you all the days of your life!

Burning Ember
by David Newcombe

Burning ember burning so bright, burning before God's glorious sight.

Burning ember burning so deep, from my heart to guide my feet.

Burning ember extinguish not, burning ember always burn hot!

Burning ember always be true, give me love, joy, peace, patience, and kindness too.

Burning ember, you are mine, scent, aroma, light so fine!

Burning ember burning so bright, burning before God's glorious sight!

I could have said, "That's how God made me!" But it would be a lie from hell, as God has made me in His image. I struggled not only with the sin of unbelief but also my choices of sin. Both made my life a cesspool of perversion! To elaborate on the bondage and captivity of sin is sinful. It is not healthy to address the details of my sin with you. I do not know the sin you as a reader may be struggling with in your life.

Know that any action opposed to God and His will is sin. When you recognize it, repent and eradicate it from your life. All I can say is, I was in bondage, and now my chains are gone. I've been set FREE! PRAISE GOD. THANK YOU, JESUS! Take my word for it. The testimony you have read about me is true! I know where I came from, and I know where I AM going! Jesus made this promise to me a long time ago. The promise I am referring to is John 14:3, which says, "If I go and prepare a place for you, I will come again and receive you to Myself, that where I am, there you may be also."

There is a memorable testimony in God's Word speaking volumes to me. It is the testimony of a man with blindness. It's found in John 9:25: "one thing I do know, though I was blind, now I see." I can relate to the man who was blind. He could not understand how he received his eyesight, and neither can I. I was born spiritually blind, and I cannot tell you how God gave me eyes to see, but He did, that's all I know. If this is you, and you can relate to my story of grace, and God has given you eyes to see, then you are rejoicing too! If not, know this truth is available to you. You also can live a life free from the bondage of sin, in Jesus! You have read the words of John 8:36; believe me, they're true.

Remember, as Jesus's disciple, the more you disciple, the more joy and gratitude you will have because God will fill the cups of joy in your life! If you are looking for purpose in your life, the most purposeful work you can ever do is the will of the Father.

When you encounter difficulty and uncertainty, look to Jesus for His wisdom and direction so that you will walk according to His plan for your life. One of the amazing things you could look forward to is when God moves and turns you toward Him and opens your eyes to see His beauty, wonders, works, love, and power. I can testify that your life will never be the same, ever again! You will press on in your journey as His disciple, loving God, others, and doing the will of the Father, just like Jesus! Amen? The only true God is the only One who possesses the inherent ability to see all a person needs in their life. So you must trust that the Holy Spirit is working and will equip you to do the work ordained for you from the foundation of the world. Remember, Jesus's disciples are to be light in darkness, salt for blandness, love for hate, water for thirstiness, and food for hunger.

Iron Sharpens Iron

God made us to be in relationship with one another, like the relationship of the Trinity. Living in the world is hard, and God places people in our lives to love, encourage, reprove, train, and teach us. In the flesh there are rough spots to sand out and make smooth. We need buffing at times, as well as a drink when we are thirsty. We need people in our life who will sharpen us as we wage war against our flesh and the evil in this world.

Let me tell you about four specific people God placed in my life and are a blessing to me from Him, believe that! I pray that when you read my words to them, you will write a note to those in your life. Thank them for their faithfulness to God, and you! I could not end this segment or the book without acknowledging *Bonnie, Keith, Geoffrey, and Mike.*

Bonnie, thank you for your love, patience, and support. Your encouragement throughout the writing of *Walking, The Way* blessed me. You are the helper suitable for me, as God promised, and He knows I need Him and you! Thank you for your faithfulness to God, and your inspiration during our time in this book

"Then the Lord God said, 'It is not good for the man to be alone; I will make him a helper suitable for him.'"

Genesis 2:18

and in God's Word. Your "in other words," has given me great insight. I see the work of the Holy Spirit as you continue growing in knowledge and understanding of His truths. I AM thankful to God for restoring our marriage. God's love is flowing through you to me! THANK YOU, Jesus! I love you, Bonnie!

Keith! Brother, I am still living in amazement over how God brought us together over forty-four years ago. Before August 1975, we were strangers. I never knew you existed. Yet God did, and we have lived out our Psalm 139:16 moments in our lives. Over the years, your mom and dad, Joyce and Stanley loved me

"A man of too many friends comes to ruin, But there is a friend who sticks closer than a brother."

Proverbs 18:24

like I was their own. They demonstrated the love of God to me. God knew how much I needed parental love at that time in my life. They were His vessel to me! I am eternally grateful for them! How they loved me is how you love me. You have been with me through the ups and downs, happy and sad, and the good and bad. You are a friend who sticks closer than a brother, and that's biblical! God's Word confirms this truth in Proverbs 18:24. We have become brothers in the flesh and have the mark to prove it! We are brothers and disciples in Christ and have the lives to prove it. I pray our relationship founded in Christ continues to grow, seasoned with salt, and God's richness is always welcomed. Keith, you enrich my life! I am thankful God brought us together! I pray and ask God to continue to make us His useful vessels to do the will of the Father as His disciples in this world. Love you, brother!

"so that the man of God may be adequate, equipped for every good work."

2 Timothy 3:17

Geoffrey, we were strangers living over nine thousand miles away—you in Uganda, Africa, and me in Texas, USA. Yet one day, being led by the Spirit, God brought us together. Praise God! I still remember the day and will always remember you raising your hand to be my interpreter. Little did we know God was forming a relationship with us through Him. Our relationship was already formed from the foundation of the world and will last through eternity. It was our Psalm 139:16 moment, and we've had them for over ten years now! Thank You, Jesus! You are a blessing from God. It brings immense joy when you encourage, teach, train and reprove me. Second Timothy 3:17 comes to life in you to me! I am blessed to have a disciple like you in my life! And even though we are thousands of miles away, I love our calls. I love the times when we can see each other's faces as we live out this ordained relationship. Miles cannot diminish God's work in our relationship, nor can they interfere with our prayers. God is confirming His work in you and me because our relationship, founded in Christ, is standing the test of time. As I was finishing the book, I remembered your prayer after the discussion about writing it. The one request you asked of God continues to echo in my heart—that God would take me to another level. Little did I know the full extent of it. Know, God answered your prayer! I AM living out spiritual growth, knowledge, understanding, and maturity. I see through the power of the Holy Spirit the power of prayer and the importance of walking by the Spirit! Thank you, my brother, for your heart-felt prayers, love for me and my family, and your love for God and His people! I look forward to the day we, as you say, "bump chests again!" I love you, Geoffrey. May the Lord bless and keep you!

Mike, over the past two years there have been hours and hours of conversation. Thank you for sharing the valuable commodity of time with me. I am thankful God placed us where He did. When we meet at the restaurant, I am nourished in my body and spirit. It is wonderful to break bread every time we meet, and the restaurant has become our office and gathering spot. Do you think they ask themselves and others what those two men could be talking about for hours? You know the amazing thing? When Jesus is at the center of your life and words, one could go on and on about Him! And since He is not bound by time, when we are in the Spirit,

"Iron sharpens iron,
So one man
sharpens another."
Proverbs 27:17

we aren't either. No matter what we talk about in our discussions, it always ends up on the importance of God's work and truth in our lives. God has made known to both of us His calling on our lives and we live it out daily. God does bring fulfillment through you to me. God's love through you to me is evident. I am in awe of how you love me. Your words are encouragement. You have sound biblical knowledge, wisdom, and training in the truth of the only true God. You are an example of God's Word in my life as you live out Proverbs 27:17. You are also the light of Jesus in my life! I could write a page and a half on all I've learned from you. It would be boredom for some, but encouragement for a whole lot of others. When they have a disciple relationship like we have, they should cherish it. Our lives, too, are Psalm 139:16 moments; thank You, Jesus! I pray and ask God to continue to grow our relationship, that we, too, prove the intimacy of the Trinity in our lives, family, and all we encounter. I look forward to the day we see and spend eternity together in the presence of our God, celebrating eternal life with our Lord, Savior, and King, Jesus Christ! Love you, Mike!

For you readers, do you want to be a part of something bigger than yourself? If you do, then look to Jesus! Jesus's life is the model for how we live as His disciples.

Read the whole Bible, but you could start in the Gospels. They tell about the life of Jesus. But know this, He's the subject of the whole book! The Bible will confirm for you how far we fall short of God's glory. You will see God's love, mercy, grace, and provision throughout. You will come to know your calling as His disciple as the Holy Spirit illuminates your mind.

There is only one way to eternal life. Do you desire to find *the Way*? You will come to know *the Way* in John 14:6: "Jesus said to him, 'I am the way, and the truth, and the life; no one comes to the Father but through Me.'" Eternal life and living in God's presence is through His Son, Jesus Christ! May the love and Spirit of God come upon you though Jesus Christ! Love you in Christ!

Before I pray, I want you to know I've always said one of the best ways to pray to God is to use His own Words.

A Prayer for You:

ABBA, I am thankful for You bringing, Ted S., Timothy T., Jarrett A., CD., David W., John E., Kenneth B., David G., Craig L., Jim K., and Cutter T. into my life. I pray You will work mightily in their lives. ABBA, You know how meaningful their relationships are to me because You brought our lives together! You also know how much I cherish them! They are a blessing to me! Equip, nourish, and grow them, like You have equipped, nourished, and grown me. Give them direction, wisdom, and discernment so that they will be obedient to Your command to "Go and make disciples." I pray, as Your disciple, that You would continue to equip me so that I lead them as You lead me, so they too live out Your truths, and so that Your truth and Words are passed on to everyone they encounter, wherever they travel. In that way, Your plan for discipleship goes on and on and on! Thank You for the courage and confidence to act on any intentional eye contact. Thank You for providing me with eyes and a heart to recognize the spiritual need in others. For all I do encounter, create a time for any spiritual conversations to occur, and allow me to fulfill the ministry You have ordained for me.

So my prayer for you men, and for all who are reading this book, is Colossians 3:1–17.

"Therefore if you have been raised up with Christ, keep seeking the things above, where Christ is, seated at the right hand of God. Set your mind on the things above, not on the things that are on earth. For you have died and your life is hidden with Christ in God. When Christ, who is our life, is revealed, then you also will be revealed with Him in glory.

Therefore consider the members of your earthly body as dead to immorality, impurity, passion, evil desire, and greed, which amounts to idolatry. For it is because of these things that the wrath of God will come upon the sons of disobedience, and in them you also once walked, when you were living in them. But now you also, put them all aside: anger, wrath, malice, slander, *and* abusive speech from your mouth. Do not lie to one another, since you laid aside the old self with its *evil* practices, and have put on the new self who is being renewed to a true knowledge according to the image of the One who created him— *a renewal* in which there is no *distinction* between Greek and Jew, circumcised and uncircumcised, barbarian, Scythian, slave and freeman, but Christ is all, and in all.

So, as those who have been chosen of God, holy and beloved, put on a heart of compassion, kindness, humility, gentleness and patience; bearing with one another, and forgiving each other, whoever has a complaint against anyone; just as the Lord forgave you, so also should you. Beyond all these things *put on* love, which is the perfect bond of unity. Let the peace of Christ rule in your hearts, to which indeed you were called in one body; and be thankful. Let the word of Christ richly dwell within you, with all wisdom teaching and admonishing one another with psalms *and* hymns *and* spiritual songs, singing with thankfulness in your hearts to God. Whatever you do in word or deed, *do* all in the name of the Lord Jesus, giving thanks through Him to God the Father."

ABBA, I am humbled by your love, goodness, faithfulness, lovingkindness, grace, and mercy. Humbled by all of You! I am so thankful You have made me a new creature, given me a new heart, and placed Your Spirit in me. I thank You for this breath of life to give You the praise and glory. I thank You for Your words of truth. I thank You for Your Spirit, because I know without Him I would not be doing this work.

I pray and ask You to lead all of those You desire to read this book, and that You move mightily in their lives. I pray You disclose Yourself to them, giving them a new spirit, as You did this sinner saved by Your grace! Thank you for Your Spirit, Word, and life! I thank You and am so grateful, so, so grateful, for Jesus, and it's in Jesus's name I ask and pray, AMEN!

Remember, when you are *walking* in the light of Jesus Christ by the *power* of the Holy Spirit, you will be the *disciple* God *called* you to be. You too will *live out* the wonderful work of God every day the *rest your life* on this planet now, and forever!

I desire to be a disciple God inspires either to do or to say extraordinary things; revealing the will of God the Father and His Son Jesus Christ by the work, power, and teachings of the Holy Spirit; experiencing true joy of bringing the gospel to wherever and whomever the Spirit leads or directs me. I pray God places a desire like this on your heart.

Remember, you will be less likely to stumble in the dark if you're walking in the light of Jesus!

I look forward to every Psalm 139:16 moment, for whoever it may be that reads this book and we meet, *Walking, The Way!*

Reflections